IMAGES
of America

CONNEAUT LAKE

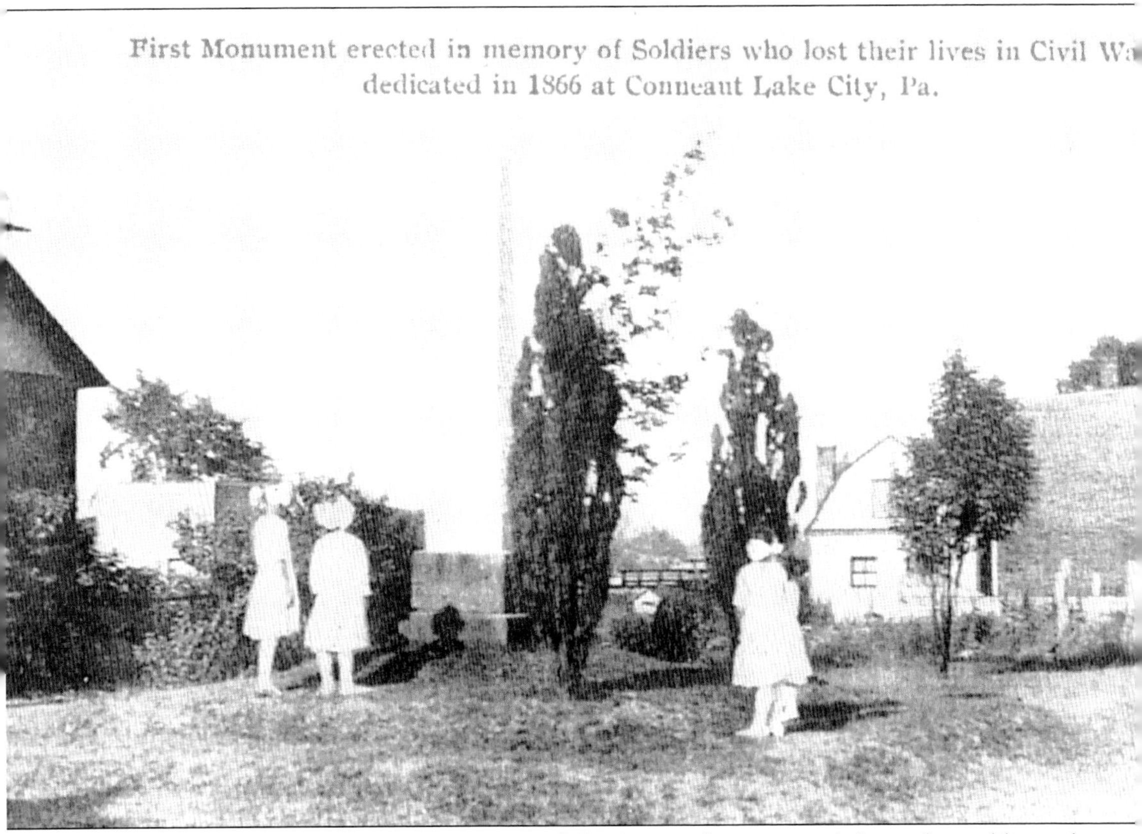

Erected in 1866, this monument is one of the first in the country dedicated to soldiers who lost their lives in the Civil War. It is located in Memorial Park in the center of Conneaut Lake Borough, where traditional Memorial Day services are conducted by the Conneaut Lake Kiwanis Club. (Courtesy of Conneaut Lake Area Historical Society.)

On the Cover: This 1958 photograph shows members of the Conneaut Lake Ski Club as they perform their special routine during a ski show on Conneaut Lake. (Courtesy of Conneaut Lake Area Historical Society.)

IMAGES
of America

CONNEAUT LAKE

Jane Smith on behalf of the
Conneaut Lake Area Historical Society

ARCADIA
PUBLISHING

ISBN 978-0-7385-9285-5

Published by Arcadia Publishing
Charleston, South Carolina

Printed in the United States of America

Library of Congress Control Number: 2012933855

For all general information, please contact Arcadia Publishing:
Telephone 843-853-2070
Fax 843-853-0044
E-mail sales@arcadiapublishing.com
For customer service and orders:
Toll-Free 1-888-313-2665

Visit us on the Internet at www.arcadiapublishing.com

To all those who love Conneaut Lake and its rich heritage
and to the volunteers who work to keep it alive

Contents

ACKNOWLEDGMENTS

Since the Conneaut Lake Area Historical Society was organized in 1999, the wonderful, rich history of the Conneaut Lake area has been brought to life for residents and visitors alike. This publication was made possible because of the support of the board of directors, which allowed its archives to be accessed. Many images in this book were provided by the historical society. However, were it not for the generosity of members Julia Catalano, Susan Luty, Kate Hilton, Hale Jenkins, Pam Harned Mullen, Jeremy Burgo, Bill Hrusa, Alan Moss, Glendora Adsit, and Bill Rhodes, a more in-depth history could not have been achieved.

I also wish to acknowledge my deep appreciation to those whose photography is part of the society's collection. When asked for permission to use their photographs, all responded with a resounding "yes." I give special thanks to the Harry Lowther family (HLF), the Luty Family Collection (LFC), Stanton-Rand Photography (SR), and the *Meadville Tribune* (MT). The book could not have been completed without their amazing photographs. It is wonderful to live in a community of such caring, generous individuals.

All images, unless otherwise noted, appear courtesy of the Conneaut Lake Area Historical Society (CLAHS). I also want to acknowledge Kate Hilton (KH), C. Hale Jenkins (CHJ), Pam Harned Mullen (PHM), Jeremy Burgo (JB), Bill Hrusa (BH), Alan Moss (AM), Glendora Adsit (GA), William Rhodes (WR), Doris Egyud (DE), Phyllis Martin (PM), Betty Stallard (BS), Ed Mailliard (EM), and Blood's Studio, for contributing photographs.

I also give special thanks to those who helped proofread the book, Julia Catalano and Hale Jenkins; and to my sister, Jean Shanley, for her help with research, proofreading, gathering materials, and for her patience; and to Abby Henry and the staff at Arcadia for their assistance.

Special appreciation goes to those who got me interested in history, all the early settlers, residents of Conneaut Lake, and to all the "mupheres" and "overheres," who came "up here" from Pittsburgh and "over here" from Cleveland and returned to make it their home.

Introduction

Located in northwest Pennsylvania, 40 miles south of Erie and 100 miles north of Pittsburgh, Conneaut Lake Borough is located along the shores of Conneaut Lake, the largest natural lake in Pennsylvania. The lake measures about three miles long, covers roughly 929 acres, and is said to be up to 101 feet deep in places.

As its rich history shows, the lake served many purposes. It provided employment for more than 200 men in the early 1900s, as they harvested tons of ice from the lake to be shipped via railroad to many large cities hundreds of miles away. Others gained employment on the boats that traveled the lake in the late 1800s and early 1900s to accommodate tourists. The lake continues to provide employment in 2012 for those involved in the tourist industry, as visitors from near and far converge on the lake each year.

The beautiful blue water of the lake offers that much-needed escape from reality from time to time. People not only take advantage of the boating opportunities but also swim, fish, ski, and hunt—all available to the public free of charge. Tourists were attracted to the area in the late 1800s when an amusement park, first named Exposition Park and later Conneaut Lake Park, opened on the west side of the lake. This book will not tell the history of the park itself, as it has already been recorded in a previously published Arcadia book, *Conneaut Lake Park*, but because the park was ultimately responsible for some of the early development of the town and the surrounding areas, it remains a significant part of this history.

Although records date only as far back as 1793, Conneaut Lake's history started centuries before. In 1958, local men dredged a portion at the southern end of the lake to build new docks for boat launches. They found what they believed to be tree trunks, but discovered they were in fact woolly mammoth and mastodon bones, determined by anthropologists to be at least 10,000 years old.

Abner Evans, a blacksmith, settled in the area in 1793. In 1796, the town was named Evansburg in his honor and remained Evansburg until 1892, when it was changed to Conneaut Lake to reflect the name of the lake itself. Legend has it that the name was changed because so many people talked of going to Conneaut, referring to the lake, instead of referring to the town, Evansburg. Conneaut is from the Seneca word *kon-ne-ot*, meaning "snow waters," because the snow stayed on the lake longer than it did other places. Evans opened a gristmill in 1795. The small town began to flourish as more than 20 other mills of various types were established within a year. Channellock, Inc., a worldwide distributor of quality hand tools, got its start in Conneaut Lake in 1886.

Although a small town, the area had many interesting visitors. One special visitor was the famed author Mark Twain. An account printed in the *Meadville Daily Messenger* in 1903 told of Twain's visit 24 years before, in 1879. Residents did not know him as Mark Twain, nor even as Samuel Clemens. He was "Mr. Turner" during the two weeks he spent in retirement at the cabin of a friend, Phil Miller, on the west side of the shore of the lake. Miller introduced Twain at a debating society and goaded him into taking sides. At one point, Miller, who was debating a local schoolmaster, argued a point that Twain had made in his story "Innocents Abroad," about whether a college education is essential to success. The master replied, "That has no weight. It is from one of those alleged funny books of Mark Twain's." To remain incognito, Twain could offer no comment. It was not until just prior to his death, in 1885, that Miller told the true identity of his visitor.

Many commercial buildings, street scenes of downtown Conneaut Lake, and homes of early residents are depicted in this volume. Of particular note is the fire hall, constructed by volunteers in 1931. The building later became a community hall, home to many community events, including high school graduations prior to the construction of a new high school with an auditorium. In 2003, the former fire hall became home to the Conneaut Lake Area Historical Society Museum.

Photographs of the community's annual traditions include the Kiwanis Snowball Festival, Memorial Day observance, and Fall Pumpkin Fest, which draws thousands of visitors to the area. Other celebrations include the 2008 sesquicentennial celebration, when the mayor and his wife did the "Sesquicentennial Stroll." Photographs of Geneva in Greenwood Township, including the schools and the post office, are also presented.

Conneaut Lake boasted many champions. The state's largest Muskie was caught here. Conneaut Lake produced two Major League Baseball players. Two champion basketball teams (the boys' and girls' teams), a girls' volleyball team and a high school wrestler won state championships, and softball teams won national championships. In addition, Conneaut Lake was home to the world champion barefoot water-skier, a 15-year-old boy.

Paintings of small-town America by famed artist Norman Rockwell, published in the *Saturday Evening Post*, may best reflect life in the borough of Conneaut Lake and surrounding townships, which comprise the Conneaut Lake area. As Norman Rockwell's paintings show life in the small towns, this book is designed to give readers a glimpse into similar life in the Conneaut Lake area. Chapters show a different part of that life, dating back to the days of early travel via canal boats and continuing through the various forms of transportation. Each chapter reflects the lives of the residents and all those who visited the area.

One

Early Years

Conneaut Lake's roots can be traced back to the days of the Native Americans, but the town itself was established when Abner Evans arrived in 1793. Evans opened a gristmill in 1795. Others soon established sawmills and carding mills, and the small town began to grow. The town was chartered as Evansburg in 1858; its name was changed to Conneaut Lake in 1892.

Beginning in the 1800s, transportation progressed from boats, pulled by mules on a towpath beside the canal, to railroads and to trolleys. When the Beaver and Erie Extension Canal was constructed, a feeder canal into Conneaut Lake was built. It raised Conneaut Lake nine feet and later an additional two feet. The canal was good for the business, but in 1840 the town was hit with an epidemic of malaria, attributed to the flooding of the lake. Many people died, and Evansburg became known as a deserted village. When the Erie & Pittsburgh Railroad opened in 1870, the use of the canal ended.

However, the natural lake continued to provide opportunities for development. In 1880, the Conneaut Lake Ice Co. was formed. The company employed 200 men in the winter to harvest ice from the lake, which was then cut into blocks, wrapped in sawdust, and stored in icehouses along the southern shore. In some years, 100,000 tons of ice were harvested and shipped via railroad to large cities. When electric refrigeration made its way into society, the ice industry became a thing of the past. The icehouses were torn down in the early 1930s.

Trolley lines made their appearance in Conneaut Lake in 1907 as the trains ran from Meadville to the lake and then to Exposition Park, Linesville, and Harmonsburg. These were also lost to progress when automobiles replaced them by the end of World War I.

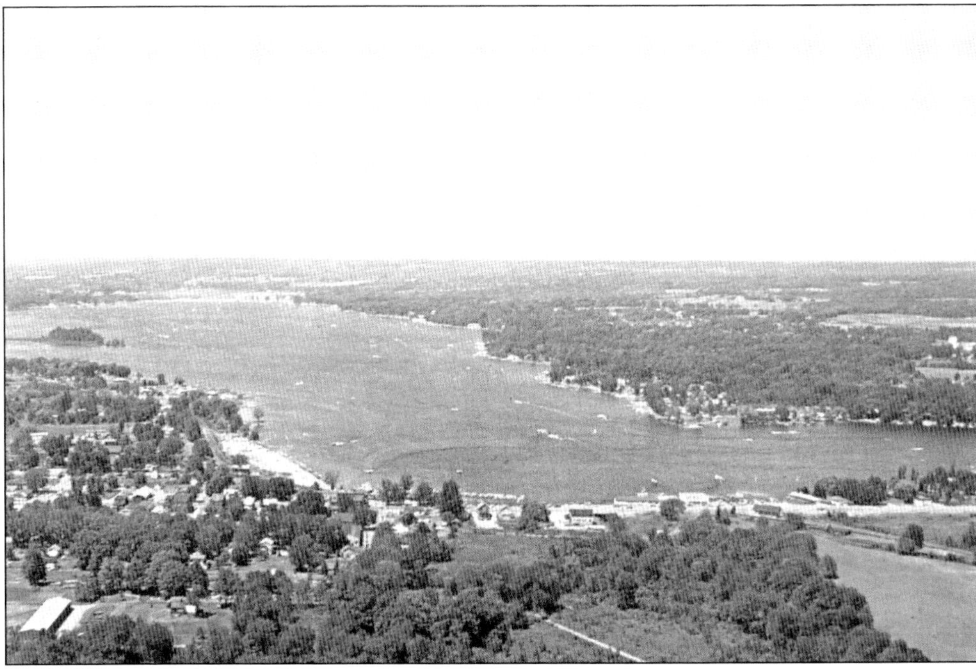

This aerial view of Conneaut Lake, along US 6 and 322 and Route 18, shows the area covered by the state's largest natural lake. The lake covers 929 acres and is 101 feet deep in some places. It continues to be a source of enjoyment for those who love water sports of all kinds.

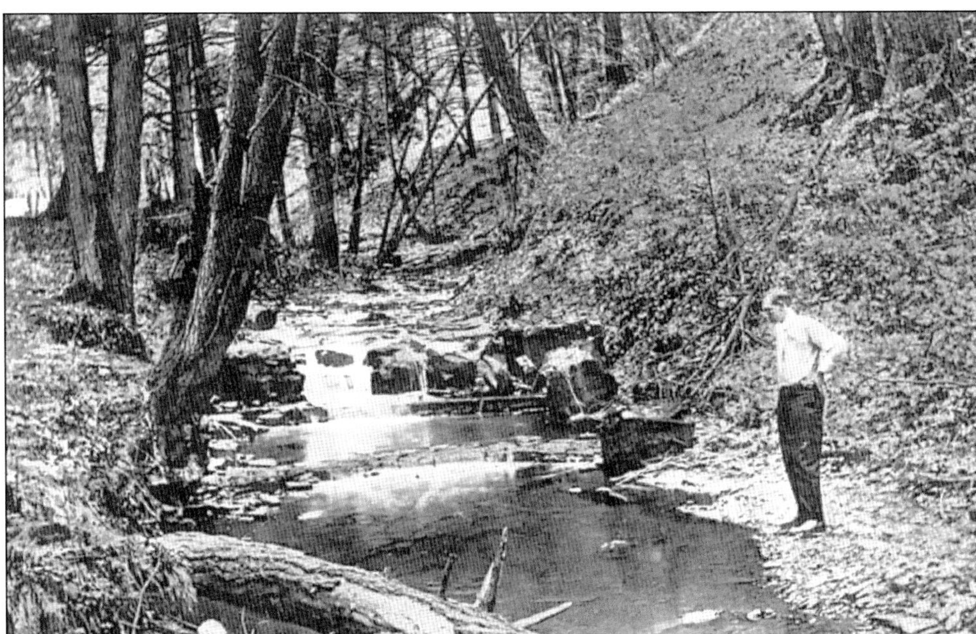

This early-1900s postcard shows a man checking the water at the head of the inlet at Conneaut Lake. The inlet was used by small crafts for fishing, hunting, or pleasure boating. (PHM.)

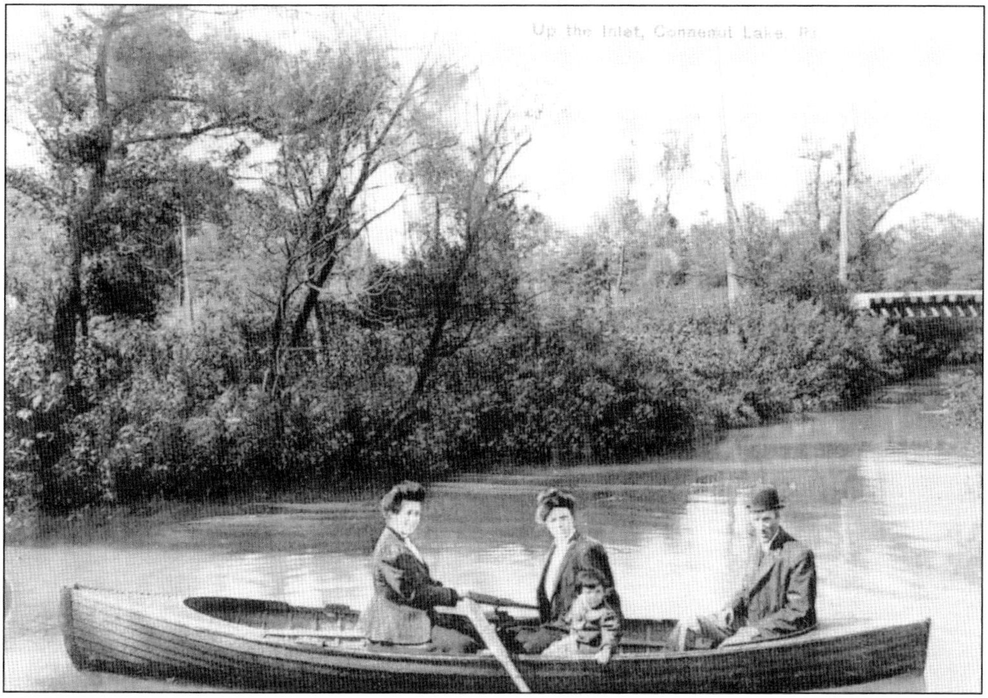

The attire worn by the people in this postcard is much different than the standards of dress a century later. Women are wearing skirts, blouses, and jackets while the man is dressed in a suit jacket, trousers, and hat. They are pictured as they canoe up the inlet at Conneaut Lake. (PHM.)

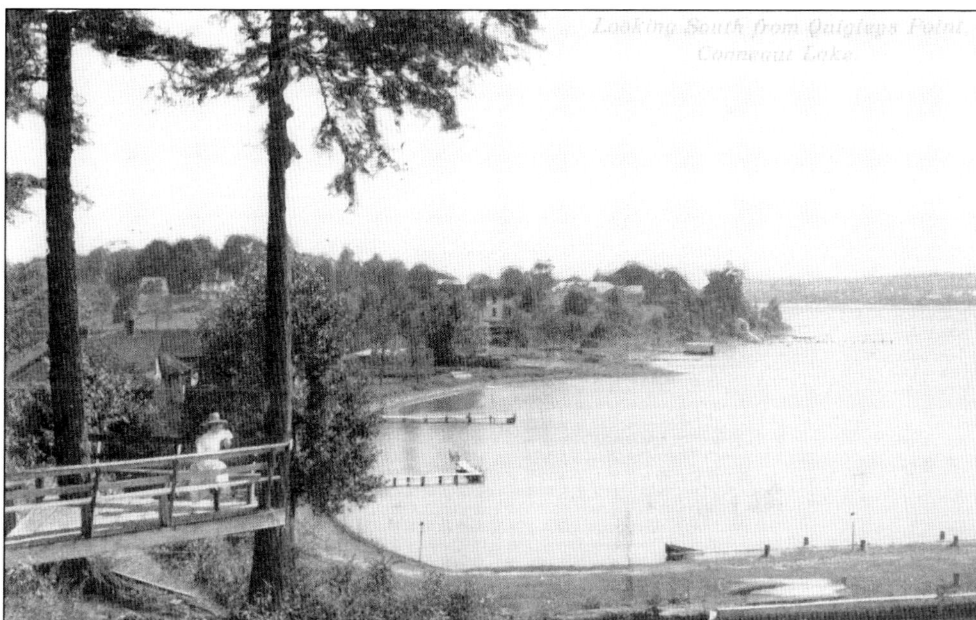

The beauty of Conneaut Lake is evident in this postcard, which faces south from Quigley Point, located on the east side of Conneaut Lake. Brothers James and John Quigley emigrated from Ireland in the late 1700s and settled on the east side of the lake.

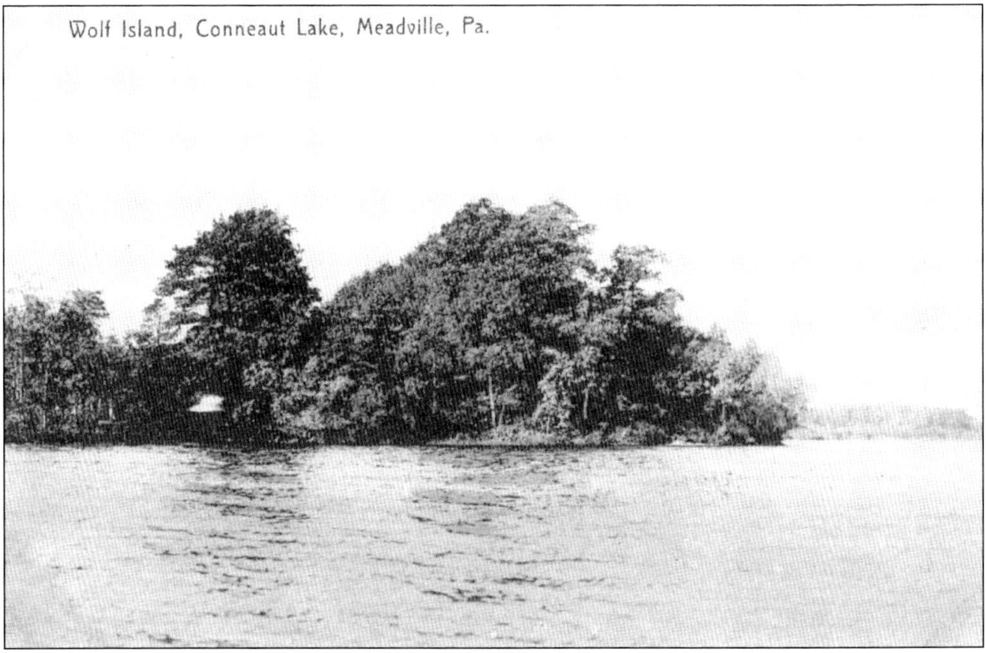

This 1909 postcard shows Wolf Island at the end of a peninsula. For a number of years in the 1800s, it was the solitary estate of a man named Phil Miller. Miller was instrumental in hosting the famed Mark Twain, who visited Conneaut Lake incognito for two weeks.

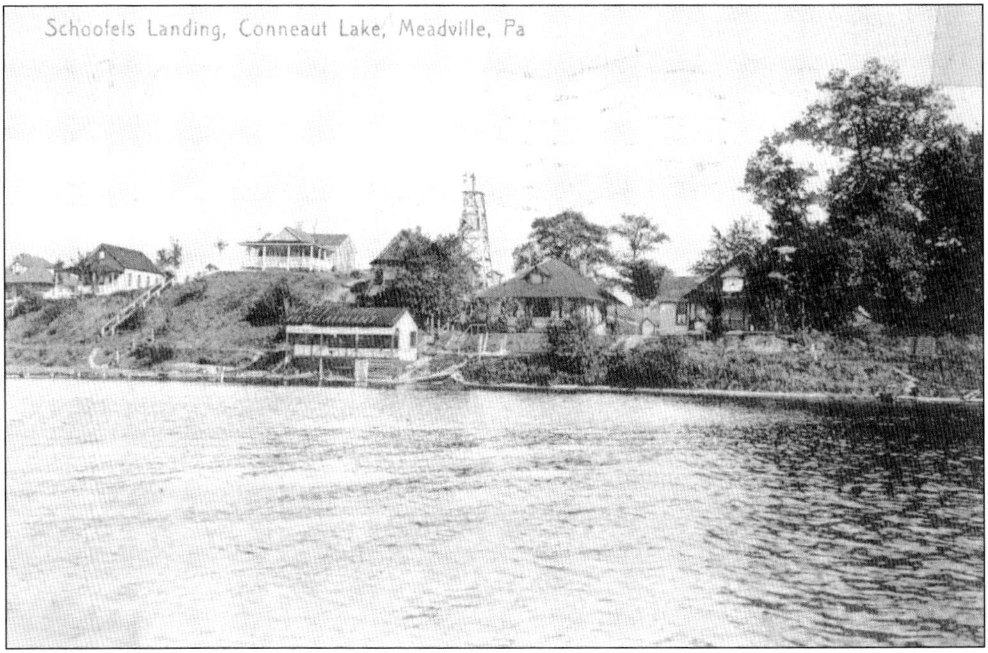

Schoofels Landing, located a short distance north from Shady Avenue on the east side of Conneaut Lake, is the subject of this 1909 postcard. Stairs on the left side allow visitors to access cottages.

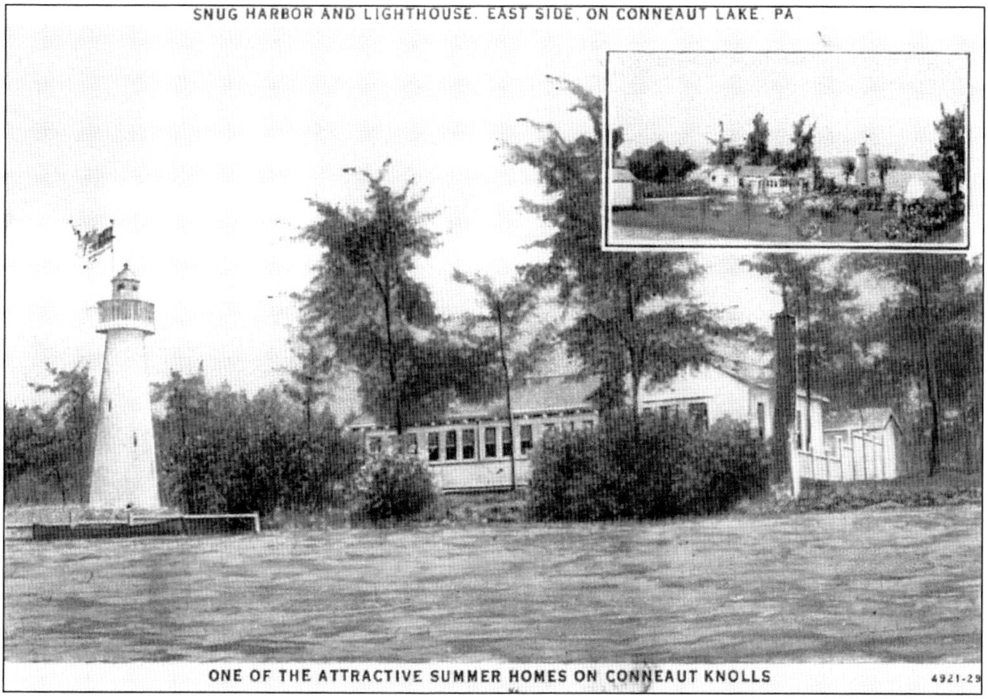

Snug Harbor and the lighthouse on the east side are well-known landmarks in the Conneaut Lake area. E.H. Shartle constructed the cottage, named Snug Harbor, in 1921 and also the lighthouse in 1924. Snug Harbor was described as a pleasant, cozy summer home on the east side of the lake.

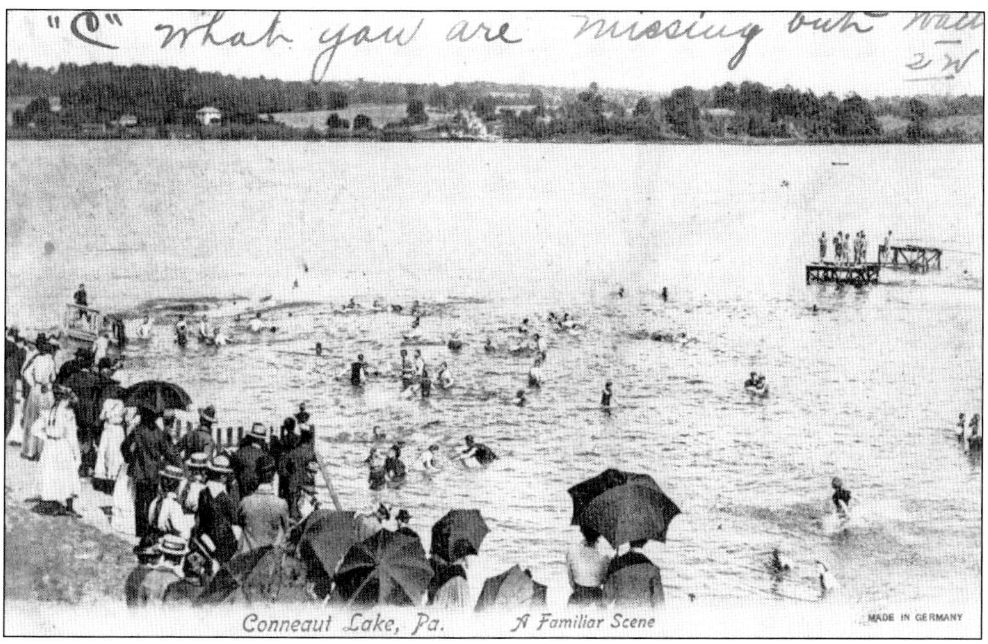

This 1906 postcard shows visitors enjoying swimming at Conneaut Lake, while others on the shore hold parasols to block the sun. Note the inscription, "C what you are missing," at the top of the postcard.

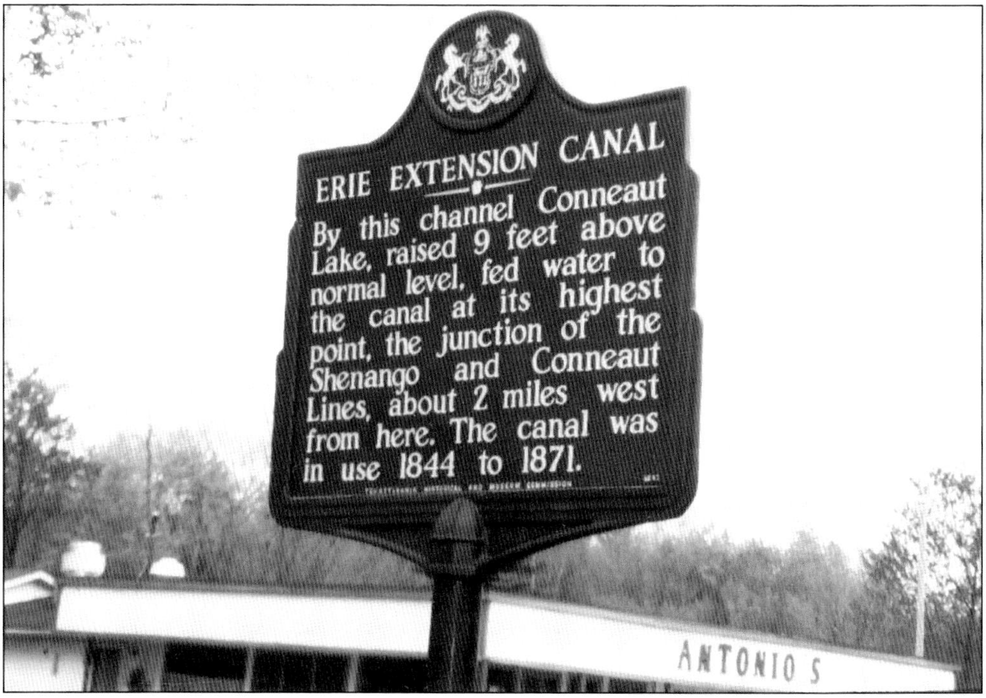

This state historical marker notes the location of the Erie Extension Canal, which was in use from 1844 to 1871. Located on Route 618, on the west side of Conneaut Lake, the inscription states that the channel raised the lake nine feet above normal level.

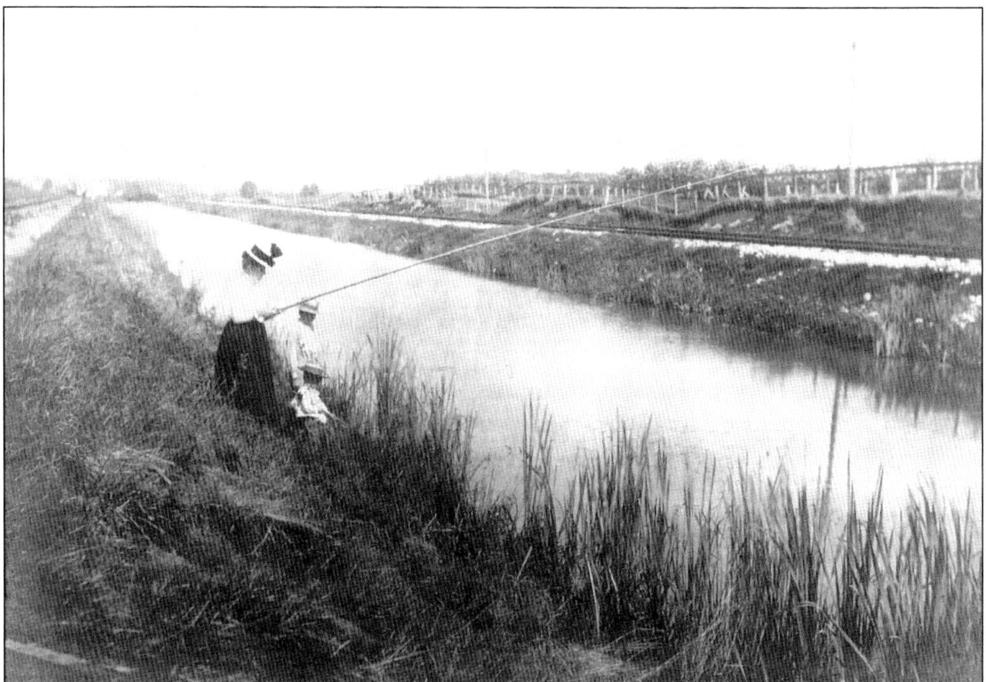

A family in the mid-1800s fishes from the towpath of the Erie Extension Canal near Conneaut Lake. Also seen at the top of the photograph is the railroad line.

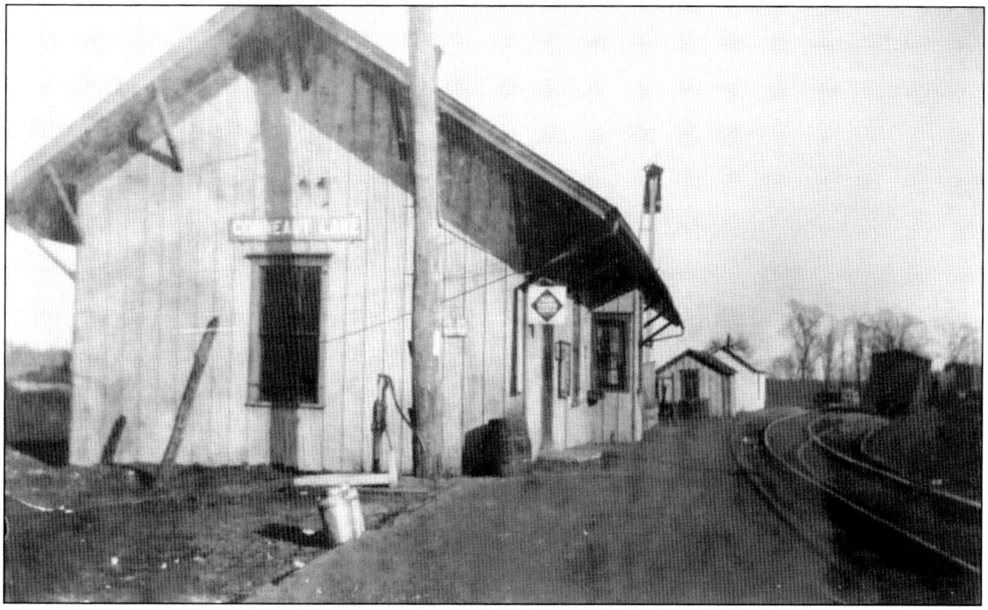

This 1881 photograph shows the Conneaut Lake Railroad Station, located at the south end of town. According to Bronson Luty in *The Lake as It Was*, the depot was described in the *Crawford Journal* as handsome. It contained three rooms: a waiting room, a ticket room, and a freight room.

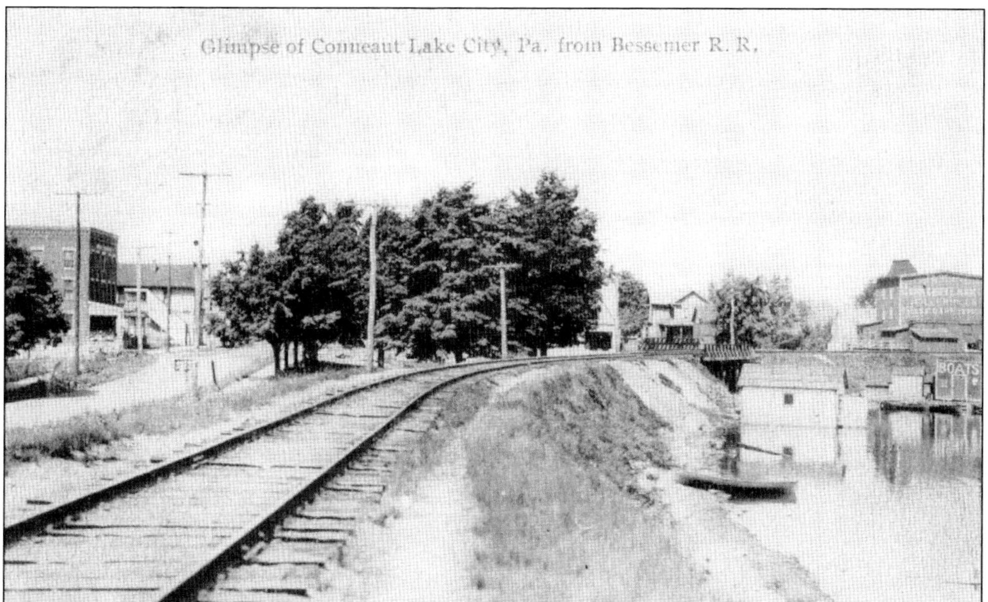

A glimpse of Conneaut Lake, from the Bessemer & Lake Erie Railroad, is seen in this 1915 postcard. Reports from 1881 show the first passenger trains in Evansburg began running October 4, 1881, and passengers were transported from Meadville to Linesville, starting with express runs at 8:00 a.m. and stopping at Evansburg at 8:40 a.m.

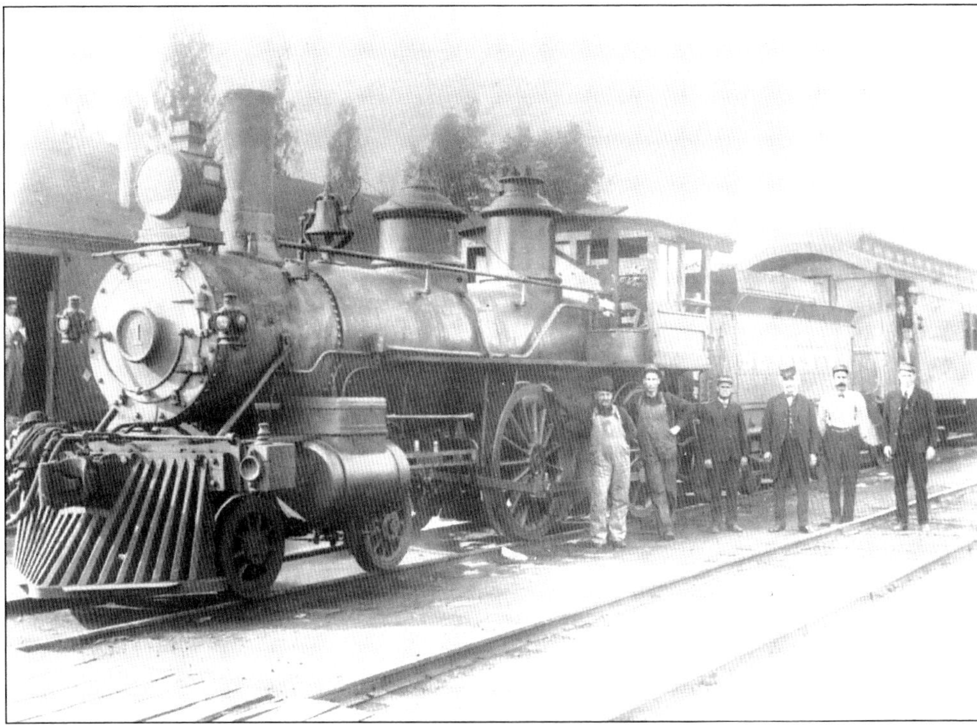

In the early 1900s, this six-man crew operated the Bessemer & Lake Erie Railroad in Meadville, prior to a run to Conneaut Lake. The last regularly scheduled train to Conneaut Lake was in 1955. (LFC.)

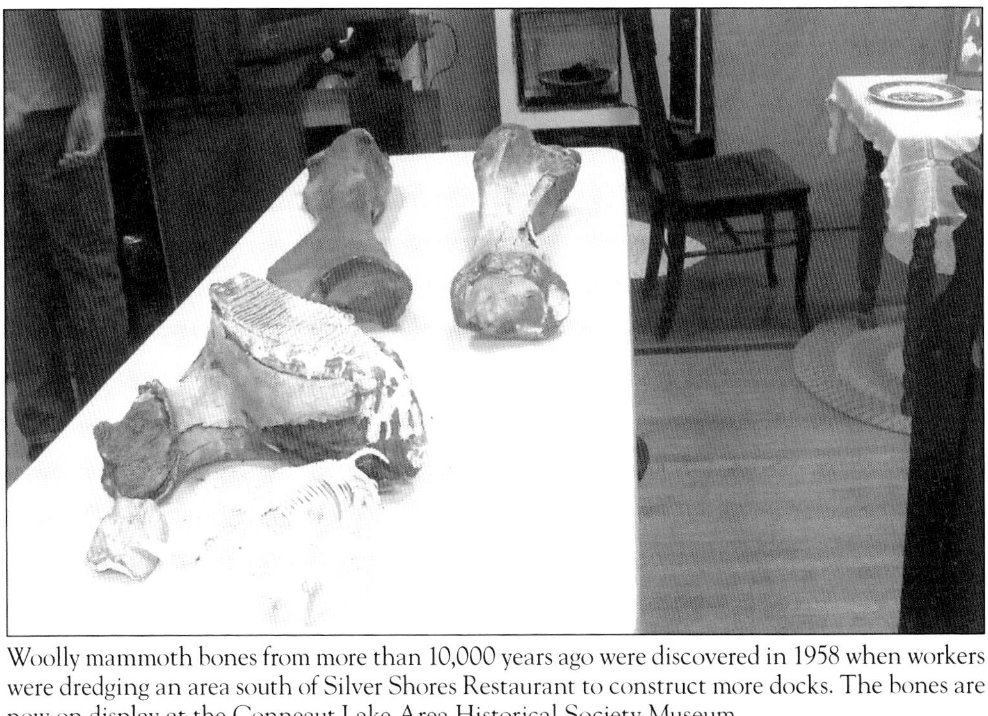

Woolly mammoth bones from more than 10,000 years ago were discovered in 1958 when workers were dredging an area south of Silver Shores Restaurant to construct more docks. The bones are now on display at the Conneaut Lake Area Historical Society Museum.

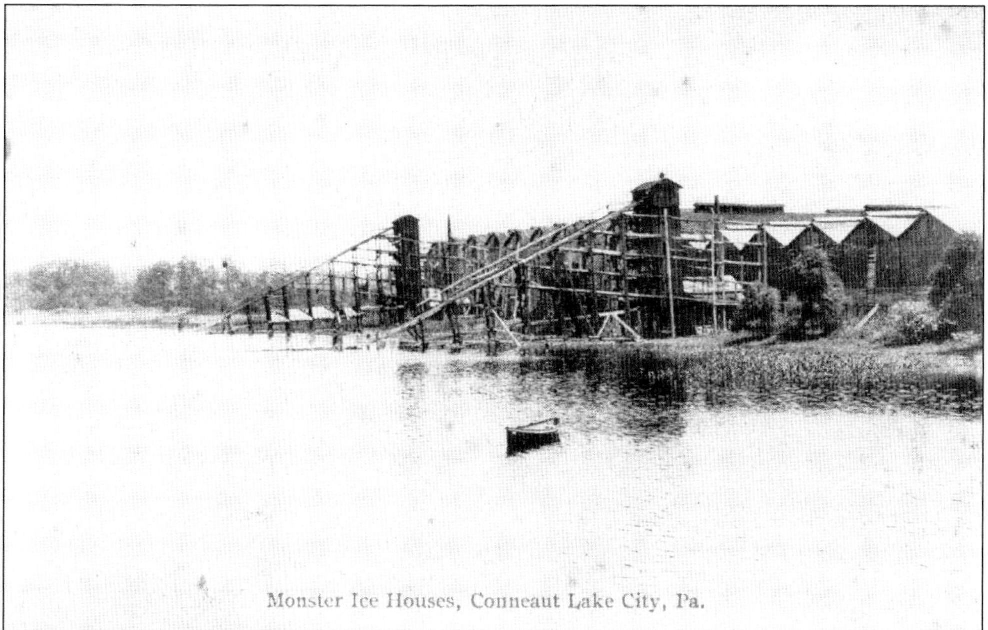

Monster icehouses, located on the south end of Conneaut Lake, were erected by the Conneaut Lake Ice Co. in 1880. They were used to store the ice harvested from the lake before it was shipped via train to Pittsburgh and other cities. The buildings were torn down in the early 1930s, after refrigeration was made available. (BH.)

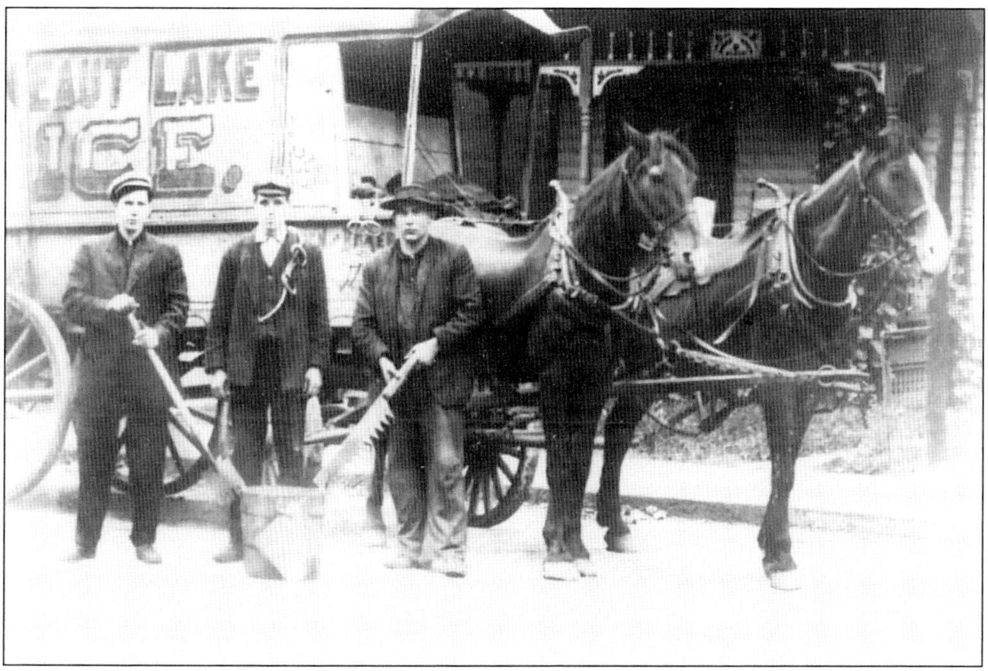

This 1910 photograph shows employees of the Conneaut Lake Ice Co. with their saws, before delivering the ice. Horses were used to harvest the ice from Conneaut Lake. The icehouses were located immediately south of where Silver Shores Restaurant now stands. (CHJ.)

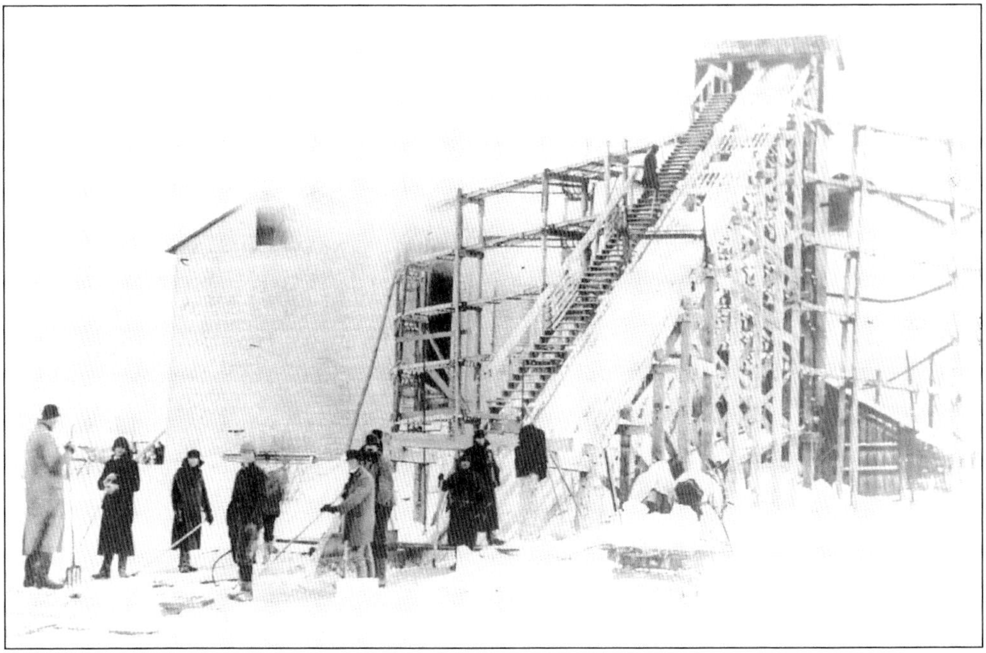

Some of the 200 employees of the Conneaut Lake Ice Co. are shown as they prepare to put the ice harvested from the lake onto a conveyor belt to store in the icehouses in the early 1900s. Employees used two-man saws to cut blocks of ice before removing them from the lake and transporting them to the icehouses for storage. (BH.)

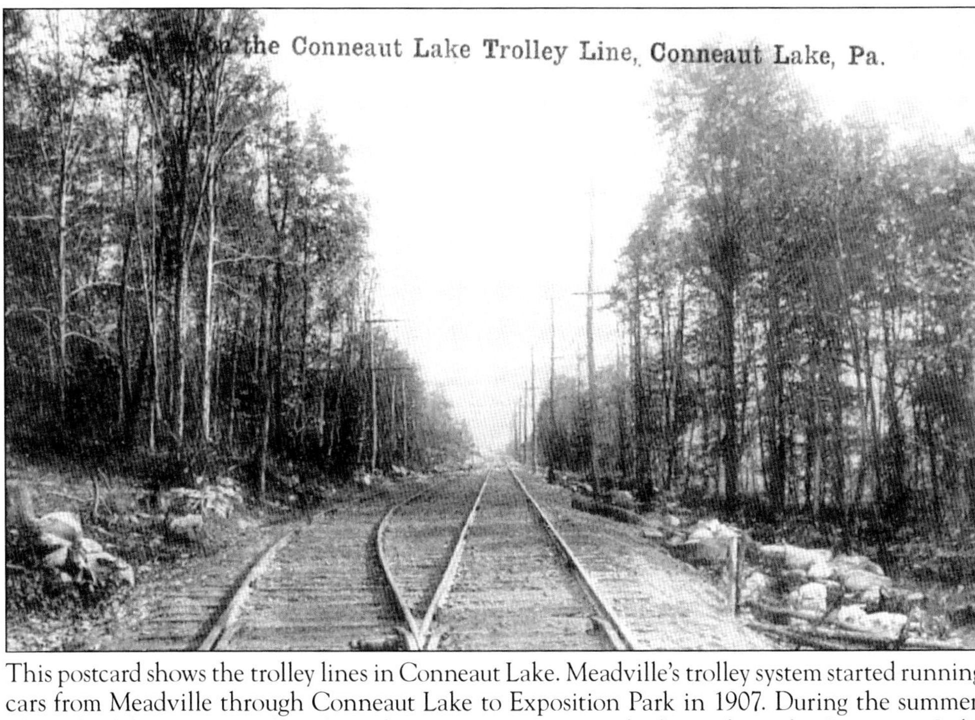

This postcard shows the trolley lines in Conneaut Lake. Meadville's trolley system started running cars from Meadville through Conneaut Lake to Exposition Park in 1907. During the summer, when the lake was open (not frozen), passengers were met by boats from the Conneaut Lake Navigation Company until midnight at the park. (LFC.)

Two

BUSINESSES

Gristmills, pliers, ice-cream parlors, lumber, and purebred horses all played a major role in the development of Conneaut Lake. Many of the businesses in the early years of the borough involved those designed to meet needs of its residents, such as gristmills, physicians, carpenters, cobblers, blacksmiths, and boatbuilders.

In 1886, George B. DeArment, a blacksmith, began hand-forging farrier's tools in a small factory in Conneaut Lake. He traveled along the railroad line via wagon, selling his tools. The reputation of the quality of the tools soon spread across the world, and the company received an order for the tools from England's reigning monarch, Edward VII, in 1902. The tool line expanded, and the company needed more space; they moved to Meadville in 1923. Today, the company, now known as Channellock, Inc., is recognized by its trademark blue handles and sells its products all over the world. British soldiers found a pair of Channellock pliers on the beach at Normandy in 1944. The company employs about 400 people in 2012.

Another major business, the Little Missouri Stock Co., came to Conneaut Lake in 1887. The company, owned by Arthur Clarke Huidekoper from the North Dakota Territory, was located one-half mile from the railroad station. They raised and trained Percheron horses, used for pulling loaded wagons. In 1887, Canada-native Fred J. Moss came to Conneaut Lake and opened an ice-cream stand. Along with his brother, he later opened Moss Brothers Lumber Co. Other businesses that started in Conneaut Lake included the Dennis Lumber Company and Associated Contractors, Inc., as well as numerous tool shops. Conneaut Lake also boasted many retail businesses, such as Ralston's Hardware Store and the Harvey Thomas Store, restaurants, service stations, and funeral homes. Infrastructure improvements included a water system in 1910, natural gas lines in 1955, and a sewage system in 1959.

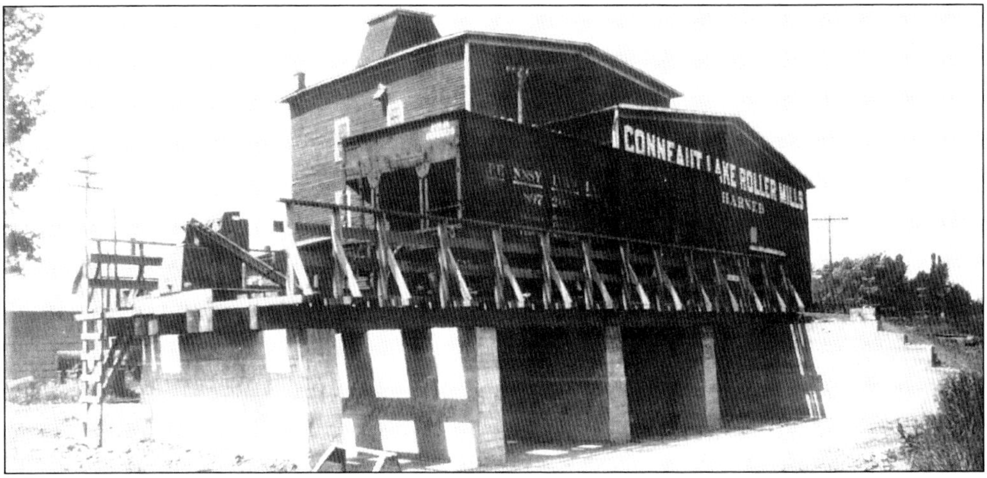

Conneaut Lake Roller Mills, opened by Charles Darrow in 1907, is pictured during the ownership of P.C. Harned. Harned operated a mill in Edinboro at the time Darrow died. Darrow's widow, Rosa, wanted their four daughters to go to Edinboro Normal School. She sold the Conneaut Lake mill to Harned, and she and the Harned family traded homes. She moved to Edinboro, and Harned moved to Conneaut Lake.

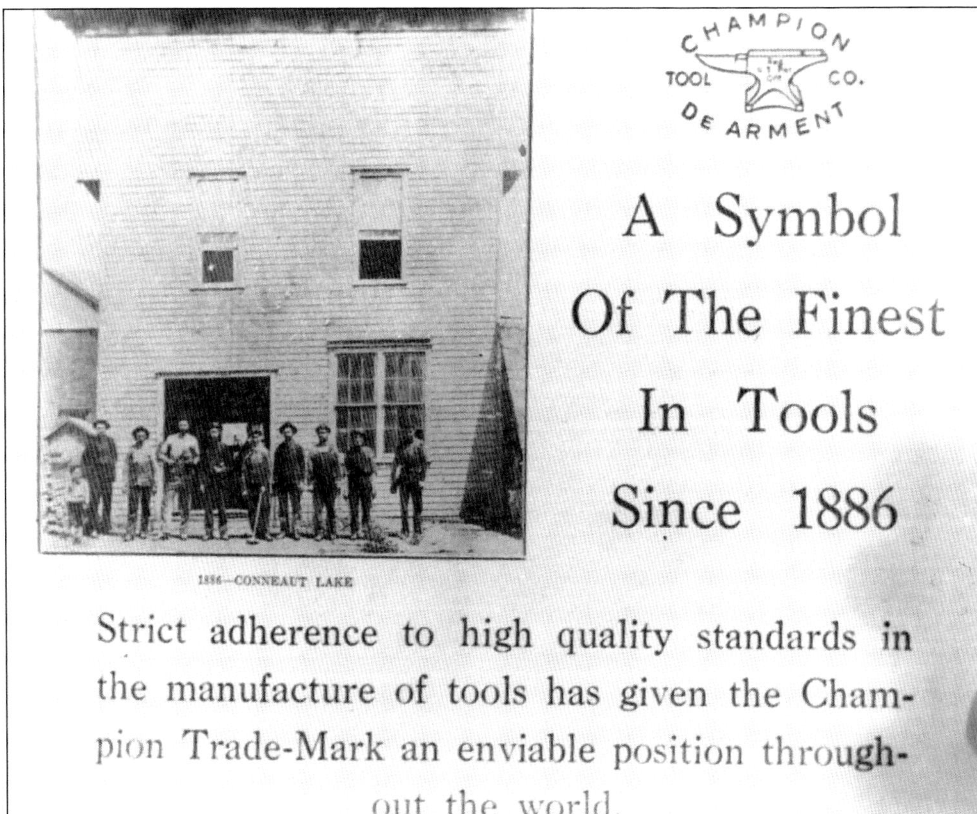

Original employees of the Champion DeArment Tool Company are seen in a building at Conneaut Lake, where the company was founded in 1886. Now known as Channellock, Inc., the company is located in Meadville and now employs about 400 people in 2012.

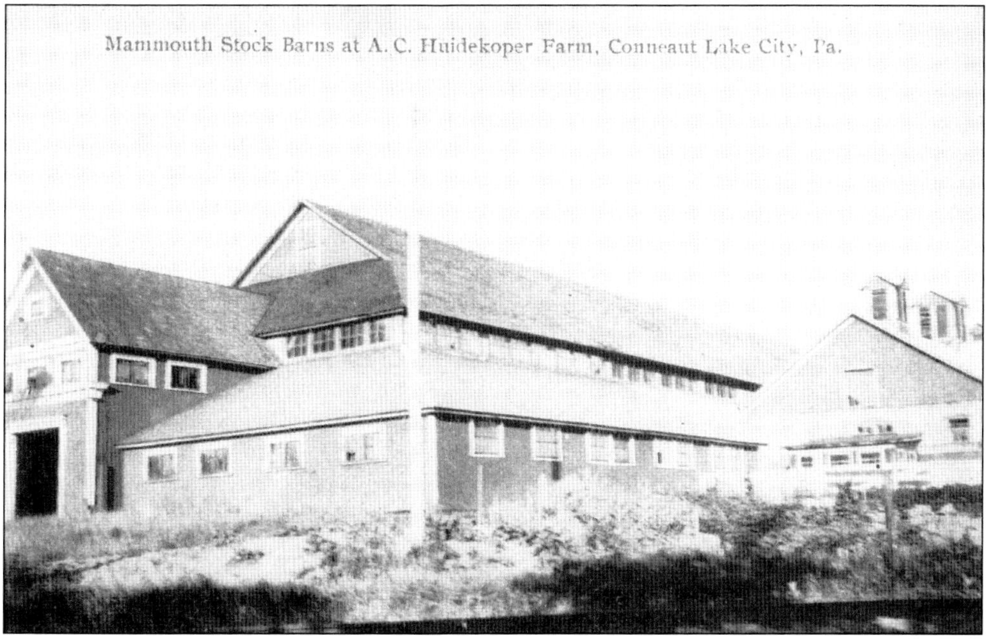

The mammoth barns of the A.C. Huidekoper Stock Farm in Conneaut Lake could be seen for miles around. This barn housed Percheron horses, brought here from the badlands of North Dakota to be bred, trained to draw heavy wagons, and sold.

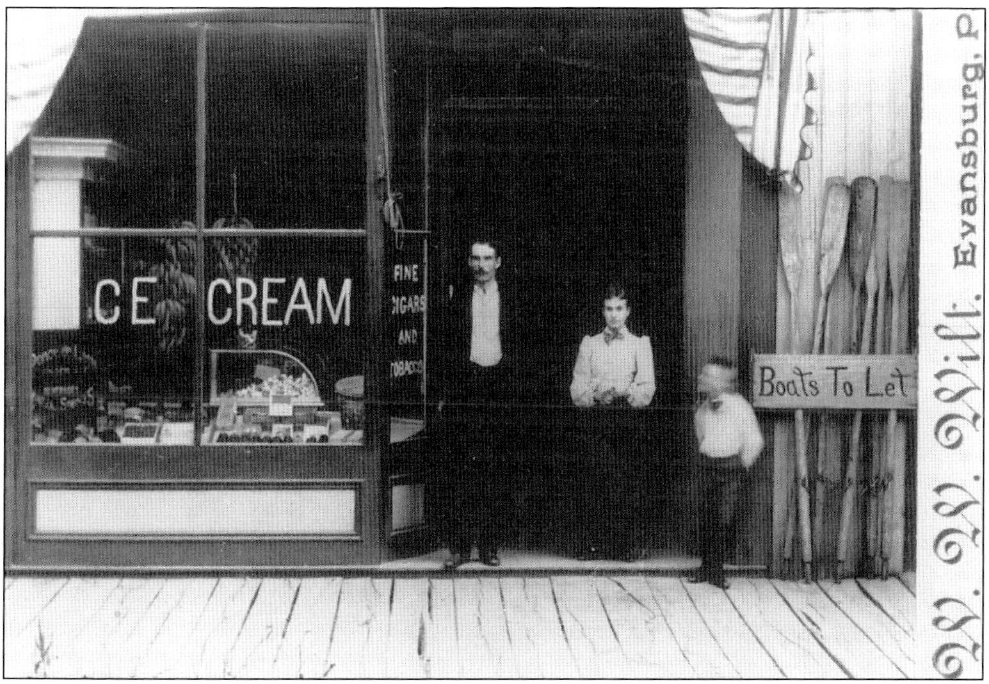

The F.J. Moss family is pictured in front of their ice-cream store in 1887. From left to right are F.J. Moss, Lillian Moss, and Harry Rodgers. (LFC.)

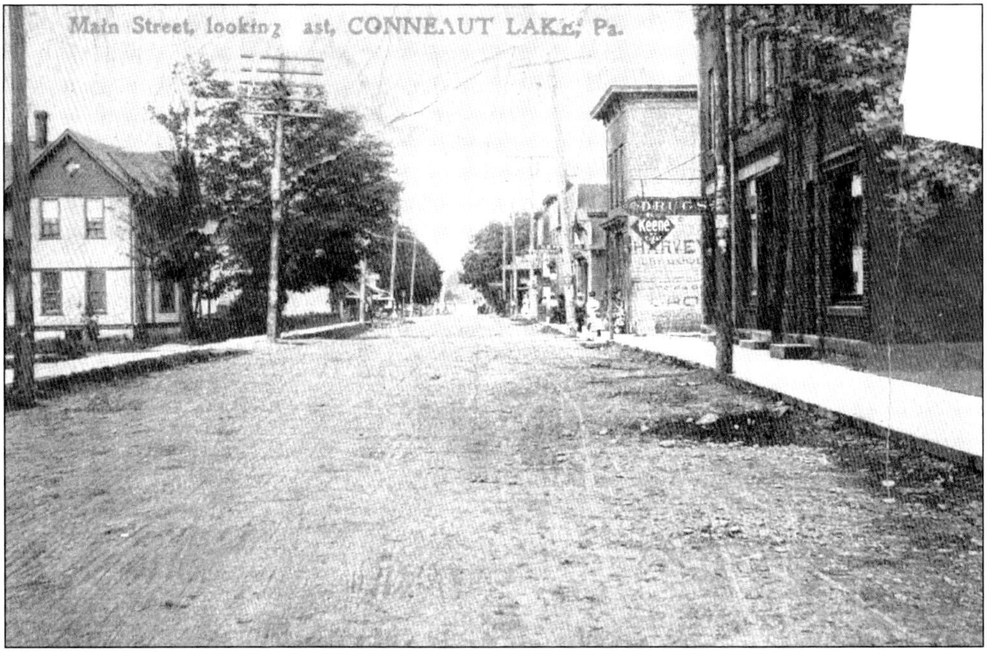

Looking east on Main Street in Conneaut Lake, this 1919 postcard shows the Harvey Thomas Store in the middle of town on the right-hand side of the picture. A drugstore is visible in the first building on the right. The streets are still unpaved.

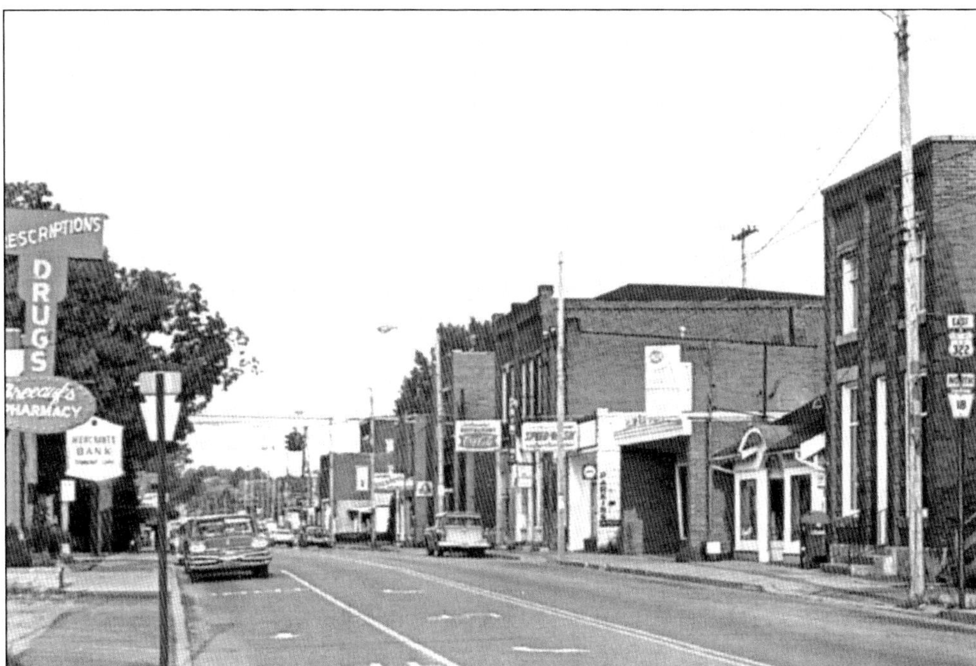

Looking east on Main Street in Conneaut Lake, this 1950s postcard shows Freeauf's Drugstore on the left with Merchant's Bank on the corner. Ralston's Hardware is in the middle of the photograph on the right. The streets are now paved. (LFC.)

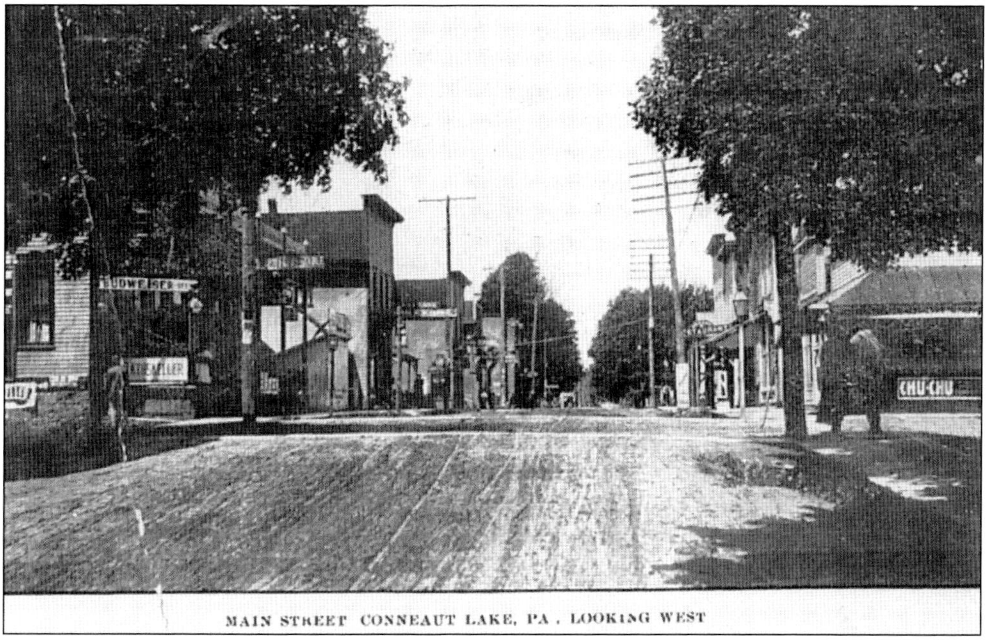

This early-1900s postcard shows Main Street to the west in Conneaut Lake. On the lower left corner is the Taylor House. Take note of the advertising for Budweiser Beer. Conneaut was not a dry town until 1907, when a liquor license was not renewed. (PHM.)

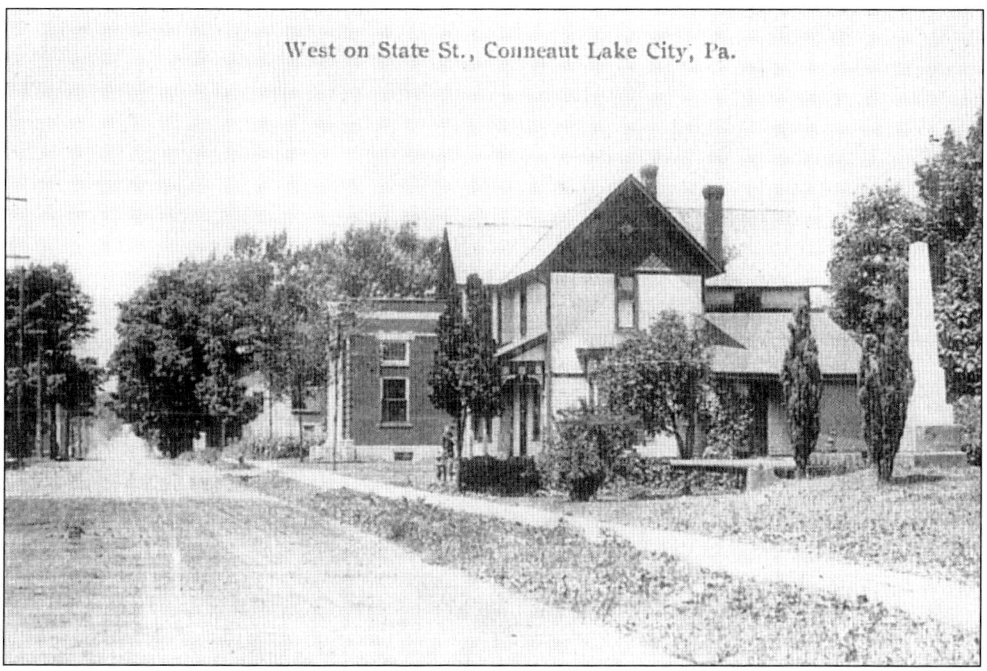

Looking west on State Street, this postcard shows what is now Water Street. On the right side, the monument is dedicated to those who lost their lives in the Civil War. It was one of the first of such monuments in the country. (PHM.)

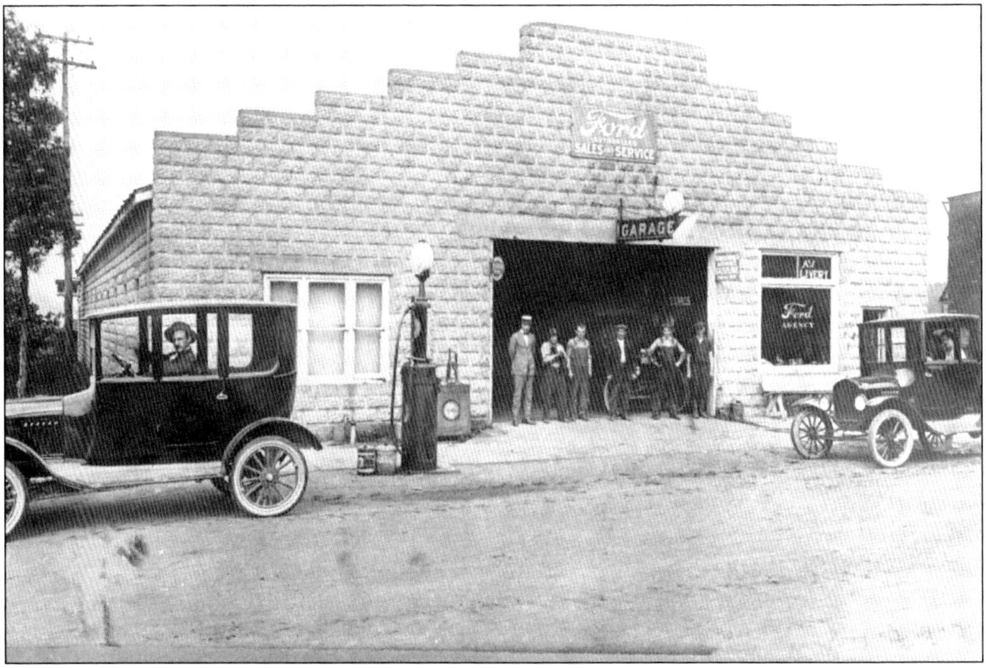

In this 1919 photograph, the Ford Garage is located on what now is Water Street, adjacent to Memorial Park. In 2012, the building was occupied by Hollywood Video and other retail stores. It was previously occupied by Harned's Oil Co.

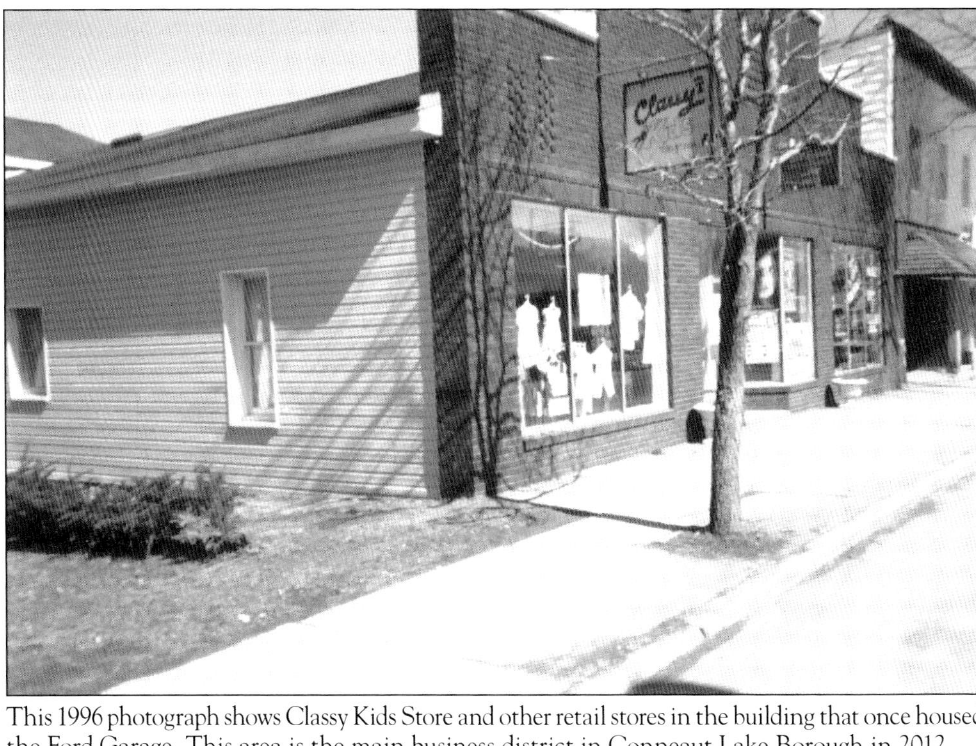

This 1996 photograph shows Classy Kids Store and other retail stores in the building that once housed the Ford Garage. This area is the main business district in Conneaut Lake Borough in 2012.

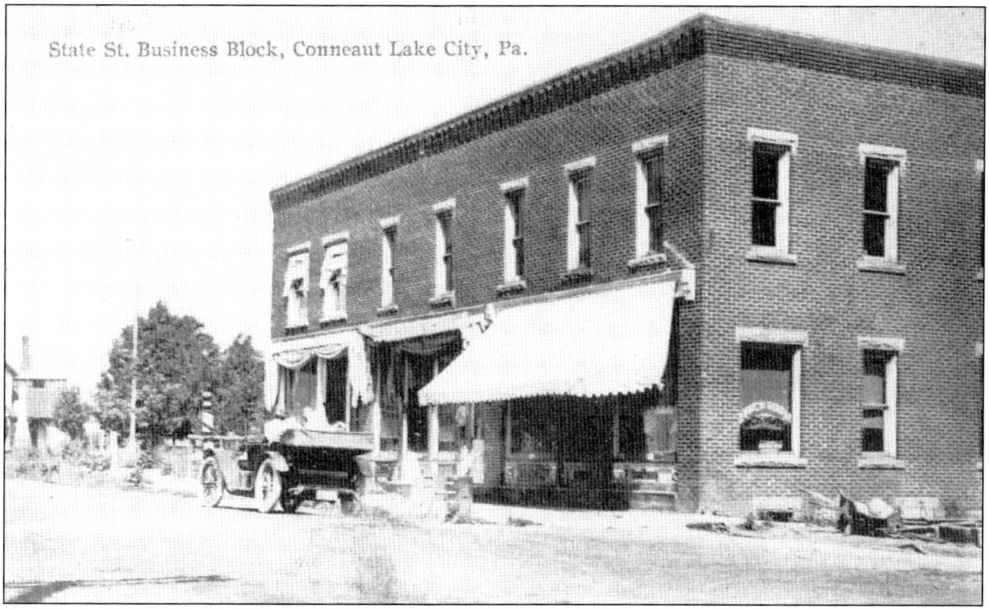

In this 1918 postcard, the business block in downtown Conneaut Lake was located on State and First Streets as one enters town from the east. In the upper right is Memorial Park.

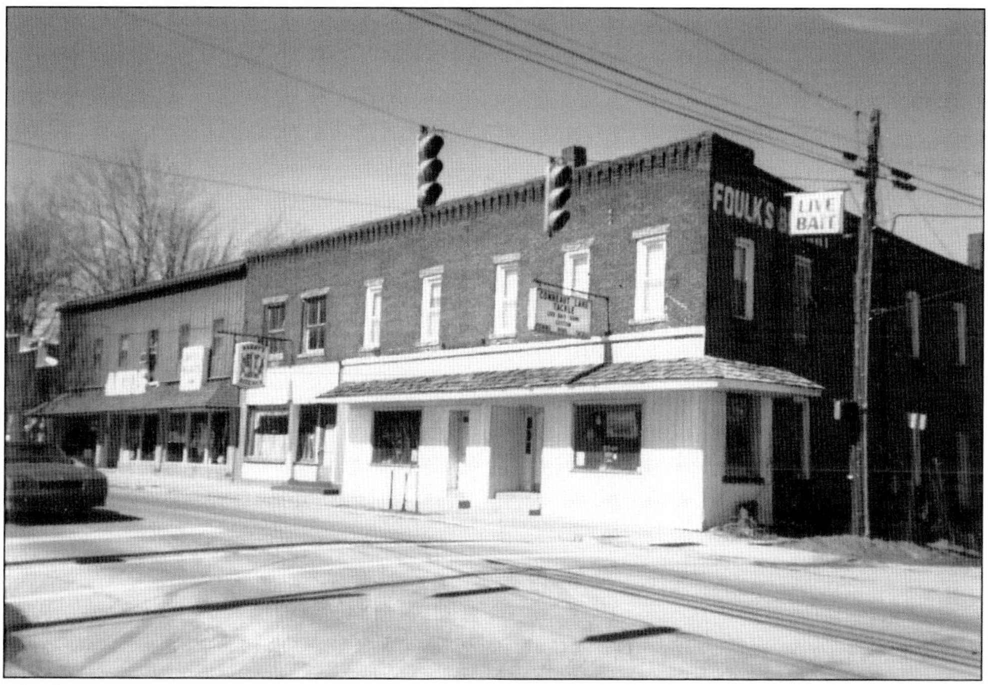

The business block in downtown Conneaut Lake, pictured here in 1996, shows the familiar Foulk's Bakery sign painted on the end of the building. By 1996, however, Foulk's Bakery was closed, and a tackle and bait shop had opened on this site. The bakery sign is still on the side of the building in 2012.

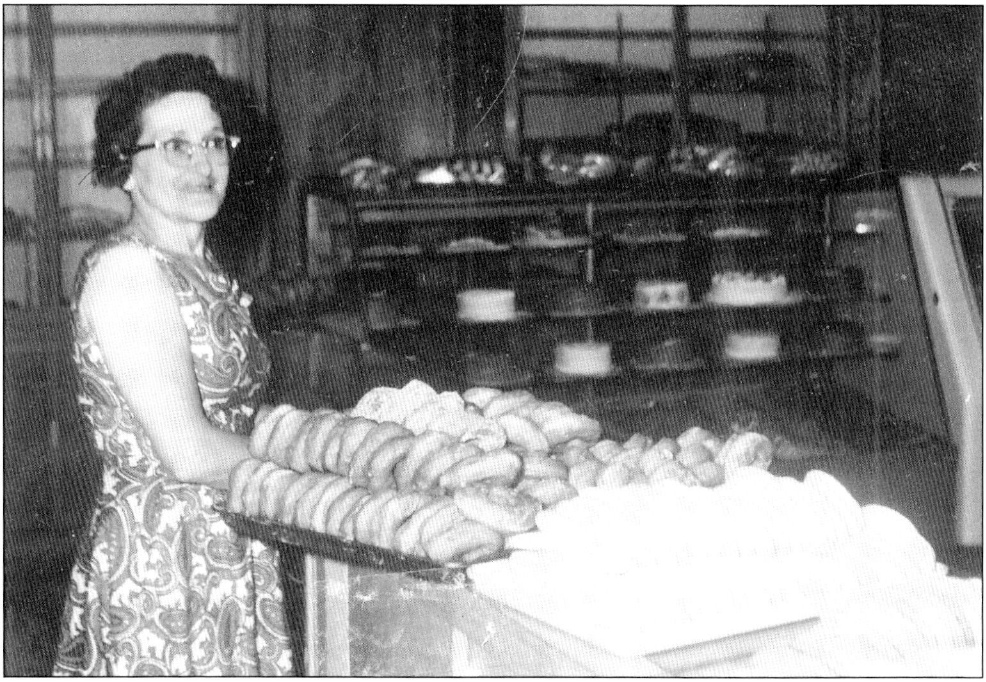

Dorothy Foulk, owner and operator of Foulk's Bakery, stands in front of her baked goods display at her shop in downtown Conneaut Lake. The bakery was located in at least three different places before it closed.

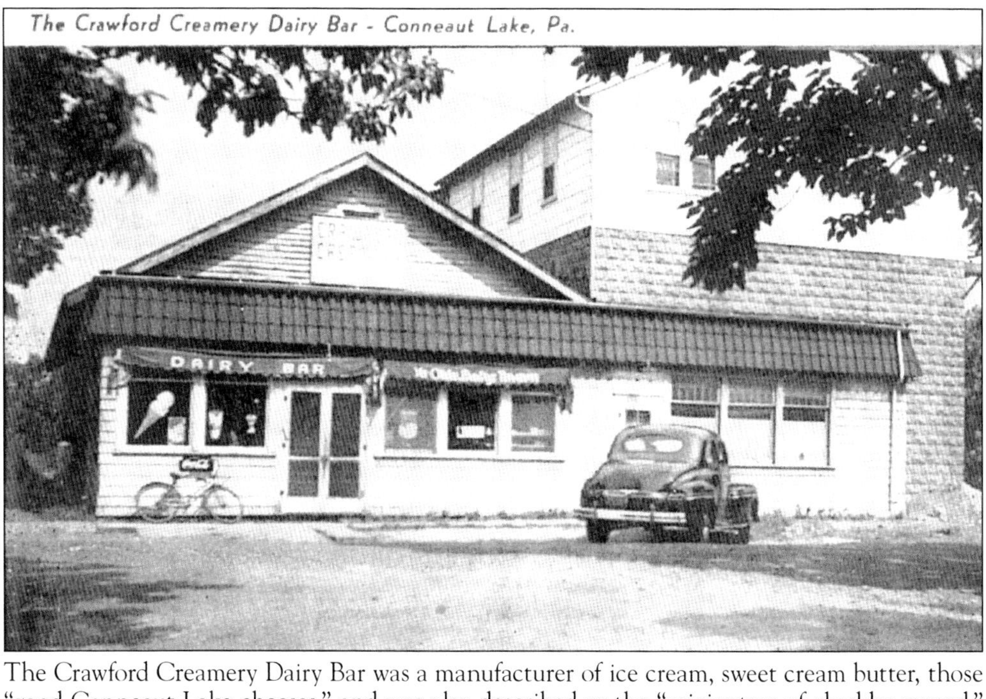

The Crawford Creamery Dairy Bar was a manufacturer of ice cream, sweet cream butter, those "good Conneaut Lake cheeses," and was also described as the "originators of cheddar spread." It was located at 126 South First Street, home to John George's Specialty Supply Co. since 1947. (PHM.)

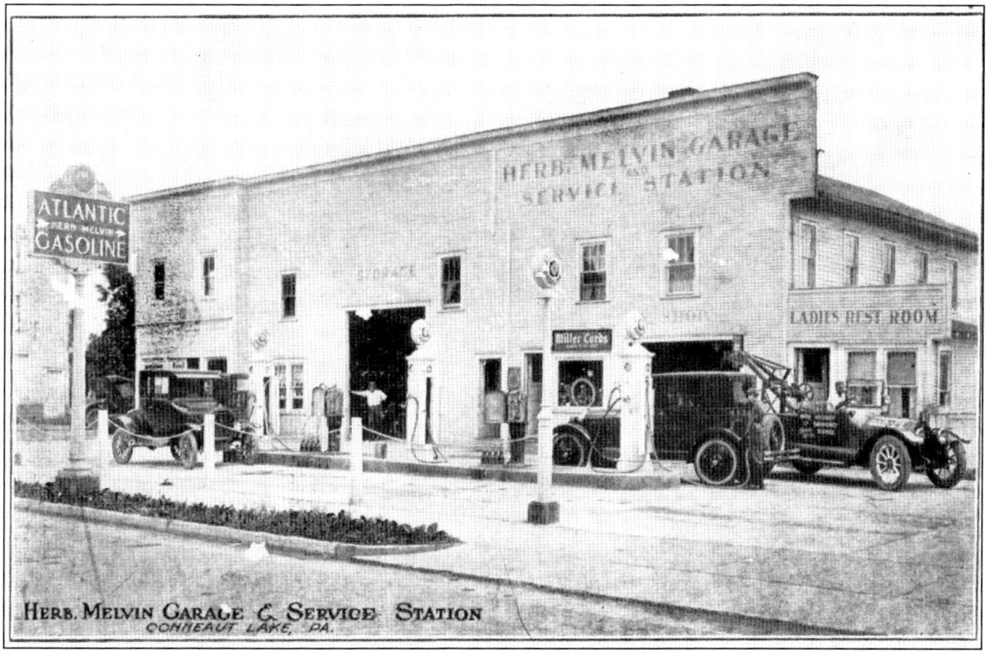

Herb Melvin's Garage and Service Station appears in this early-1900s postcard. The service station included a bakery and restaurant. Located in the center of Conneaut Lake, the building was later sold to Virgil Kean and became Kean's Garage. Note the gas tanks in the center island.

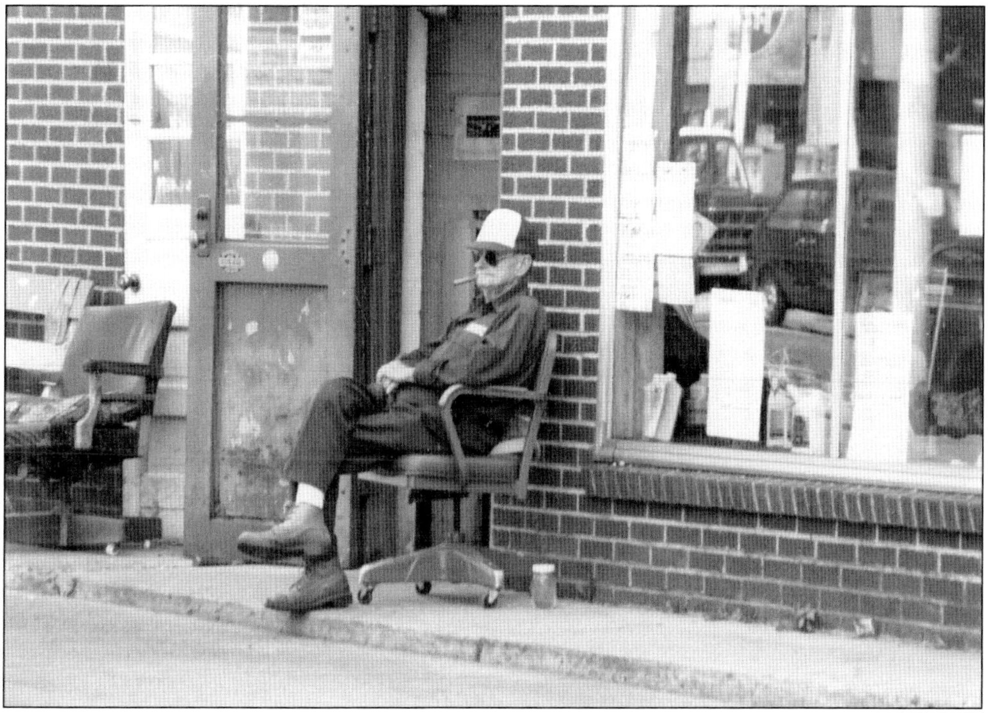
Virgil Kean, with his familiar cigar, sits in front of his garage and service station in the 1980s. Kean's was a popular meeting place for men to spend the day discussing current events and solving the world's problems. Kean retired in 1987, and the garage was sold to Sheetz for its new store.

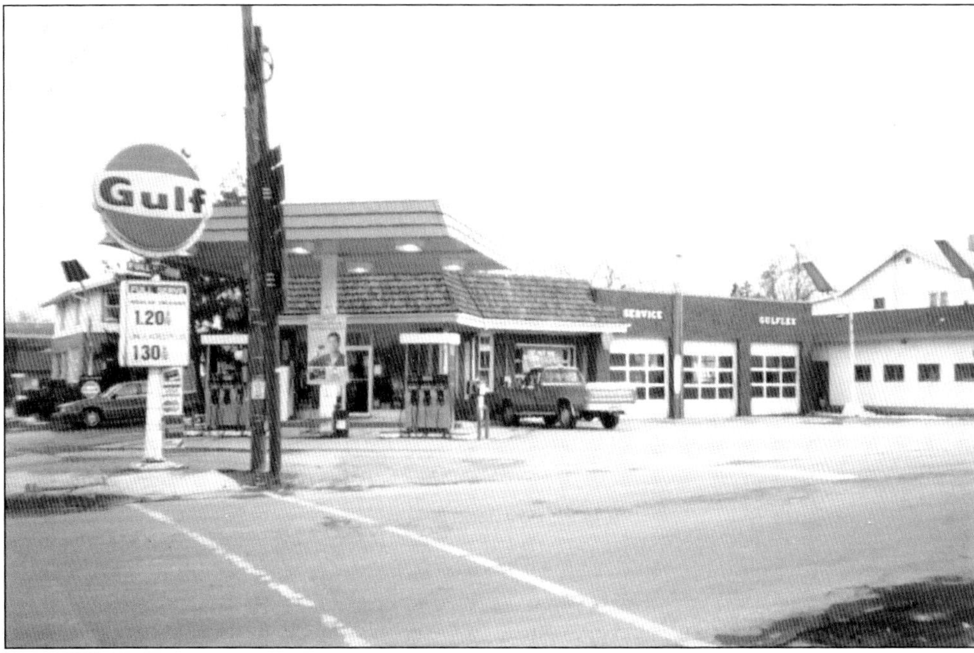

The Gulf Station on the corner of Water Street and US 322 is pictured in 1996, when the price of gasoline was $1.20 a gallon. It was owned and operated by Walter Lasch before he moved his business to the corner of Third and Water Streets. It later moved to the east side. The Gulf Station was then owned and operated by Ernie Niederriter. It since has been torn down.

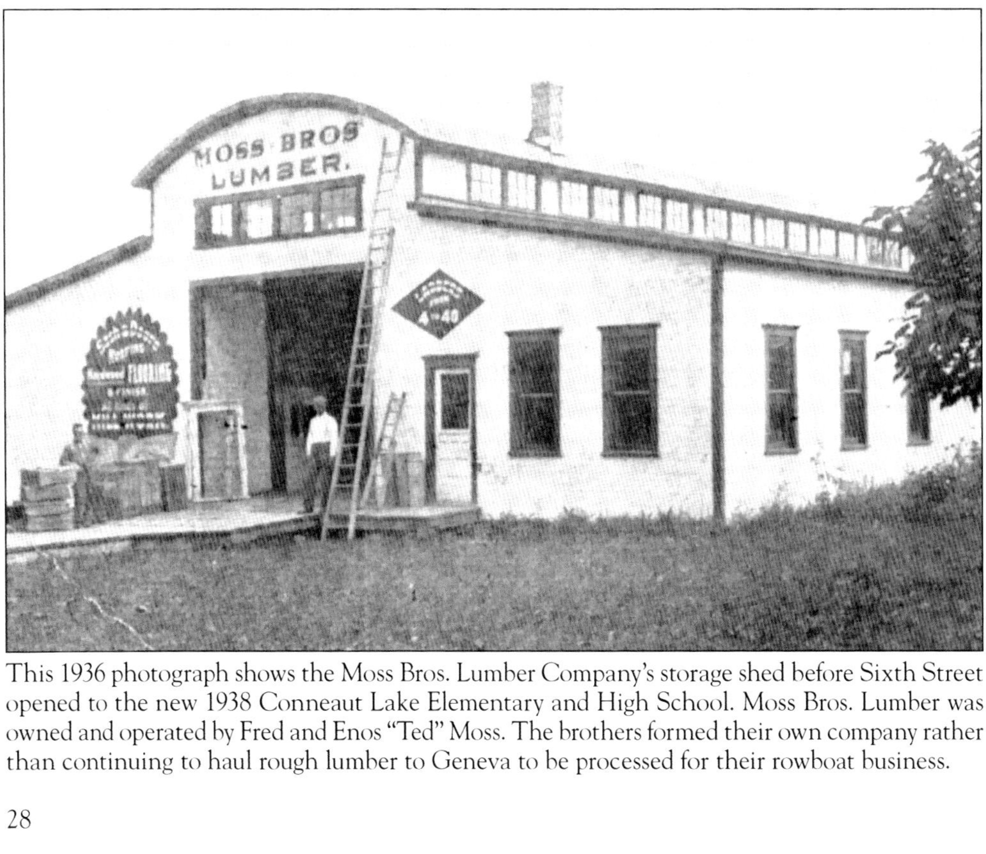

This 1936 photograph shows the Moss Bros. Lumber Company's storage shed before Sixth Street opened to the new 1938 Conneaut Lake Elementary and High School. Moss Bros. Lumber was owned and operated by Fred and Enos "Ted" Moss. The brothers formed their own company rather than continuing to haul rough lumber to Geneva to be processed for their rowboat business.

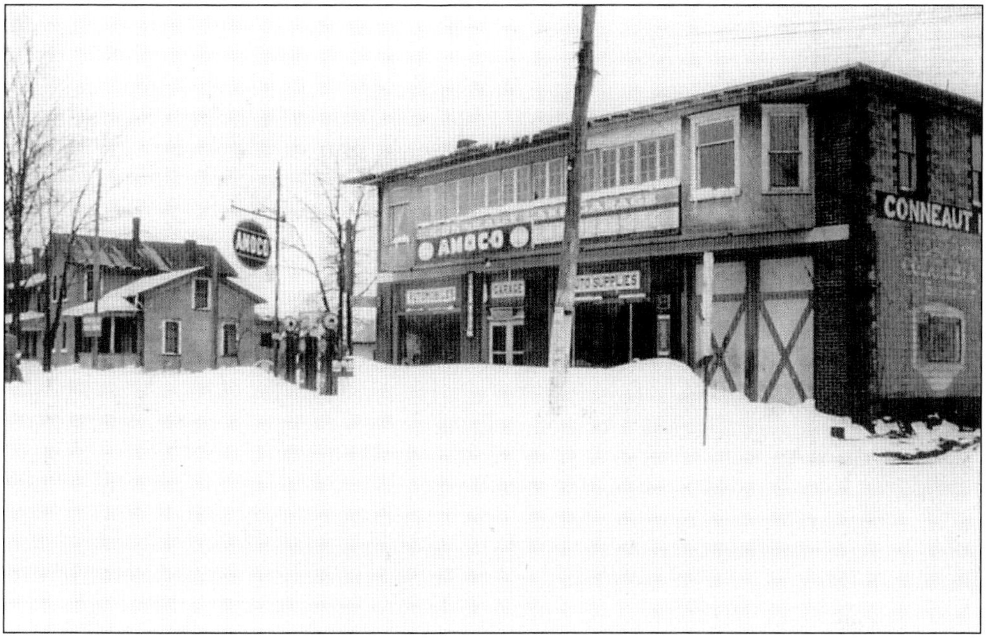

Allen's Tractor Sales, owned and operated by Everett Allen, was located on the northeast corner of Fourth and Water Streets. This 1960s photograph also shows Dillon's Grocery. The building had two rental apartments on the second floor. It was purchased by Conneaut Lake Tractor and Equipment in 1960 and was later torn down. (CHJ.)

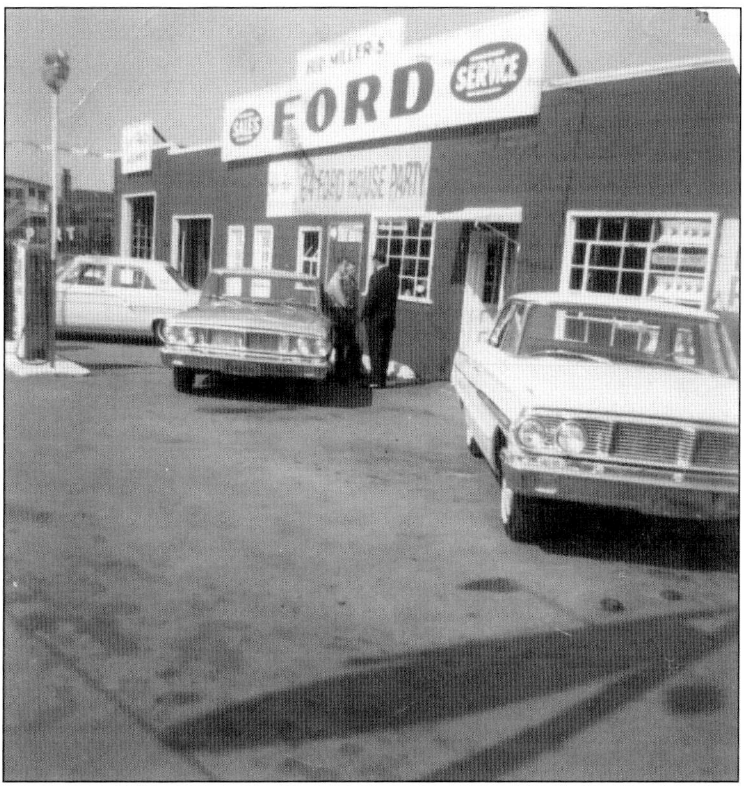

This 1967 photograph shows Bud Miller's Ford Agency, owned and operated by Bud Miller. It was located on Water Street and was previously owned by Ray Lewis. The agency moved its operation to a newer and larger building near the corner of old Route 18 and US 322 in 1968. It now is known as Lakeview Ford.

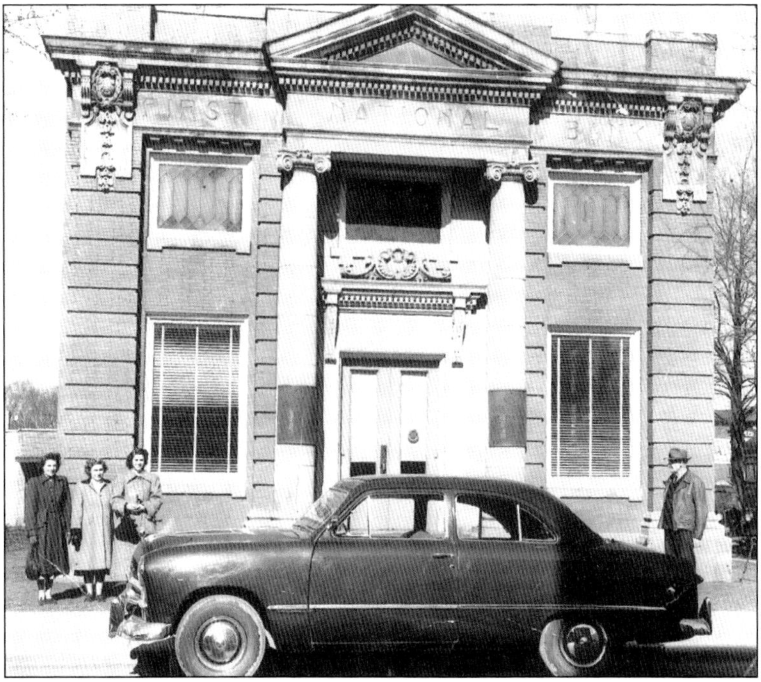

The First National Bank, shown in this 1950s photograph, was located at the corner of Second and Water Streets. Note the plaques on the front pillars, inscribed with names of soldiers from the Conneaut Lake area who died in World War II. This building houses Marquette Savings Bank in 2012. The First National Bank has moved to the corner of Third and Water Streets. (HLF.)

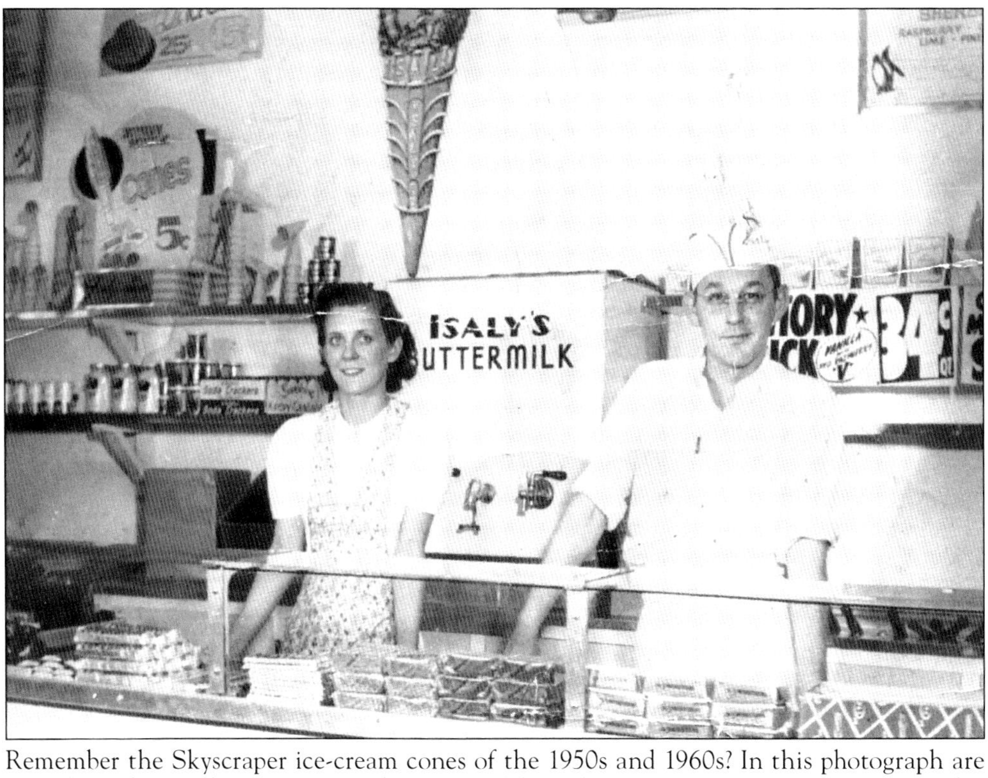

Remember the Skyscraper ice-cream cones of the 1950s and 1960s? In this photograph are Dorothy and Jim Gilmore, owner and operator of the Isaly's Store in downtown Conneaut Lake, the popular hangout where the cones were sold. Some cones cost 5¢. Milk, according to the sign, sold for 34¢ a quart.

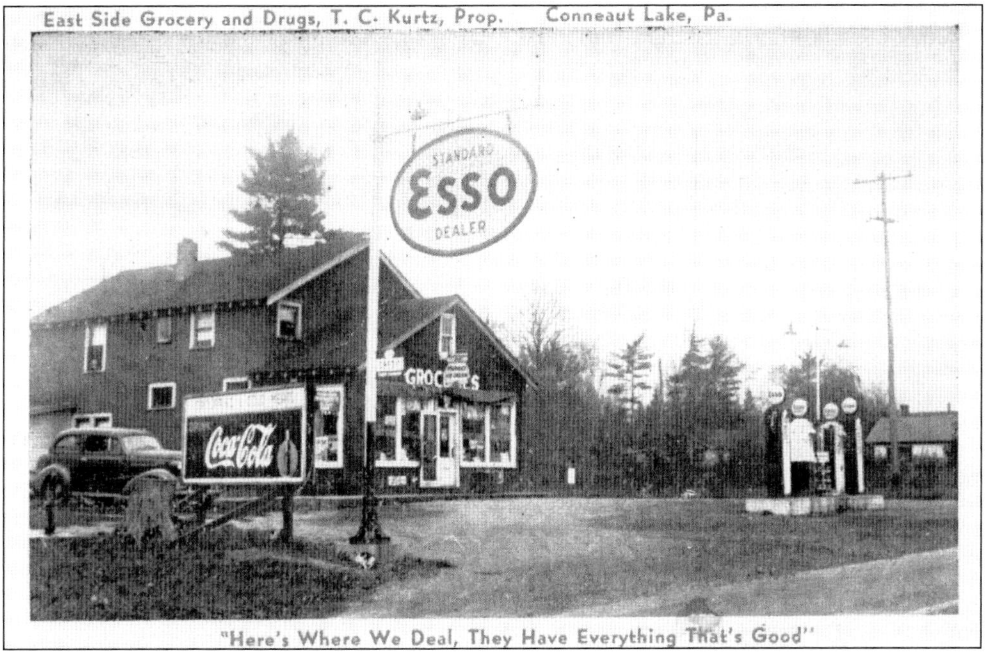

T.C. Kurtz was proprietor of this East Side Grocery and Drugstore, shown in this 1943 postcard. The inscription on the postcard reads, "Here's Where We Deal. They Have Everything That's Good." Kurtz was an Esso dealer at the station located not far from the intersection of Route 18 and US 322.

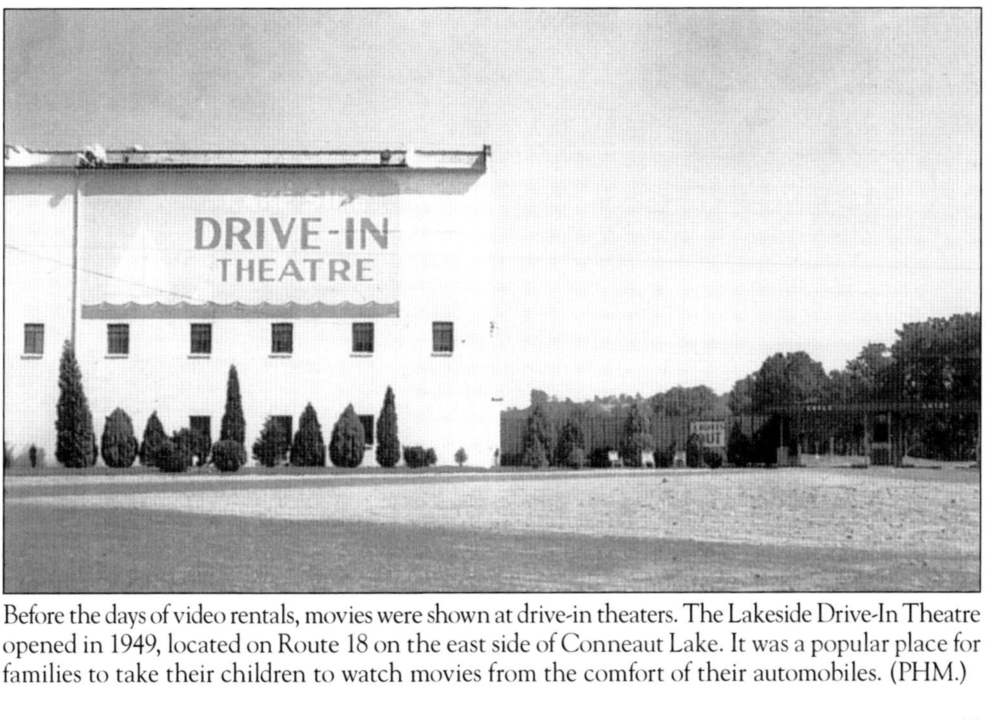

Before the days of video rentals, movies were shown at drive-in theaters. The Lakeside Drive-In Theatre opened in 1949, located on Route 18 on the east side of Conneaut Lake. It was a popular place for families to take their children to watch movies from the comfort of their automobiles. (PHM.)

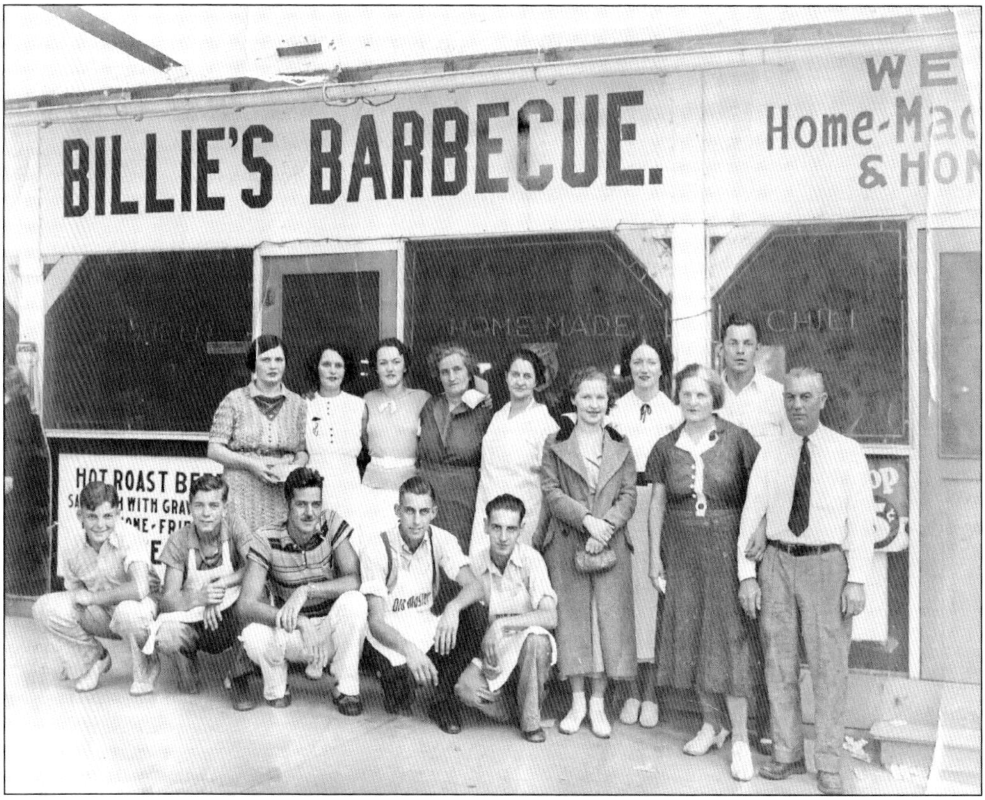

Employees and guests of Billie's Barbecue, located on the east side of Conneaut Lake, posed for this photograph in the 1940s. Although apparently named for its barbecues, the popular restaurant also featured hot roast beef sandwiches, spaghetti, and chili, according to the signs.

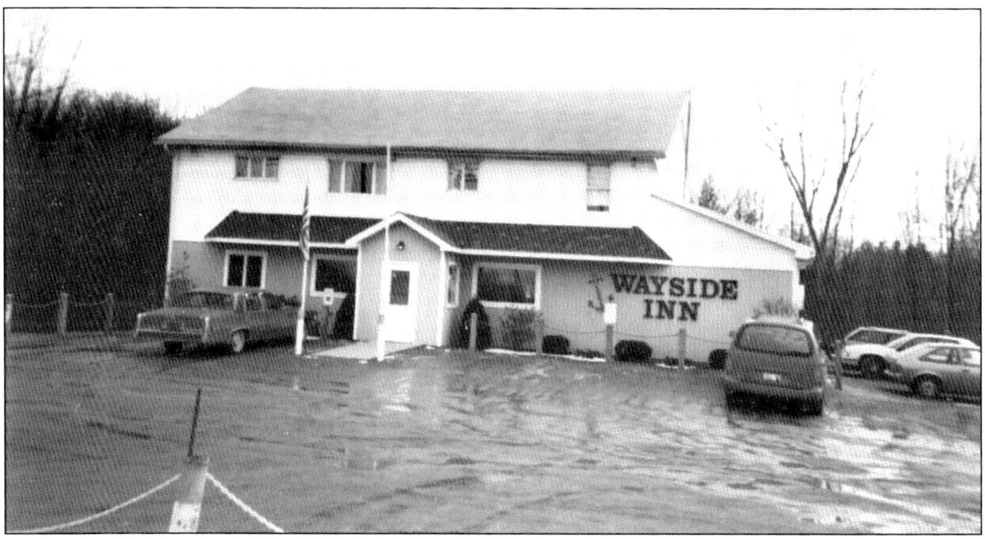

The Wayside Inn, pictured in 1996, was a popular tavern just outside the Conneaut Lake Borough line. The borough itself is dry, meaning no alcohol can be served within its limits. This building was purchased by the Conneaut Lake Volunteer Fire Department, which then burned it down to make room for its new building and club rooms.

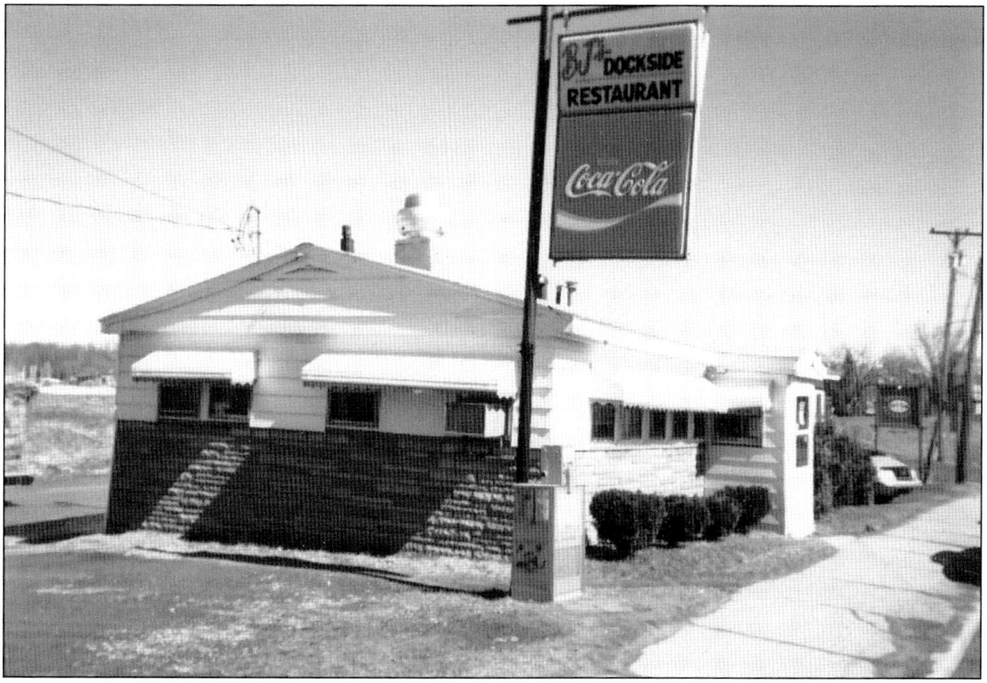

This 1996 photograph shows the Dockside Restaurant, located on the southern end of the borough. The restaurant originally was Berkey's Restaurant, which opened in the 1940s. It later was known as the Light House Diner, before it was torn down in 2008 to make way for Ice House Park. Some of its furnishings are on display at the historical society museum.

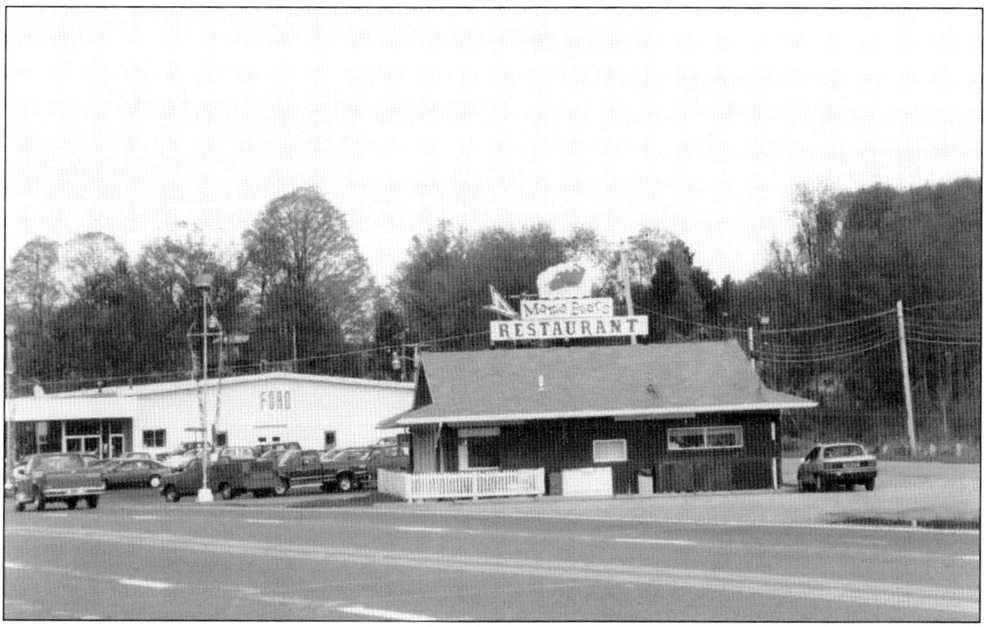

Mama Bear's Restaurant was one of the borough's most popular for residents and tourists alike. Formerly Roxie's, the restaurant was sold in 1975 to Judy Hughes, who renamed it "Mama Bear's." It was well known for its home fries and sugar cookies. Hughes subsequently sold the building to Lakeview Ford, which remodeled it and turned it into an office.

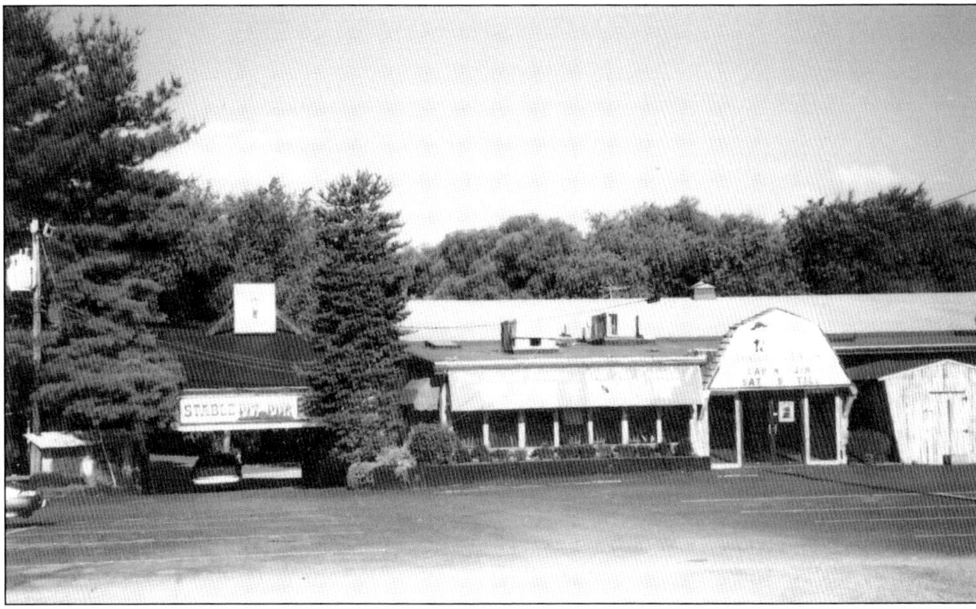

The Stable Pit and Pub, well known for its garlic toast and steaks, was located on Route 18 on the east side of Conneaut Lake. It also housed the Cow Shed, which was a popular tourist attraction in the 1940s and 1950s. The original Cow Shed burned to the ground in 1963 and was then rebuilt. The restaurant closed in 2009.

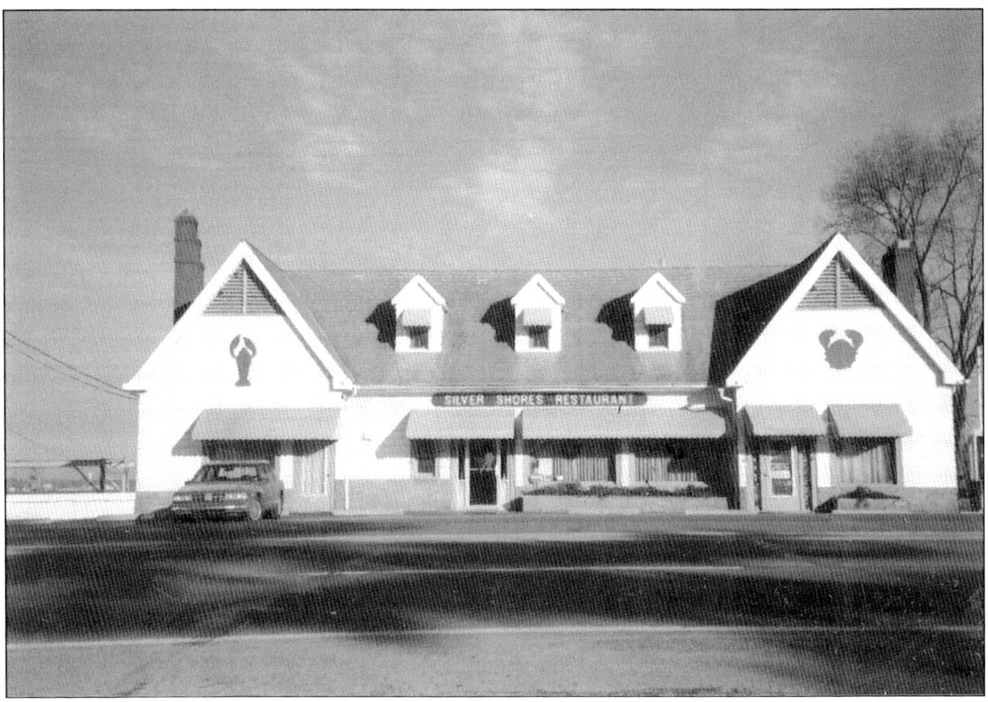

Silver Shores Restaurant, built in 1931 as a Pennzoil filling station, restaurant, and dance pavilion, across from the railroad station, is still located at the southern end of the lake. It no longer sells gasoline, but offers fine dining and a beautiful view of Conneaut Lake. It is owned and operated by Jack and Sharon Slater.

Three

Hotels

"East side, west side, all around the town," go the lyrics of the song "Sidewalks of New York." That perhaps best describes life in the Conneaut Lake area in the late 1800s and early 1900s. All around the town, thousands of people were coming to relax or to get out of the heat of the large cities and take in the cool breezes of Conneaut Lake or to visit the local amusement park. Thus, the hotel industry was born.

Hotels were erected "all around the town," from downtown Conneaut Lake to Conneaut Lake Park and to the east side. Records show no fewer than 40 hotels were in operation in the area, dating back to 1823, when the Conneaut Lake House was constructed just east of the Lakeview Cemetery. Details of many of the hotels are described in Bronson Luty's book, *The Lake as It Was*. Although many owners were men, Mary C. Lord and her daughters were mentioned often as owners or operators of several hotels in the borough, including the Lord House at the southeast corner of Water and First Streets. Hotels were more than just a place to hang a hat for a night. Luxuries such as a barbershop, ice-cream parlor, restaurant, and rowboat rentals were offered. On the west side of the lake, more than a dozen different hotels were in operation over the years.

Development on the east side of the lake included hotels, a bathing beach, park, and boat docks. Two hotels, the Midway and Oakland Beach, were familiar sights. When a new sewage system was installed in the late 1950s and early 1960s, the owners could not afford the tap-in fees and annual usage fees, so they were both demolished. All the hotels are history, except for one, Hotel Conneaut at Conneaut Lake Park. One-story motels have taken their place, most offering limited services.

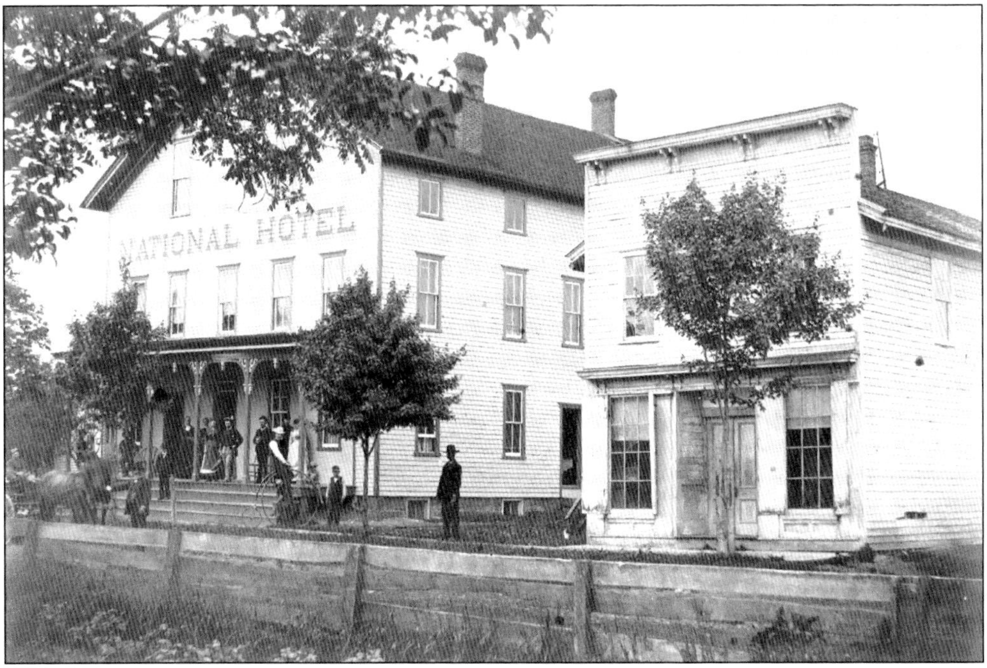

The National Hotel in nearby Geneva, Greenwood Township, was a popular establishment during the town's busiest years in the early 1900s. The small town had numerous businesses, including other hotels and a hospital. The town was close to the Keystone Ordnance Works.

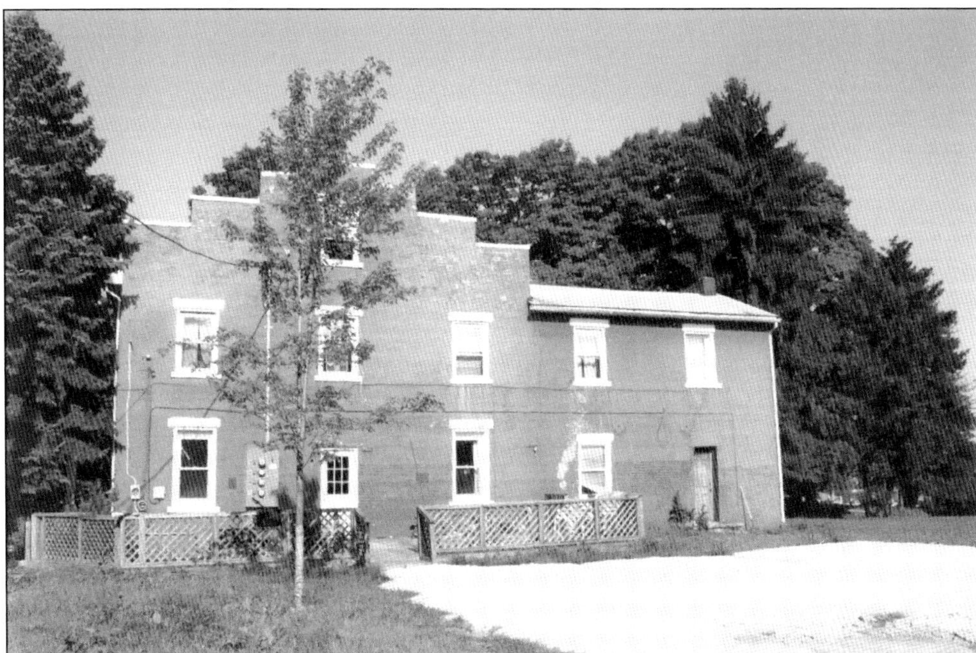

The Lake House, one of the few brick hotels, was built in 1842 by Robert and Sara Andrews Chidester near the edge of town and could accommodate 40 guests. In 1861, Mary Cordelia Lord operated the hotel, offering steaming cups of coffee to guests having picnics on the nearby grounds. Rowboat rentals were also provided.

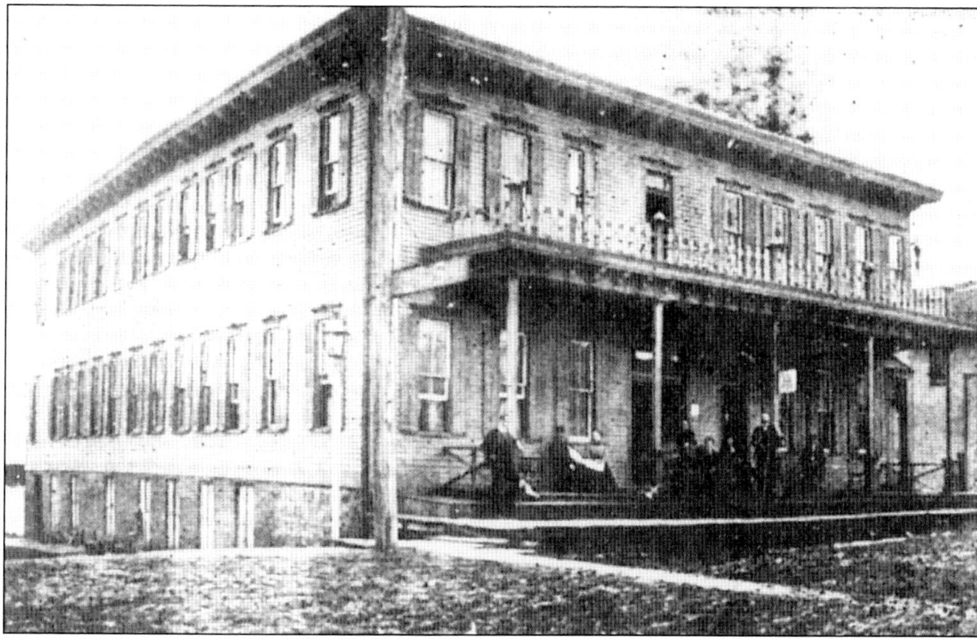

The Ramsey House was located on what is now Water Street in Conneaut Lake Borough. Owned by Charles W. Ramsey, it offered rooms for $1.50 a day and boat livery services at another place Ramsey owned in nearby Exposition Park. It was destroyed by fire in 1908. (LFC.)

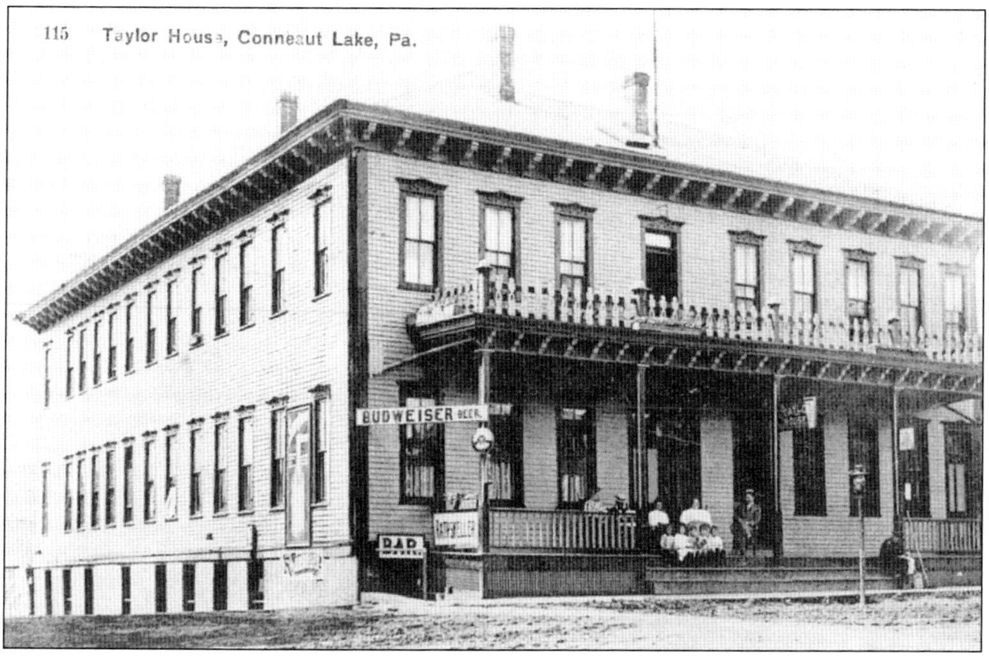

The Taylor House, built in 1885, was owned by a man from Rochester. Located at the corner of First and Water Streets, the advertising for Budweiser is proof the borough was not always dry. The Taylor House burned in 1908. (LFC.)

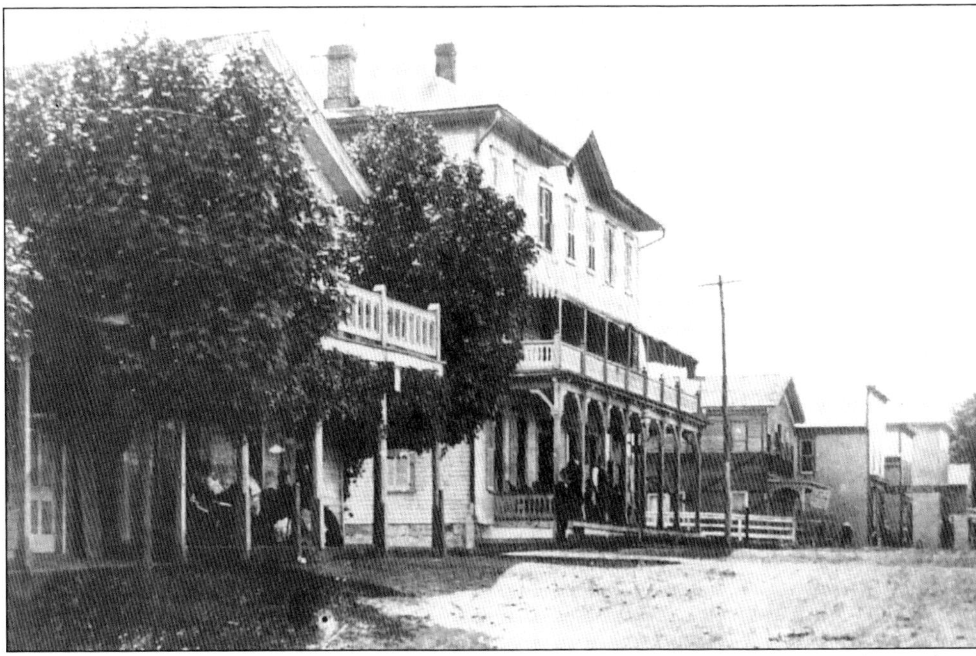

Two downtown hotels are shown in this photograph. The Lord House on left was at the southeast corner of Front (now First) Street. Beyond it at the southwest corner is the Lakeview House, a three-story hotel that offered many luxuries. Mary Lord operated the Lord House and offered to shelter and feed a team of horses for a modest fee. (LFC.)

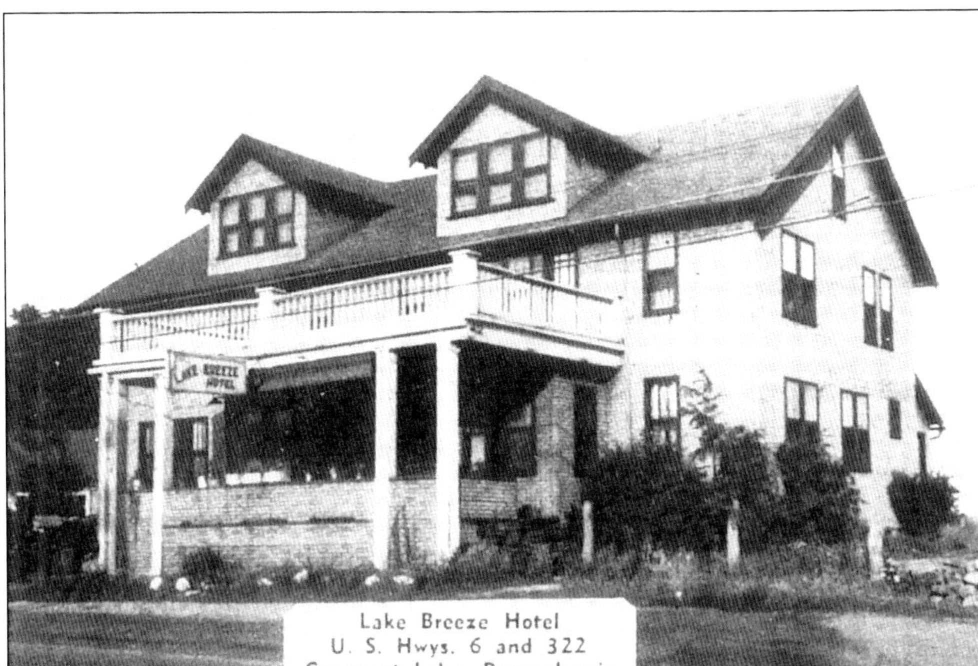

Lake Breeze Hotel, located at the intersection of US Highways 6 and 322, was not only a popular hotel in the 1940s and 1950s but was also a popular place for dining and dancing. Well-known square dance–caller Peter Groger often called for dances at this hotel on Saturday nights. (CHJ.)

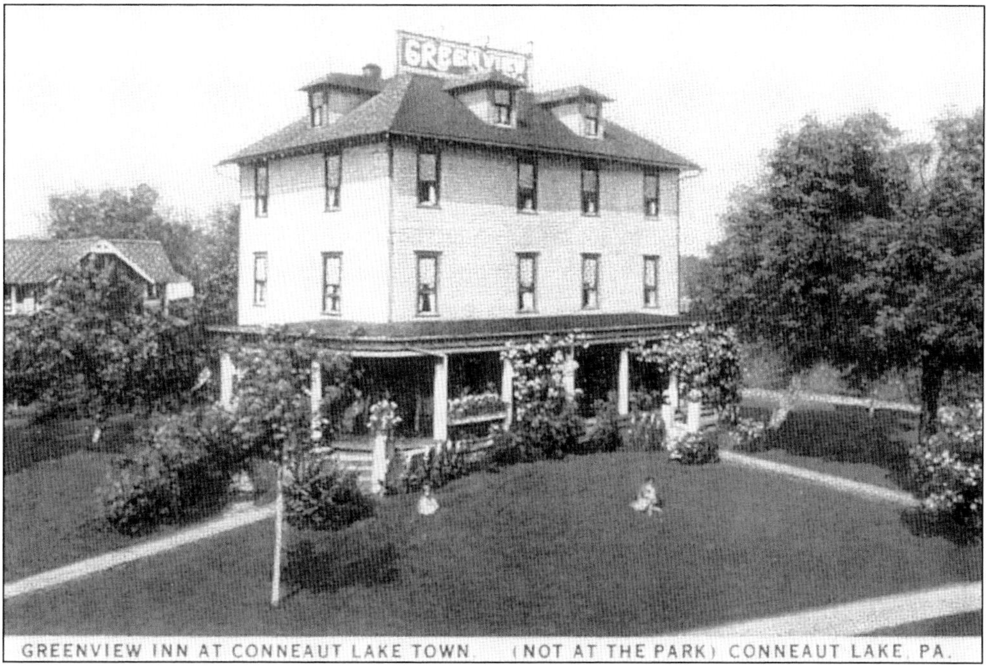

This postcard makes it clear that the Greenview Inn was located in Conneaut Lake town, not at the park, as many people believed. The two-story hotel was built in 1926 and razed in 1952. The owner of the inn obviously had a green thumb. (CHJ.)

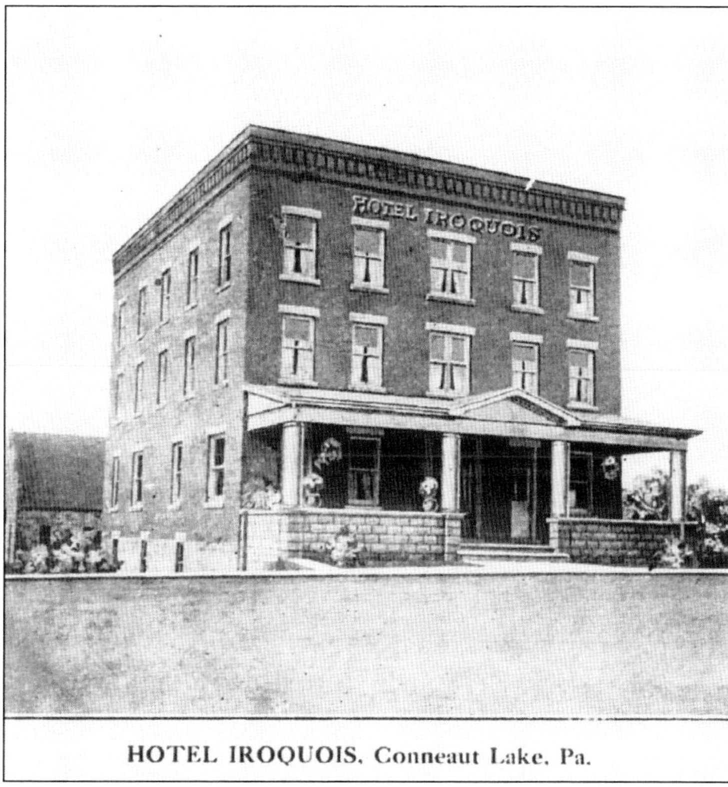

The Hotel Iroquois was the last hotel operating in downtown Conneaut Lake. Built in 1910 for Charles Ramsey, his sister Margaret Griggs, and her husband, Clarence, it was located at the corner of First and Water Streets. It was destroyed by fire in 1978 and was never rebuilt. (LFC.)

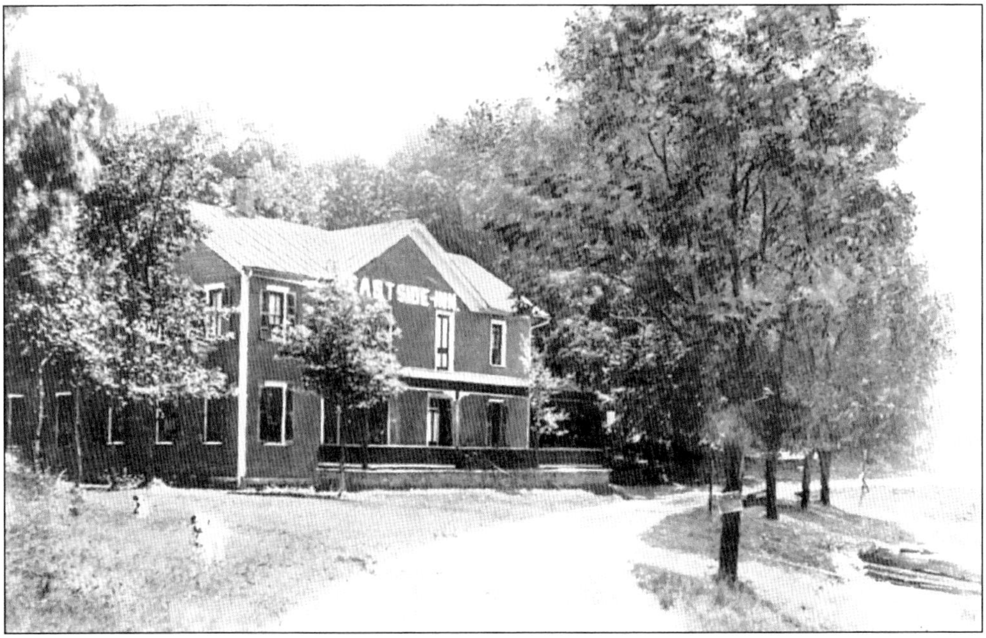

Owned by J.C. Roha, the East Side Inn, was in operation from about 1910 to 1939. It had six bedrooms and was located on the level lakefront grounds about one-quarter mile north of Oakland Beach on the east side of Conneaut Lake. It eventually became the Lake Shore Hotel, with a smaller structure for servants' quarters. (LFC.)

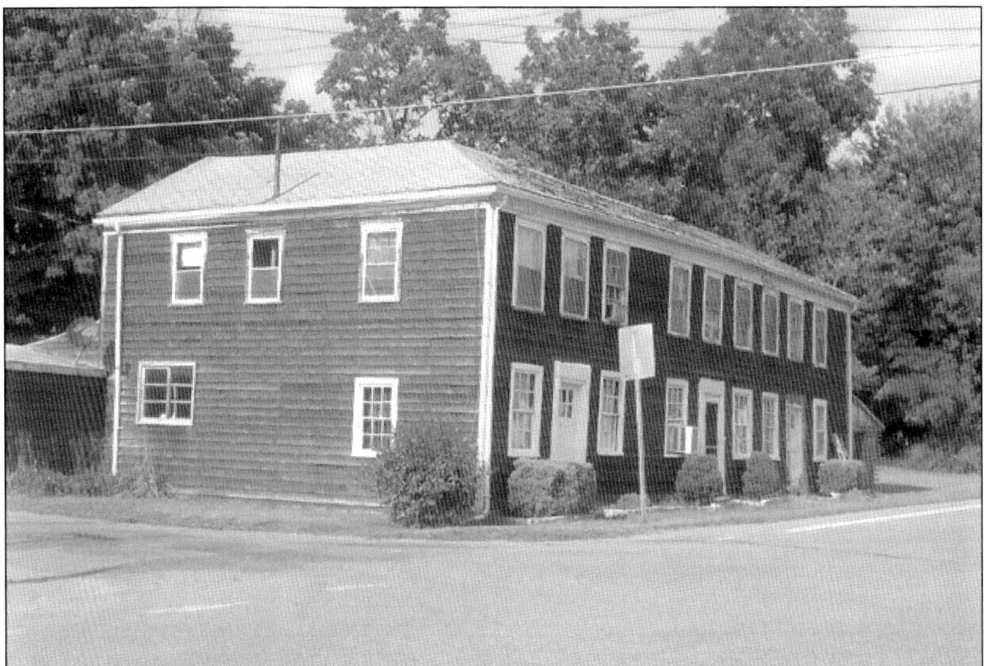

The Whiteside Inn at nearby Harmonsburg was built in 1832 and served as a stop for the stagecoach, which brought the mail from the railroad station in Conneautville to Linesville and Meadville. Legend has it that Abraham Lincoln once stayed there, but that cannot be documented.

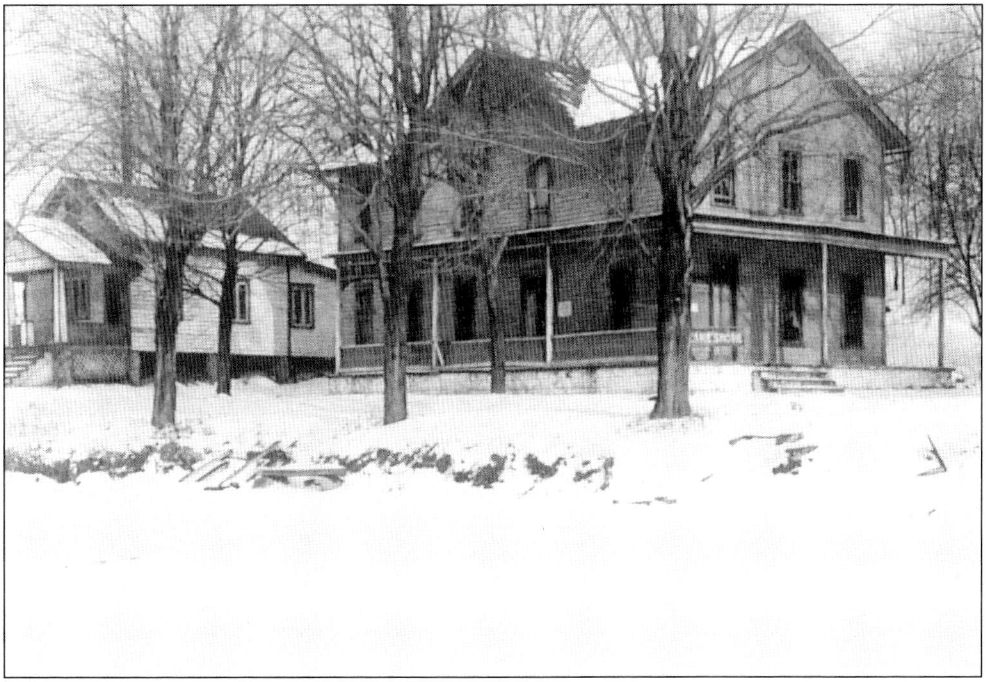

This 1940 photograph shows the Lake Shore Hotel on the east side of Conneaut Lake near Oakland Beach. The hotel was previously known as the East Side Inn. (CHJ.)

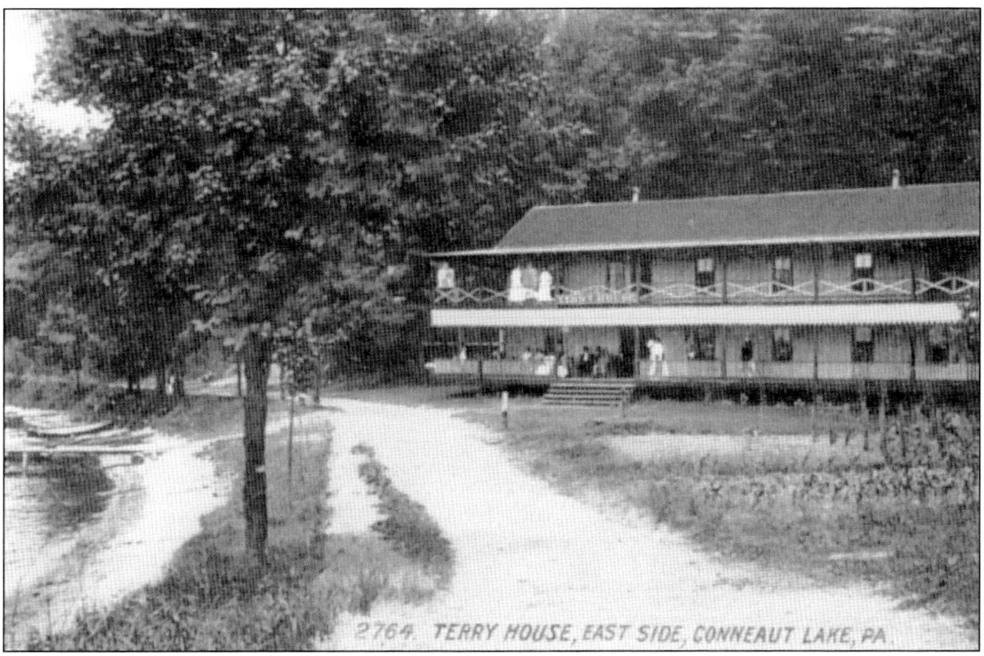

This two-story hotel, the Terry House, was on the east side of Conneaut Lake. Located just north of Oakland Beach, this facility later became servants' quarters for the Oakland Beach Hotel. The balcony was a perfect place for guests to enjoy the cool breeze off the lake. (CHJ.)

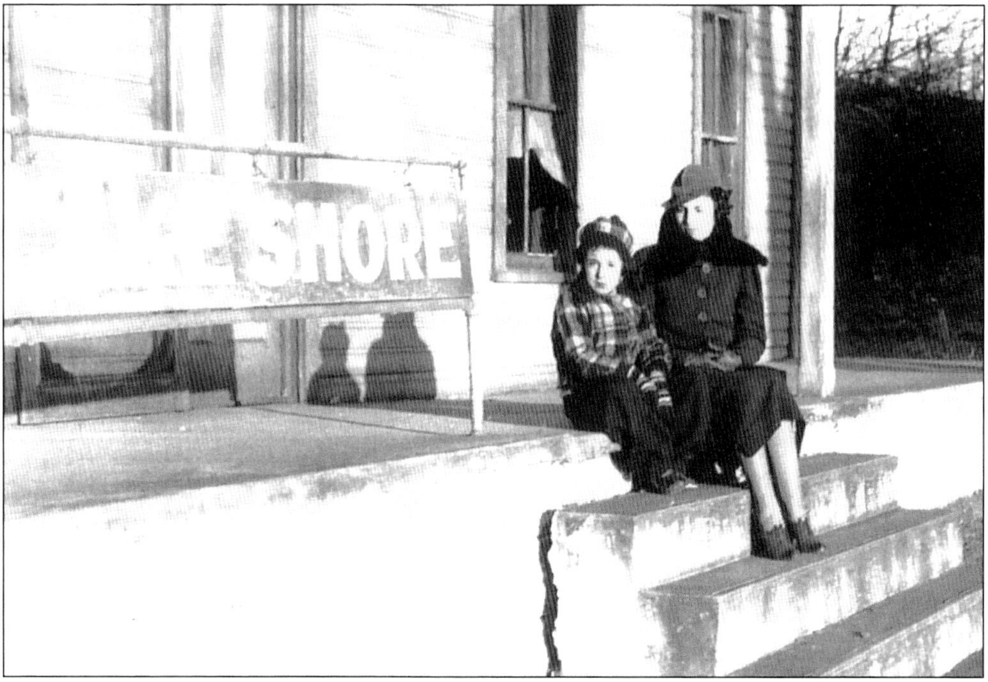

Rita Knapp Ware and her mother, Eva Mae Frantz Knapp, sit on the steps of the Lake Shore Hotel in this photograph from the 1940s. It was located on the east side of Conneaut Lake near Oakland Beach. (CHJ.)

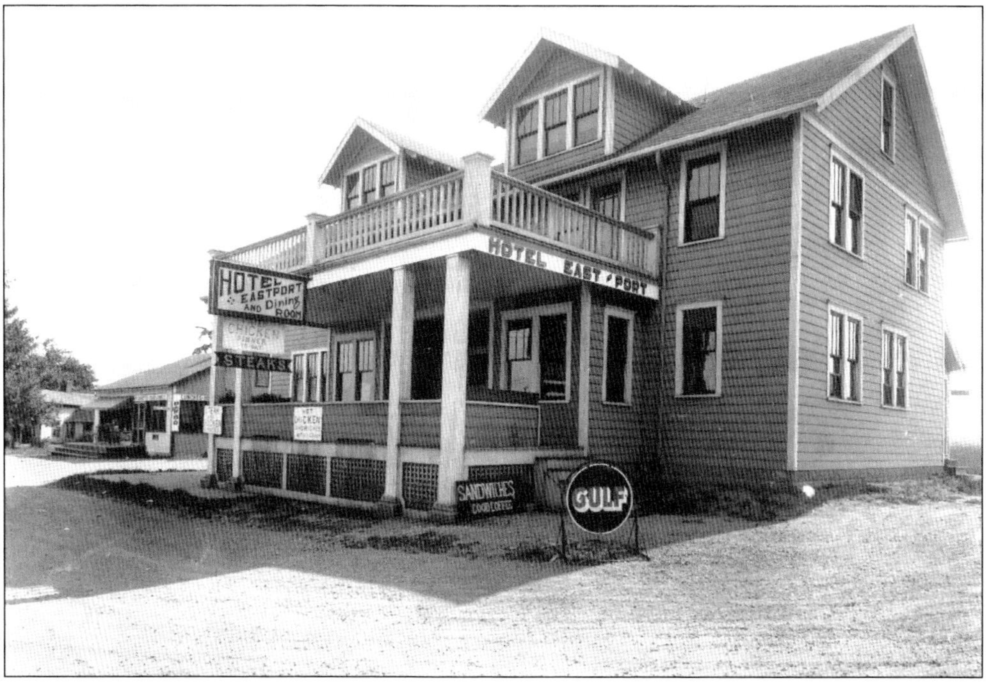

Located at the intersection of US Highways 6 and 322, Hotel East Port (and Dining Room) was previously called the Lake Breeze Hotel. It later was called the Al Jean Inn, named after the owners. The house on the left was a gas station, owned by Adam Minnis and Nettie A. Shartle.

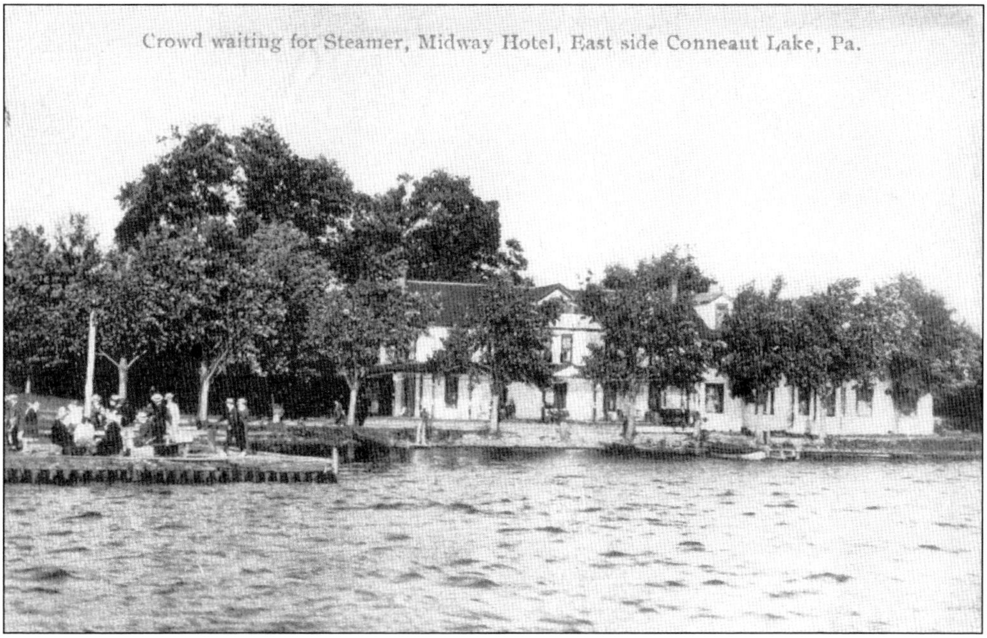

This postcard shows a crowd waiting for a steamer at the Midway Hotel and Beach on the east side of Conneaut Lake. The card notes the hotel table is supplied with "choicest food from our own farm." Located on a large bay, the hotel could house 100 guests. It was built and operated by Amos Quigley.

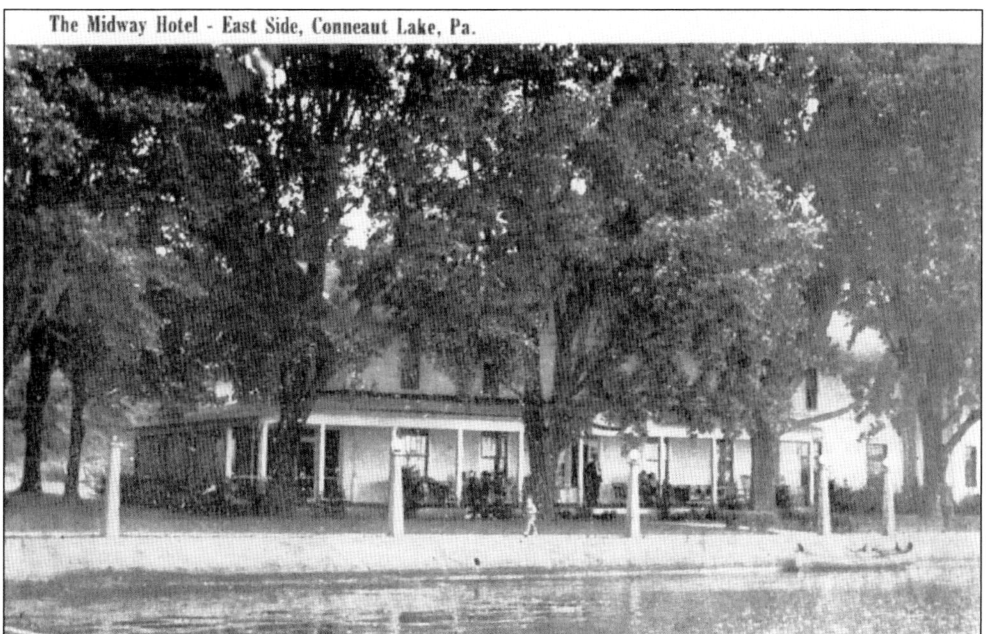

Built in 1885, the Midway Hotel was a two-story structure with two wings. The hotel was purchased by Larry Sousa and Virginia Ramsey Sousa in 1938 and operated until 1967, when it was dismantled because owners could not pay an annual sewer tax, commonly called the toilet tax.

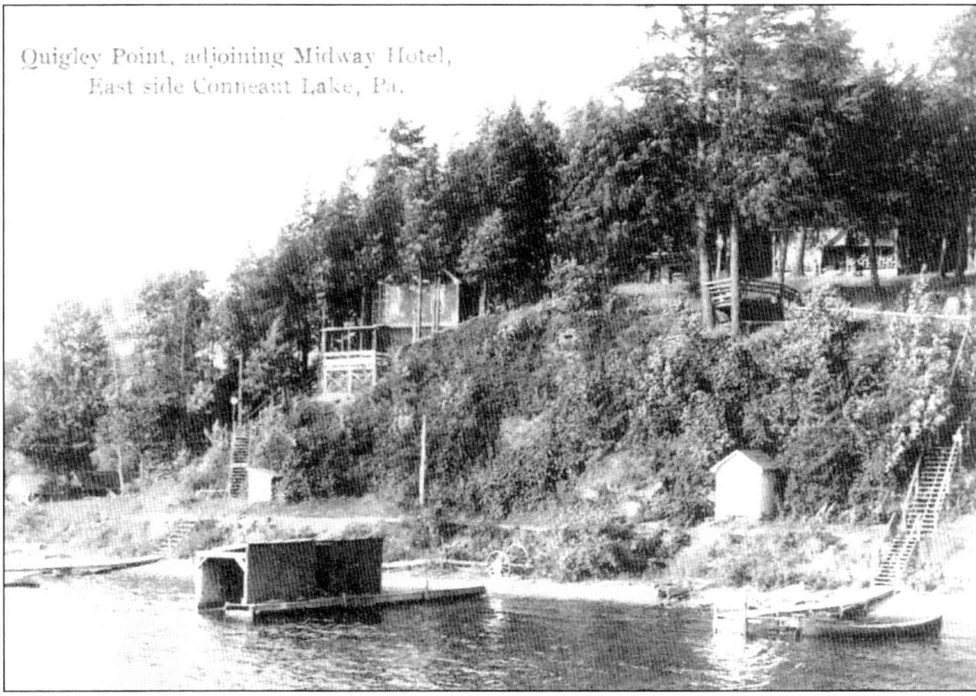

This photograph shows Quigley Point, adjoining Midway Hotel on the east side of Conneaut Lake. The Quigley family owned the Midway Hotel and made numerous improvements in that area. (BH.)

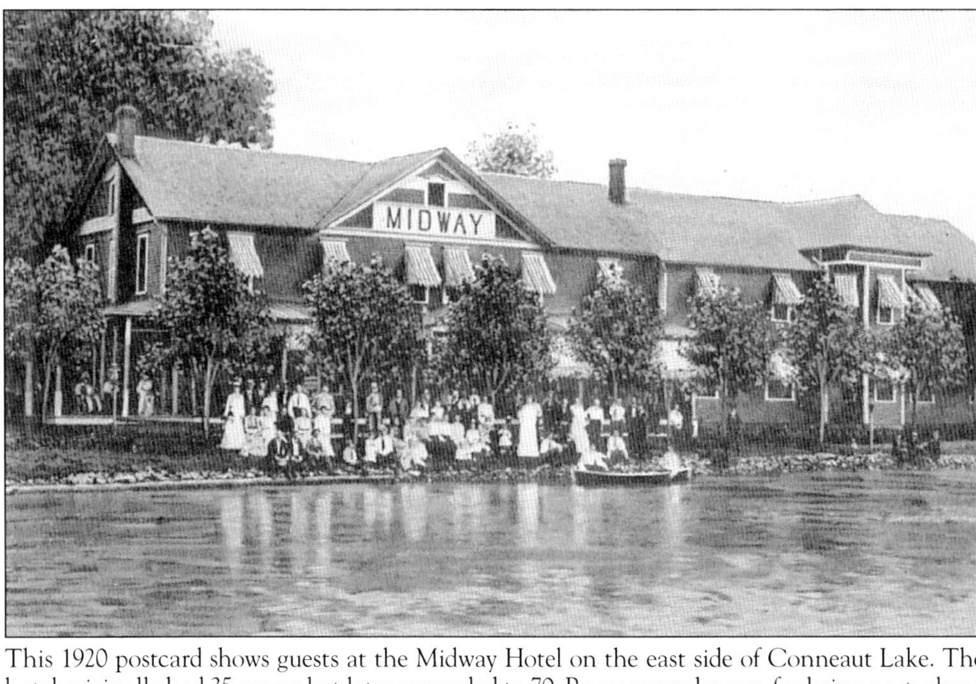

This 1920 postcard shows guests at the Midway Hotel on the east side of Conneaut Lake. The hotel originally had 35 rooms but later expanded to 70. Rooms were known for being neat, clean, and attractive. Amos Quigley, his wife, Elizabeth, and later their son Harry and his wife, Bertha, gave personal attention to their guests. (LFC.)

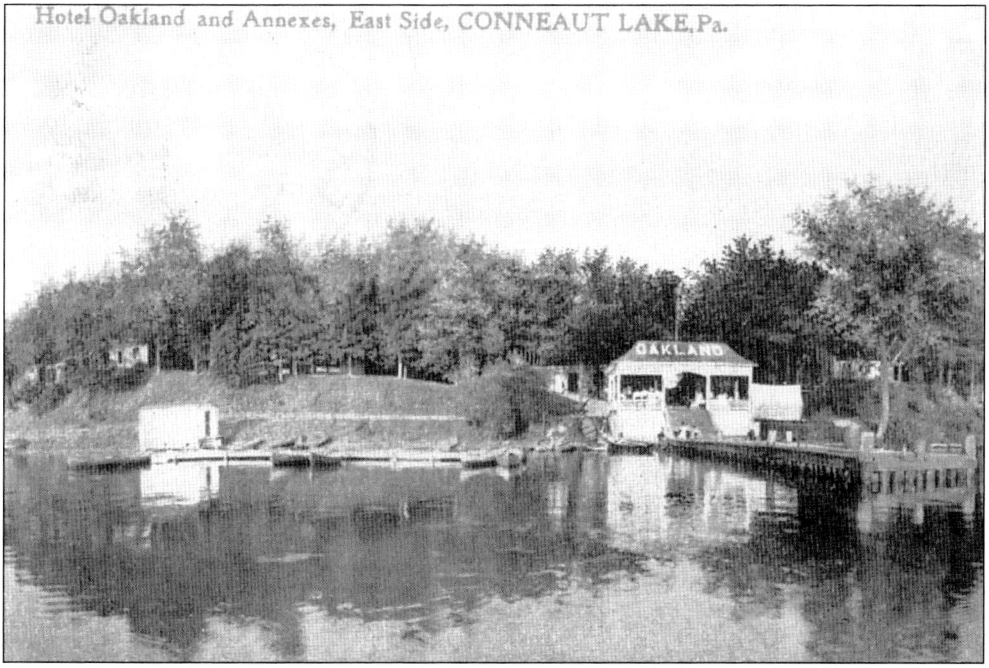

This 1910 postcard shows the Oakland Beach Hotel and annex, built by Sylvester McGuire in 1873, on the east side of Conneaut Lake. It had 28 rooms and was referred to as "The Hall." It was destroyed by fire in 1915. The Oakland Beach complex included a picnic ground, stables for horses, and a boat landing. (LFC.)

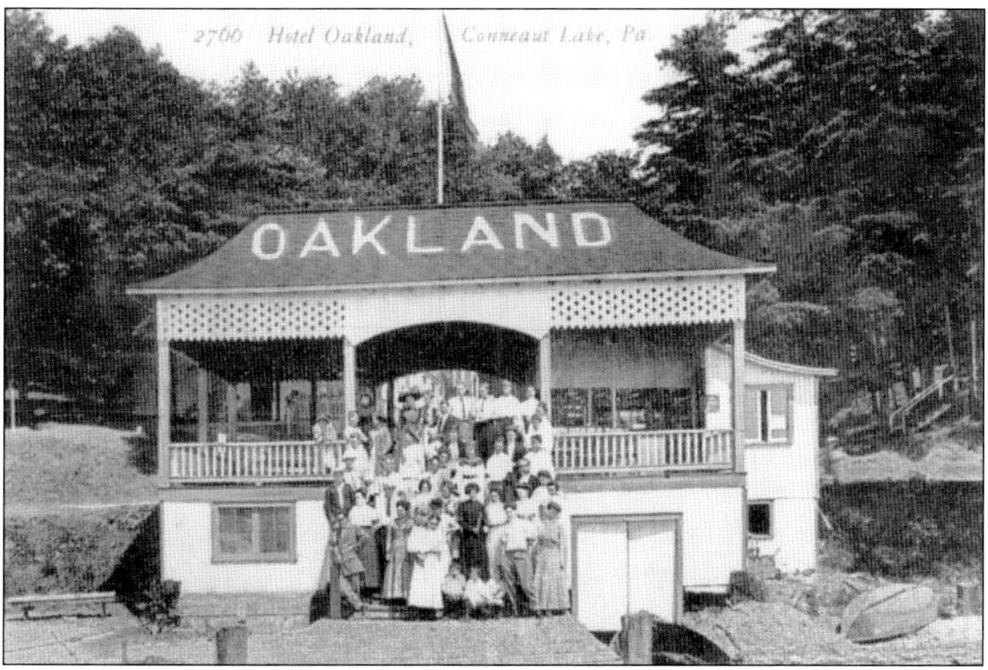

Men and women joined together for parties and dancing at the Hotel Oakland on the east side of Conneaut Lake in the early 1900s, as seen in this photograph. The resort was owned by Sylvester McGuire and his partner Frank Parker. (BH.)

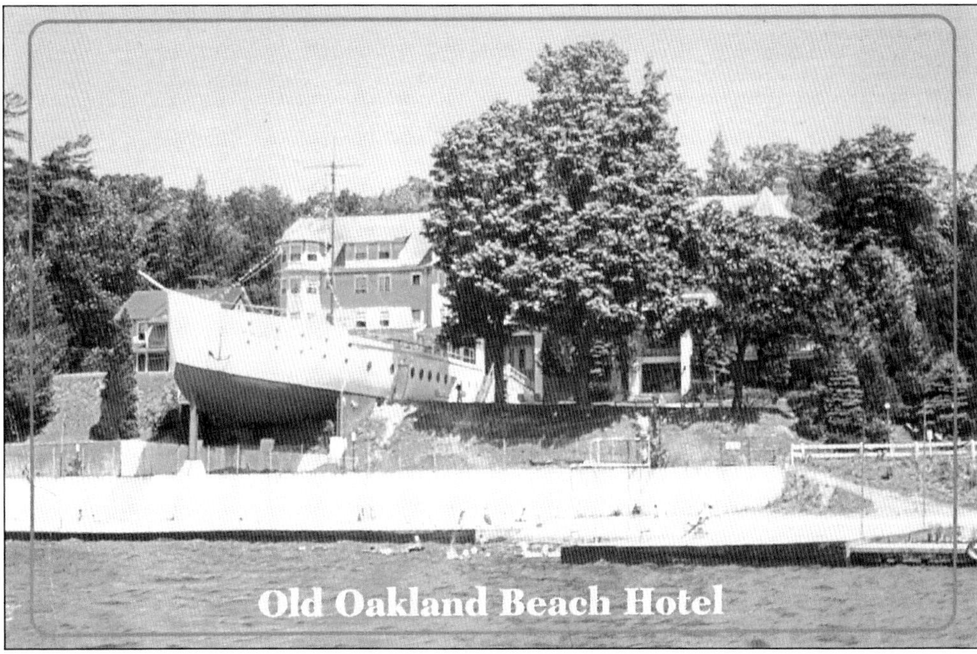

After fire destroyed the first Oakland Beach Hotel in 1915, a new hotel was erected. In 1930, a dancing pier was added with a roof that could slide back to allow guests to dance under the stars. This postcard shows a boat added in 1937 with a marine taproom and bowling alley underneath. The boat was dismantled because of liability issues.

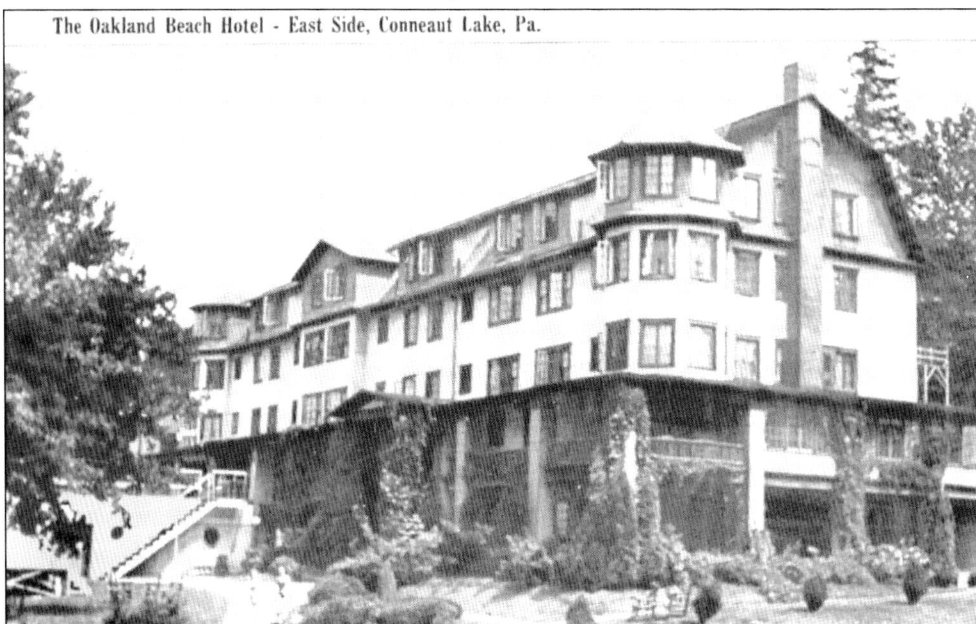

The Oakland Beach Hotel is shown in the 1960s, before the popular boat that had been connected to it was removed. The five-story structure offered 93 rooms and was surrounded by a natural park, campgrounds, and a dining area for 150. It also offered rowboats and long-distance telephone calls. It was dismantled in 1967 because of high costs associated with a new sewer system.

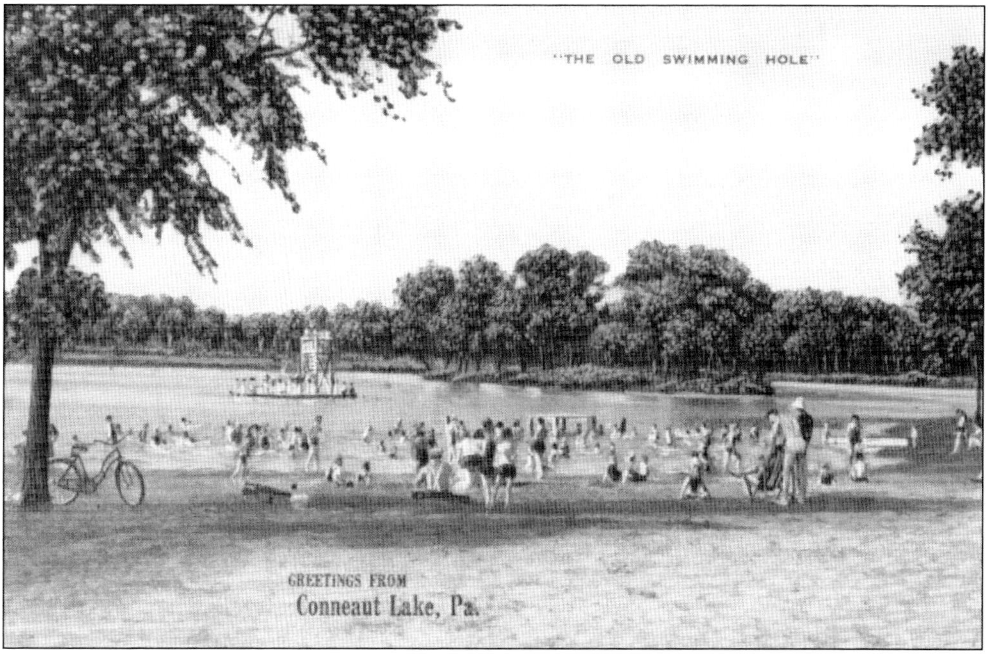

The "Old Swimming Hole" is the title of this 1950s postcard. The swimming hole is Conneaut Lake, Pennsylvania's largest natural lake. The bicycle shown on the left was one means to get to this popular place to swim.

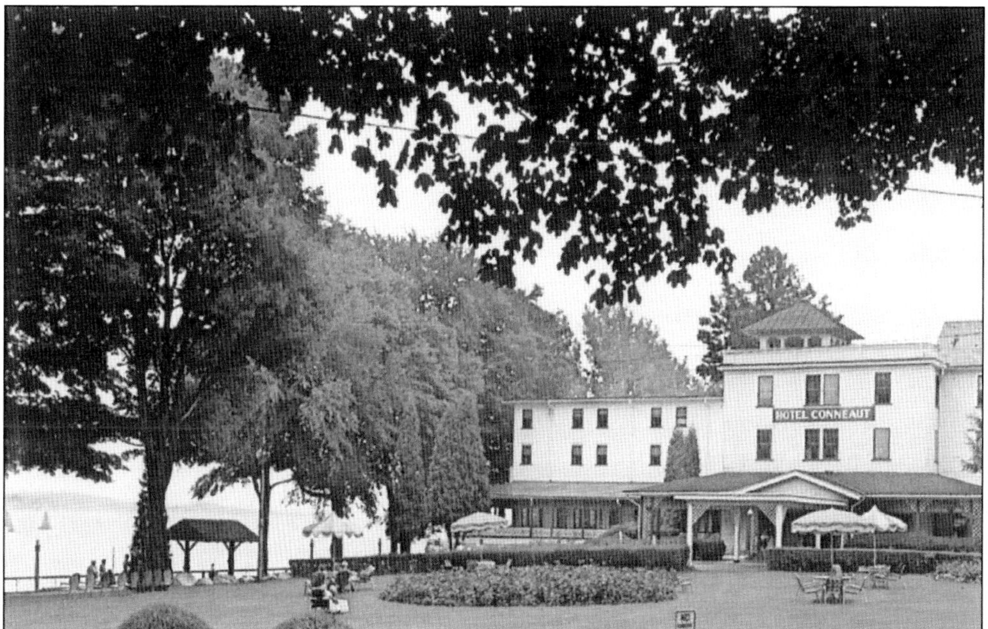

Of all the dozens of hotels in operation during the early and mid-1900s, Hotel Conneaut, erected in 1892 at Exposition Park, is the only hotel in operation in 2012. It once had 300 rooms, but a fire in 1943 caused so much damage that it was reduced to only 150 rooms. Today, it has a dining room, lounge, and ballroom. (LFC.)

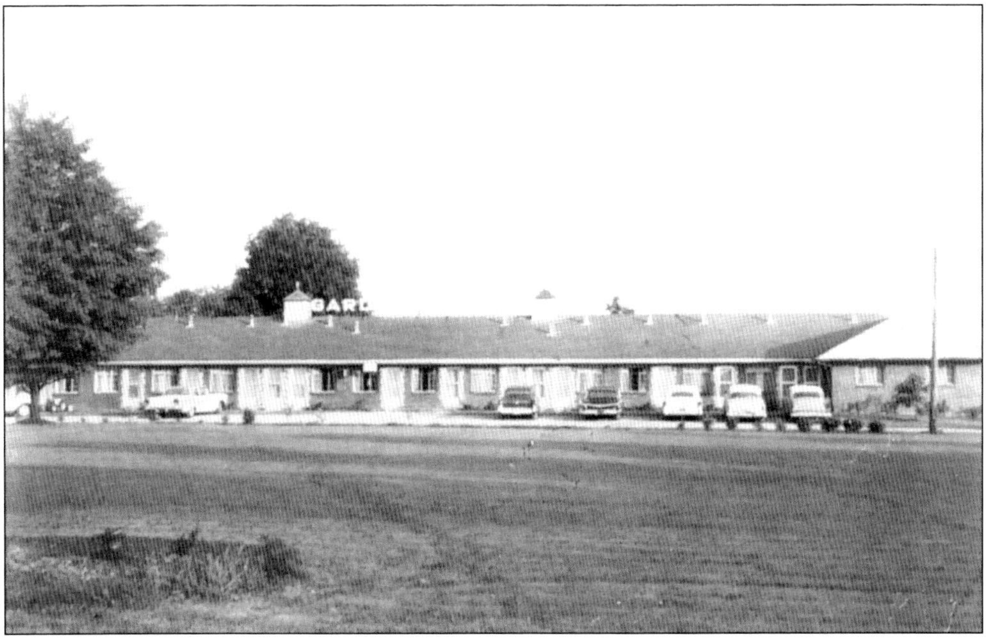

This postcard shows the Gardens Motel, located on Route 618 about one-quarter mile from Conneaut Lake Park. The motel featured heated rooms with telephones and televisions. It also featured an in-house coffee shop. The motel was a popular lodging place when the park was in full swing but has since closed and been torn down.

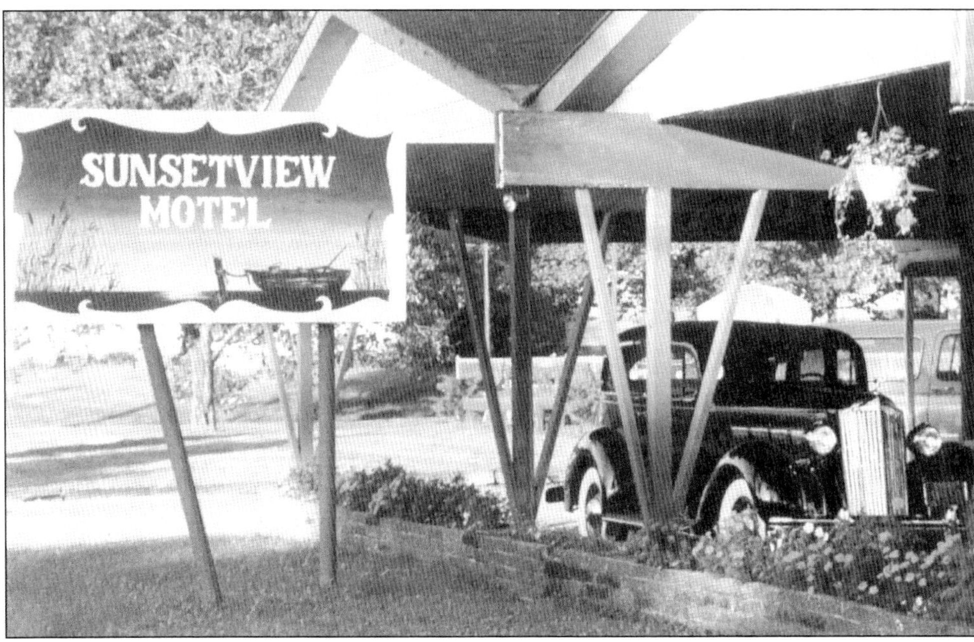

Motels have taken the place of hotels; the Sunset View Motel is one of several in operation in 2012 in the Conneaut Lake area. It is located on Route 618, just two blocks from Conneaut Lake Park. It offers a heated pool, fishing, and child care.

Four

Boats

Conneaut Lake was a beacon to water lovers of all ages. Once the lake was discovered, people flocked to Conneaut, often to launch their boats. Boats of all kinds have played a vital role in Conneaut Lake's history. From the small canoes to the large steamers, they have provided relaxation and competition for residents and visitors alike. They have also brought prosperity.

One of the first steamboats on the lake, the *Wanderer*, as listed in Bronson Luty's book, *The Lake as It Was*, best describes wanderers who traveled the lake, sometimes with no destination in mind. Passenger boats were a necessity in days before the railroad, the trolley, or automobiles. Although horses could be used for travel, many people did not have easy access to horses and buggies. *Sailing through Time*, a book written by Don Hilton, describes the many boats that have carried passengers up and down the lake.

One company that played a major role in Conneaut Lake's boat history was the Conneaut Lake Navigation Company, which operated a fleet of passenger boats managed by S.A. Harshaw. Conneaut Lake's history would not be complete without mention of *Liberty the Second*, a speedboat brought to Conneaut Lake from Pittsburgh for a race in 1922. It sank during trial runs and remained on the bottom of the lake until 1985, when it was recovered by two local divers and restored.

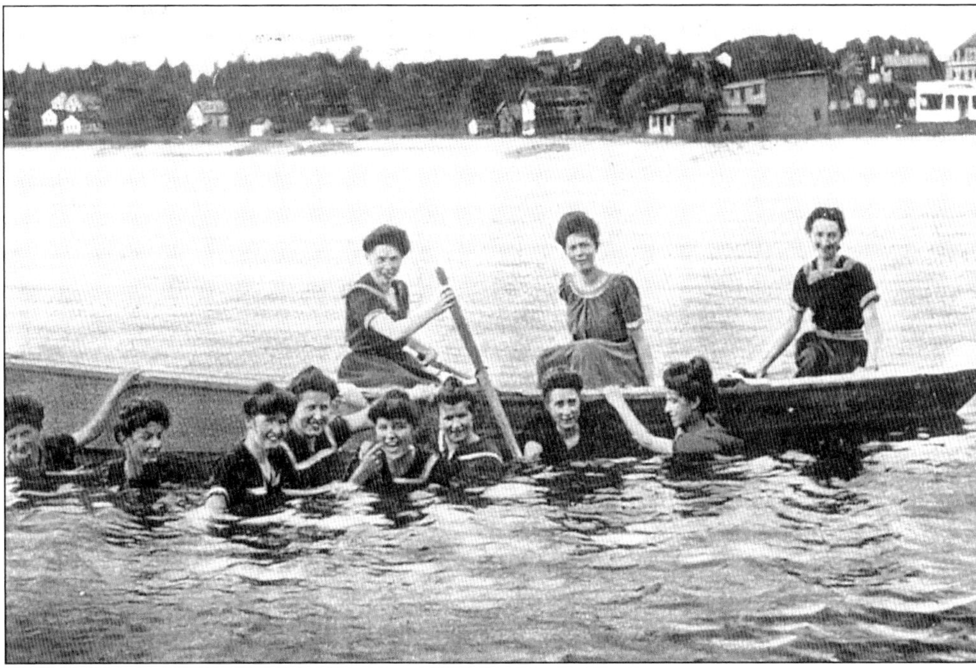

This photograph from 1907 shows a group of young women enjoying both swimming and boating in Conneaut Lake. This was a typical scene on the lake in the early days of its development as a tourist destination. (CHJ.)

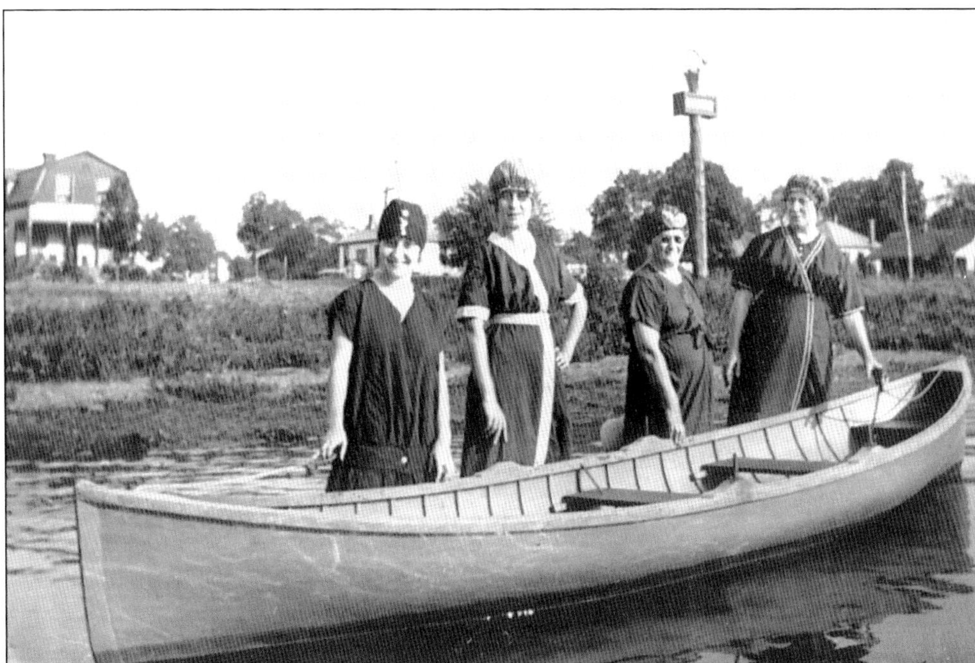

This 1918 photograph shows Carol Lauch and friends as they prepare to launch a boat off Midway Beach. Note that the women not only covered most of their bodies but also covered their hair with caps. They were holding onto the boat so it would not float away. (CHJ.)

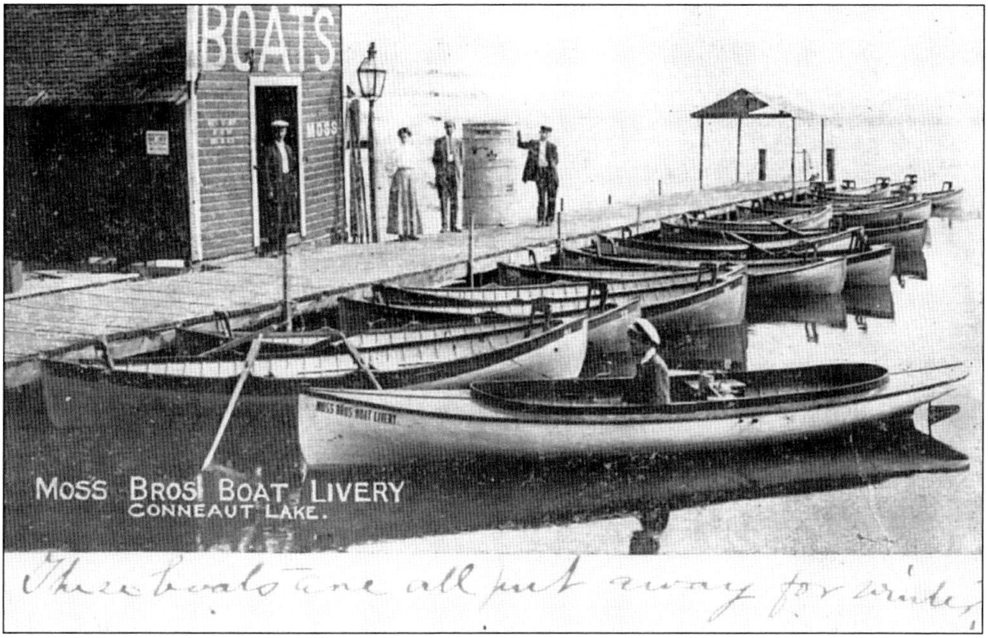

The Moss Bros. Boat Livery, with a line of boats ready for renting at Conneaut Lake, is shown in this 1909 photograph. The little red boathouse was located in front of the Lord Hotel and Ramsey Hotel in downtown Conneaut Lake. (HS.)

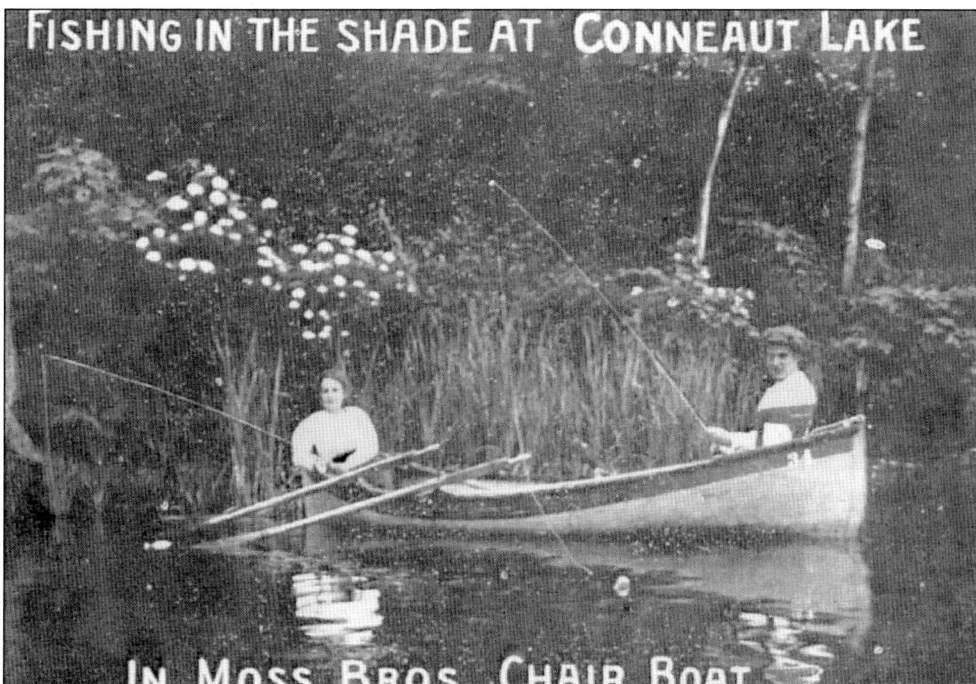

These women fish from a Moss Bros. chair boat in the shade on Conneaut Lake. The Moss Bros. Boat Livery rented both boats and oars. (PHM.)

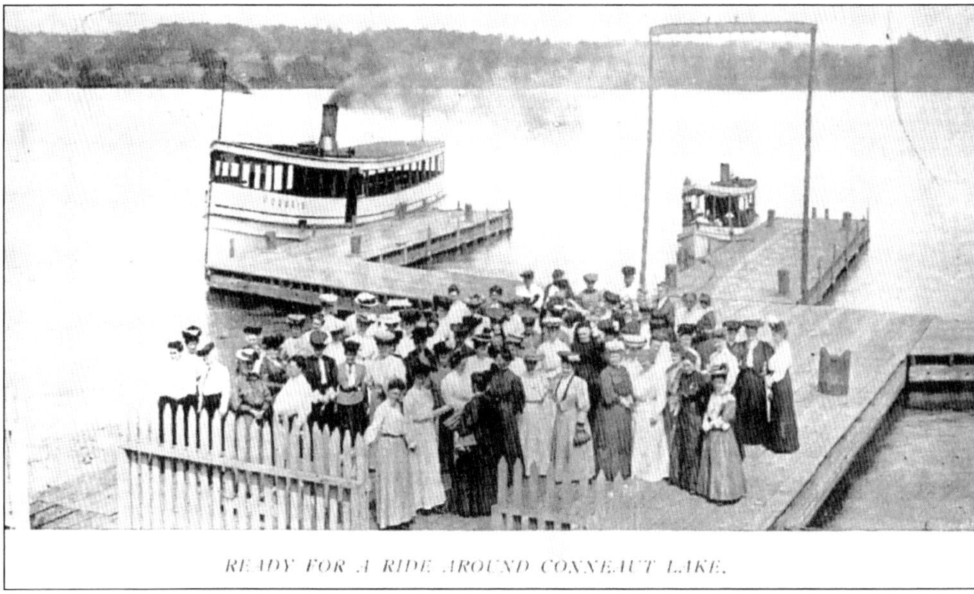

This early-1900s postcard shows passengers waiting to board the steamer *Iroquois*. The caption reads, "Ready for a Ride Around Conneaut Lake." (LFC.)

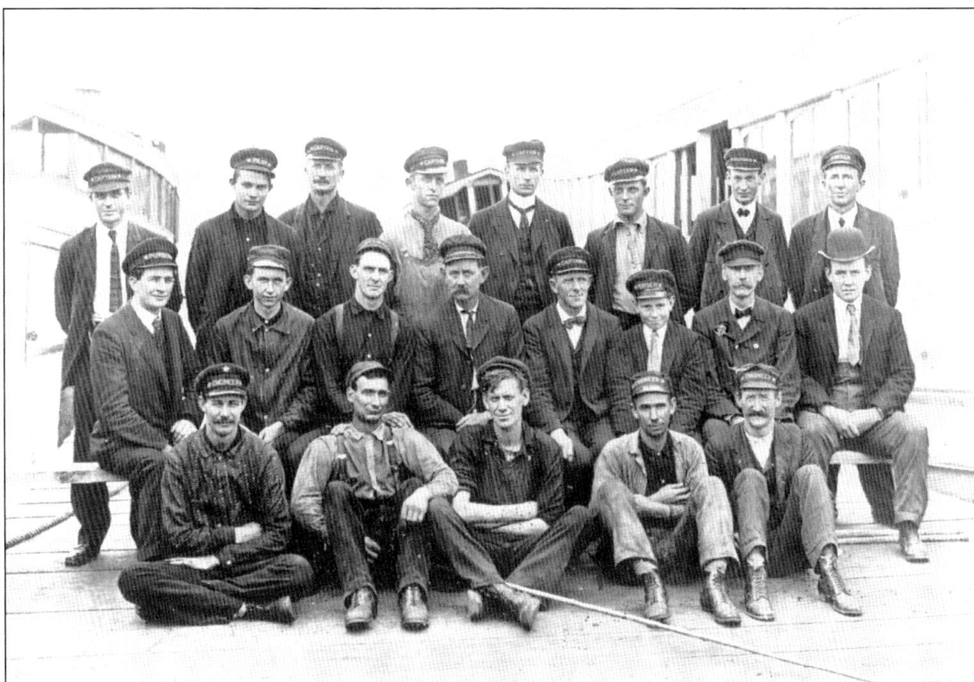

Steamboat operators from Conneaut Lake boats, from left to right, are (first row) Samual Hershelman, Free Yokes, Max Sanfod, Ray Yokes, and Hiram Ralston; (second row) Dal Shearer, Ed Moorow, "Jinks" Quigley, S.A. Harshaw, Harry Quigley, Gene Harshaw, Major Fox, and Vance Harshaw; (third row) Ed Sweet, Zack Shellito, Hiram Miller, Dan McGuire, Professor Miller, Harry Kelly, Warren Shearer, and Al First.

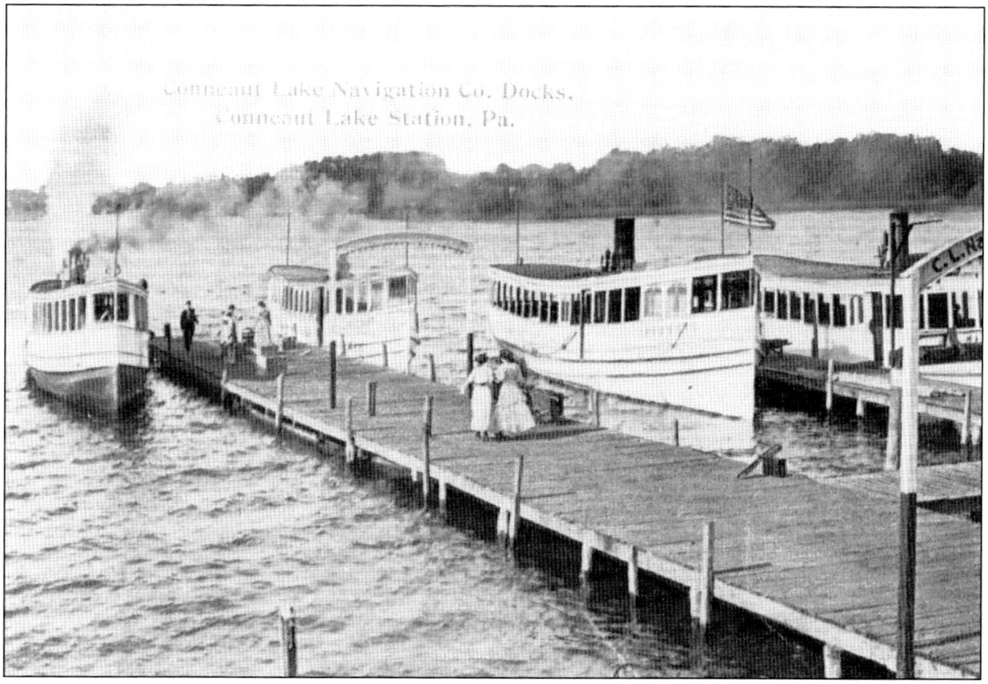

Four steamboats are shown at the Conneaut Lake Navigation Docks in downtown Conneaut Lake, waiting to take passengers to either Exposition Park or the east side of the lake. Passengers could also choose to ride around the lake, which was described as a 45-minute outing. (LFC.)

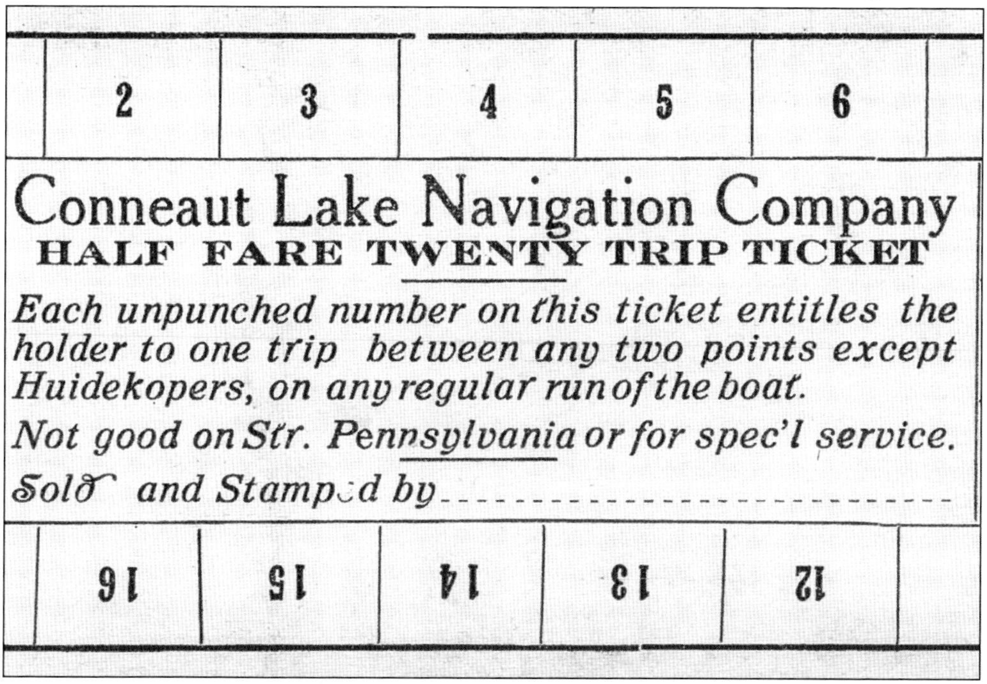

2	3	4	5	6

Conneaut Lake Navigation Company

HALF FARE TWENTY TRIP TICKET

Each unpunched number on this ticket entitles the holder to one trip between any two points except Huidekopers, on any regular run of the boat.

Not good on Str. Pennsylvania or for spec'l service.

Sold and Stamped by ____________________

16	15	14	13	12

Conneaut Lake Navigation Company in downtown Conneaut Lake provided its regular customers the following bonus: half-fare punch tickets for 20 trips around the lake between any two points, except Huidekopers. The ticket was not good on the steamer *Pennsylvania* or for special services. (BH.)

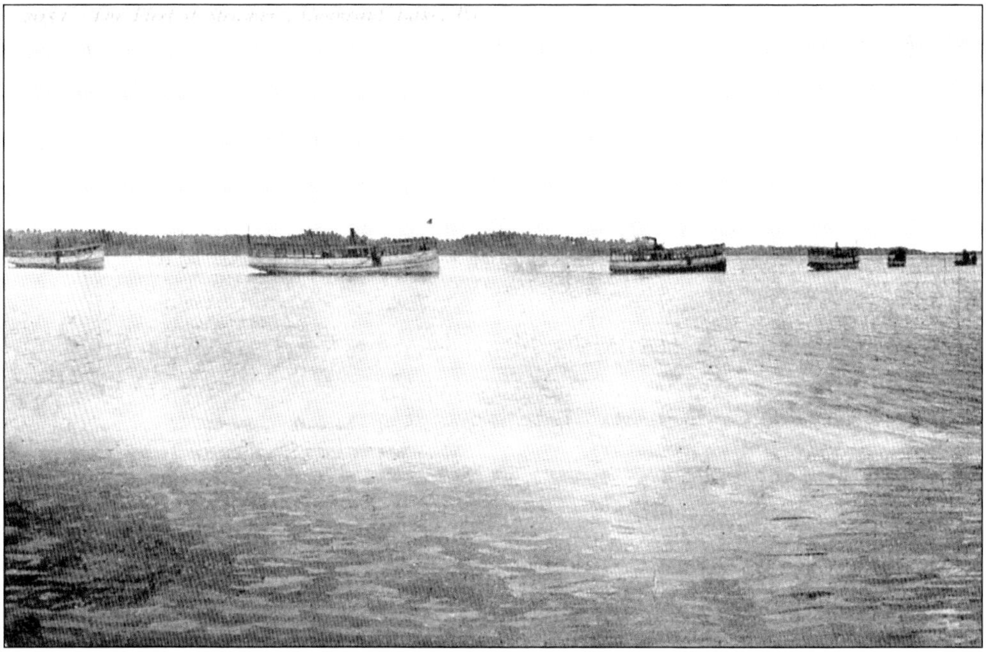

In late 1899, visitors often saw this fleet of steamers going across Conneaut Lake. Steamers include *Swan*, *Storm*, *Iroquois*, *Nickel Plate*, *Trilby*, *Conneaut*, and *Superior*. (LFC.)

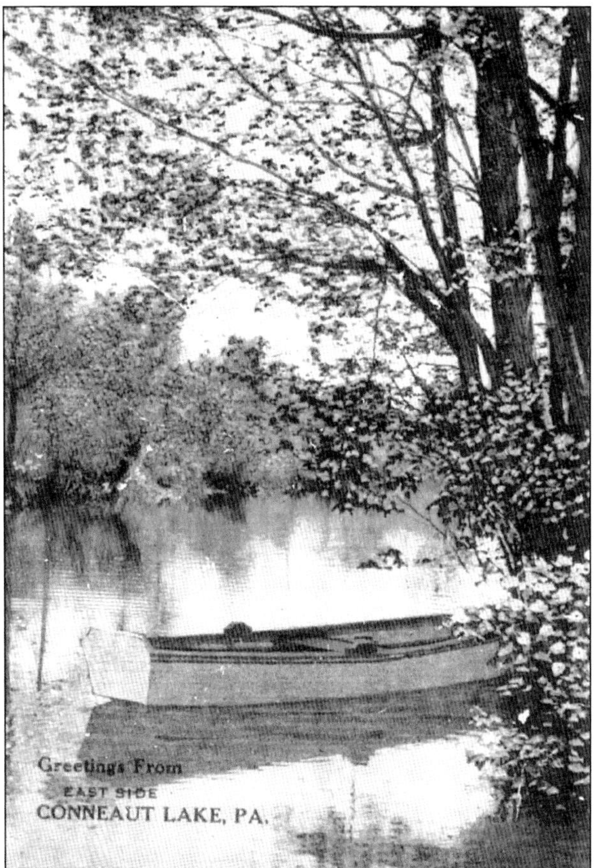

"Greetings from East Side, Conneaut Lake," reads this postcard from the 1930s, "It's Cool and Pleasant Here." Note the empty canoe. Canoes and other boats were a familiar sight on the lake as visitors took to the water to cool off. (LFC.)

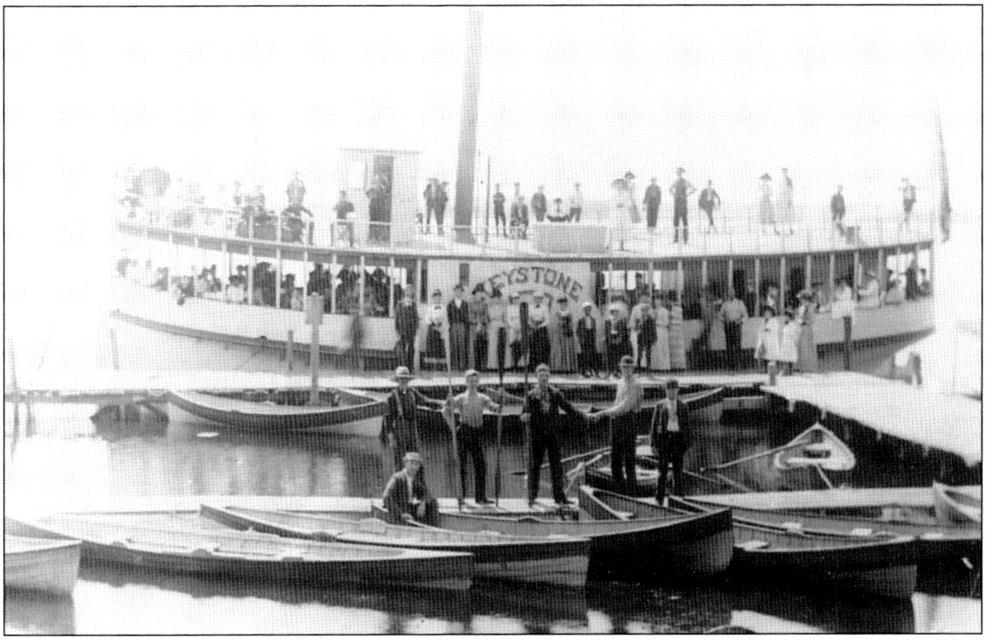

Owned by David Chidester, the *Keystone* was a double-decker boat, 75 feet long and 22 feet wide. It was kept at Lynce's Landing near the current Hotel Conneaut. It operated on Conneaut Lake from 1881 to 1895 and was described as a side-wheeler. (LFC.)

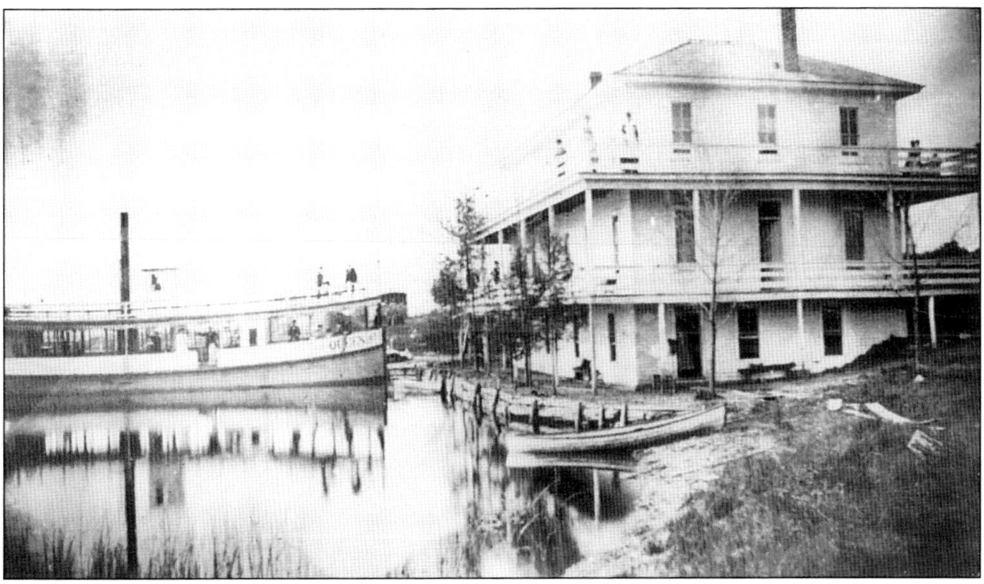

Built by Lafayette Barr in 1882, the *Queen* is docked at the Fair Point Hotel on the east side of Conneaut Lake. The steamer was a side-wheeler boat about 75 feet long with a 15-foot beam. It was sold in a sheriff's sale in 1891. (LFC.)

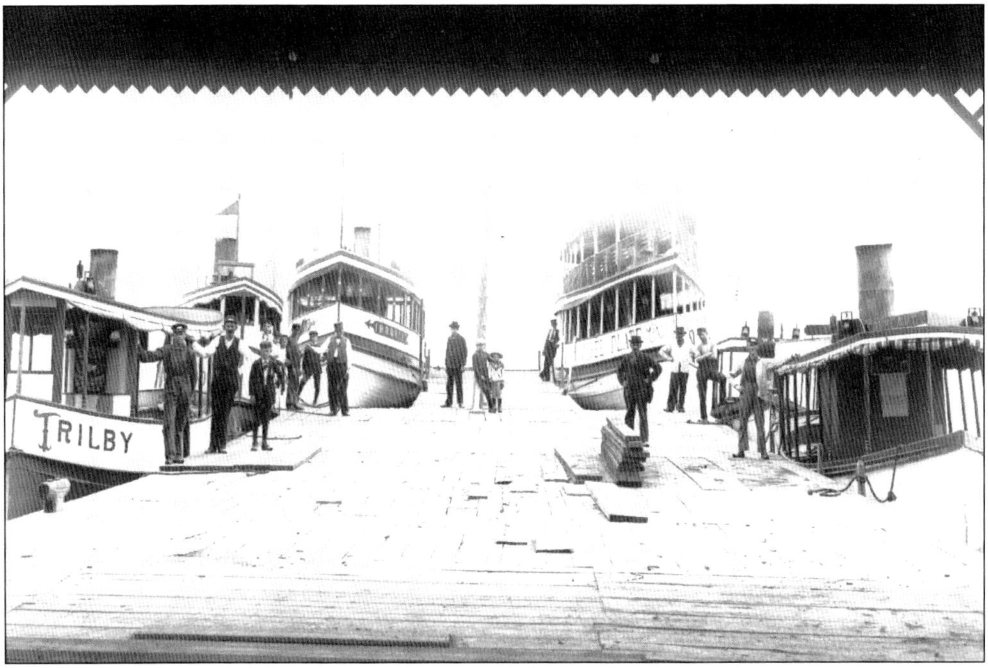

This photograph shows four steamers, the *Trilby*, *Conneaut*, *Iroquois*, and *Nickel Plate*. The *Trilby* previously made runs on the old canal. Her name, according to *Sailing through Time* by Don Hilton, was from a novel. It came to mean "safe and easily controlled." The *Iroquois* was owned by Amos Quigley at the Midway Hotel. The *Nickel Plate* had a capacity of 300 people and a speed of 16 miles per hour.

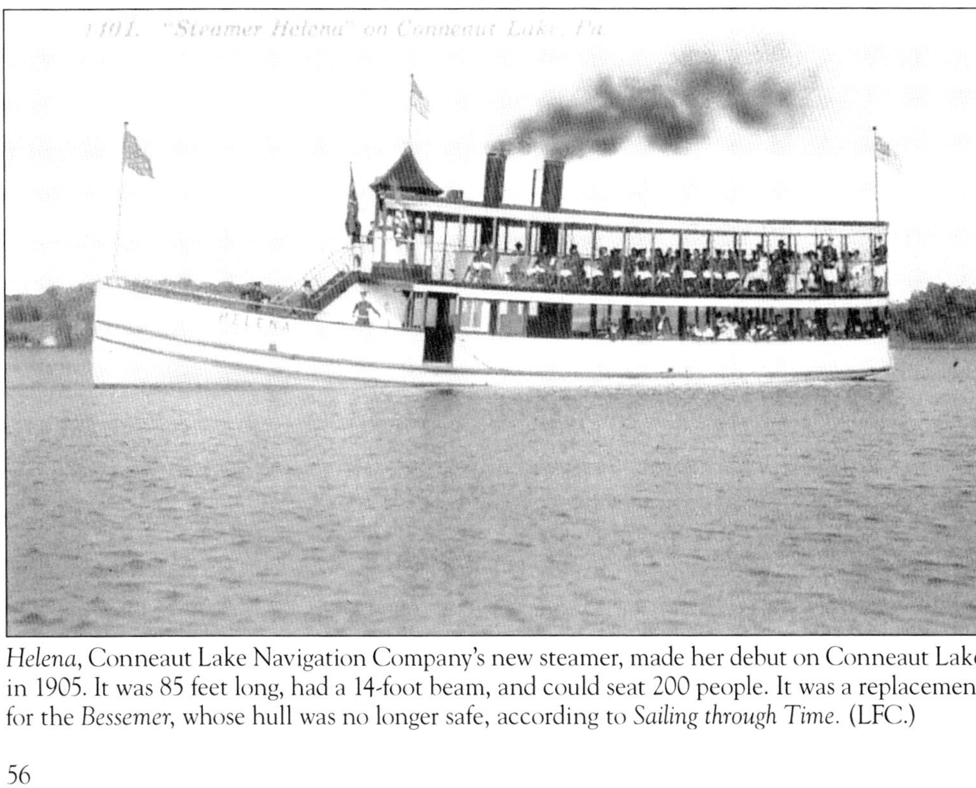

Helena, Conneaut Lake Navigation Company's new steamer, made her debut on Conneaut Lake in 1905. It was 85 feet long, had a 14-foot beam, and could seat 200 people. It was a replacement for the *Bessemer*, whose hull was no longer safe, according to *Sailing through Time*. (LFC.)

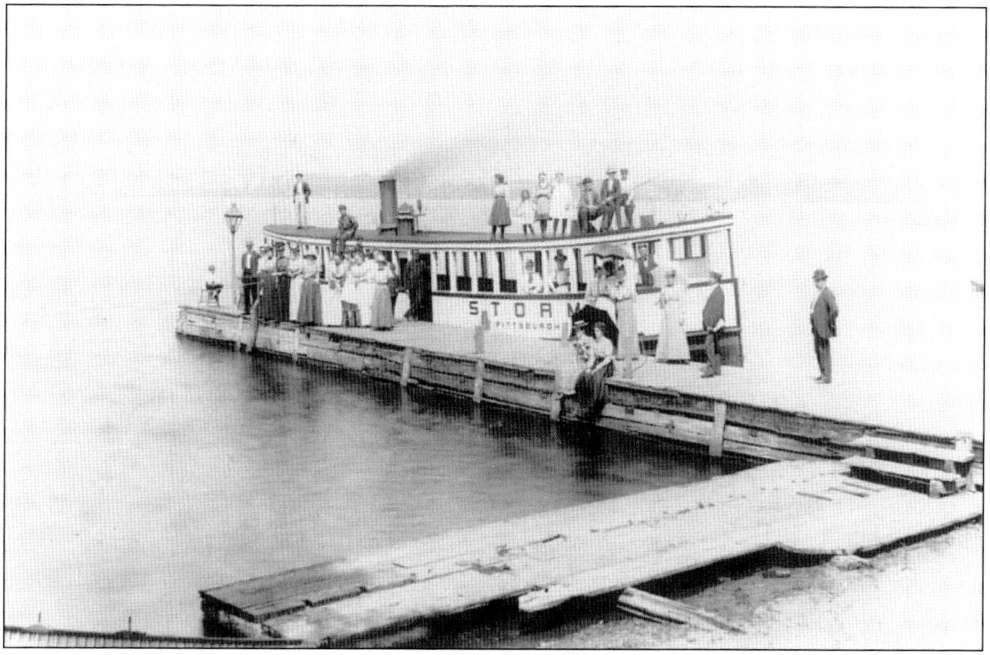

The *Storm of Pittsburgh* previously was named the *Oriole of Pittsburgh* and renamed after the owner brought it from Pittsburgh to join the Oakland Beach facility, according to *Sailing through Time*. It also was known as the *Storm of Pittsburg*, without the letter "h." Like many of the large steamboats, it burned; its remains are on the bottom of Conneaut Lake. (LFC.)

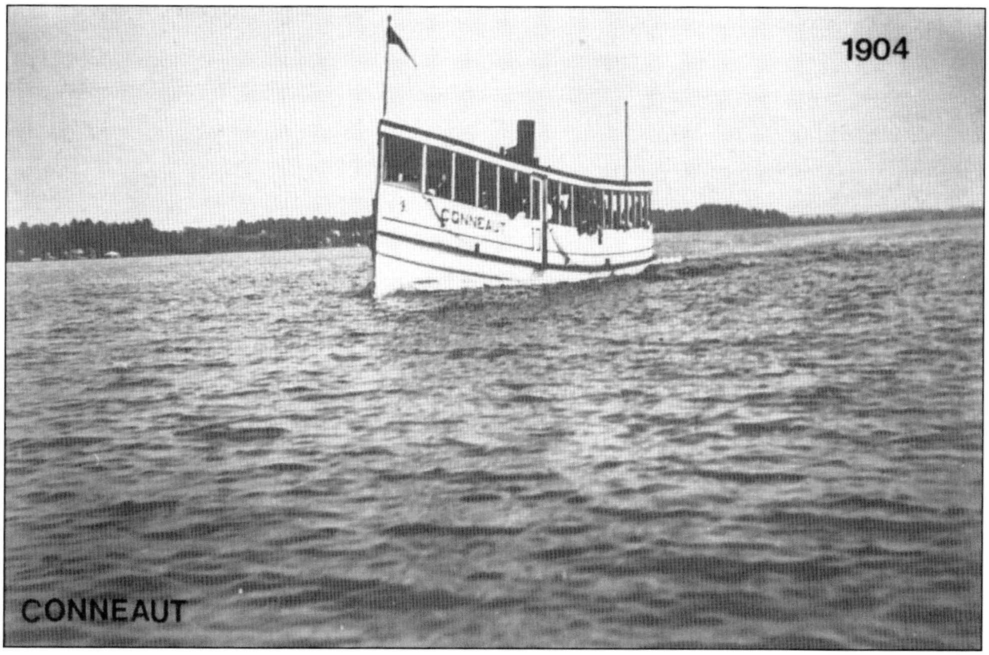

This 1911 postcard shows the steamer *Conneaut*, described as "newly rebuilt and enlarged" after it caught on fire in 1902 while sitting at the dock. The earlier version was criticized as "running much too fast and a danger to other boats on the lake," according to *Sailing through Time*. It operated on Conneaut Lake from 1885 to 1913. (LFC.)

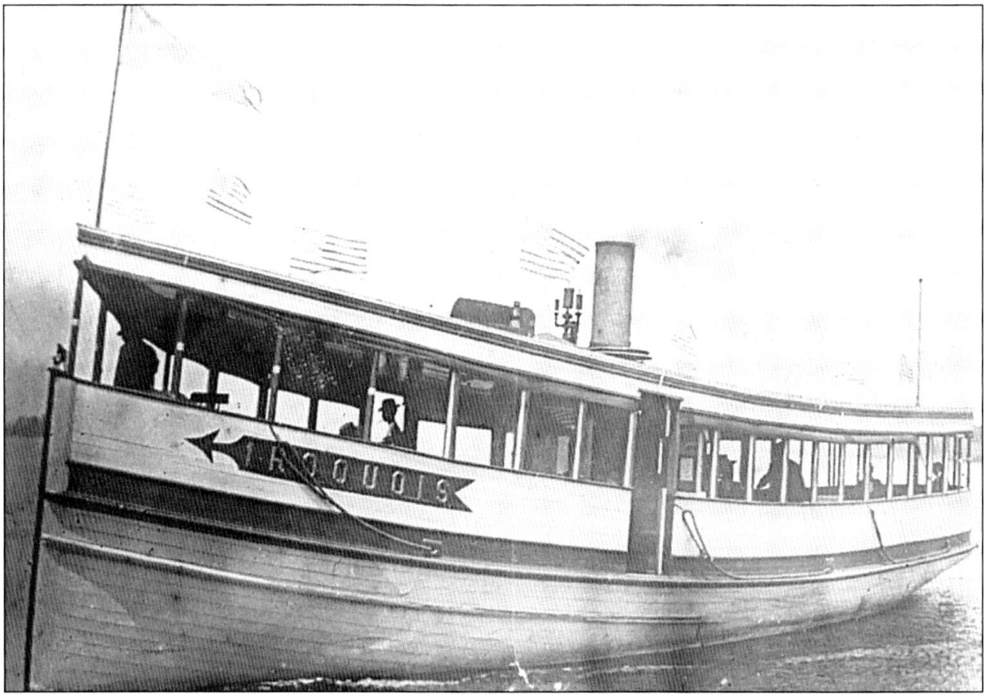

This 1902 photograph shows the *Iroquois*, owned by Amos Quigley at the Midway Hotel. It was the first boat on the lake to have electric lights and among the first to have glass in the windows. *Sailing through Time* chronicles the history of the boat, which operated from 1893 to 1928. (CHJ.)

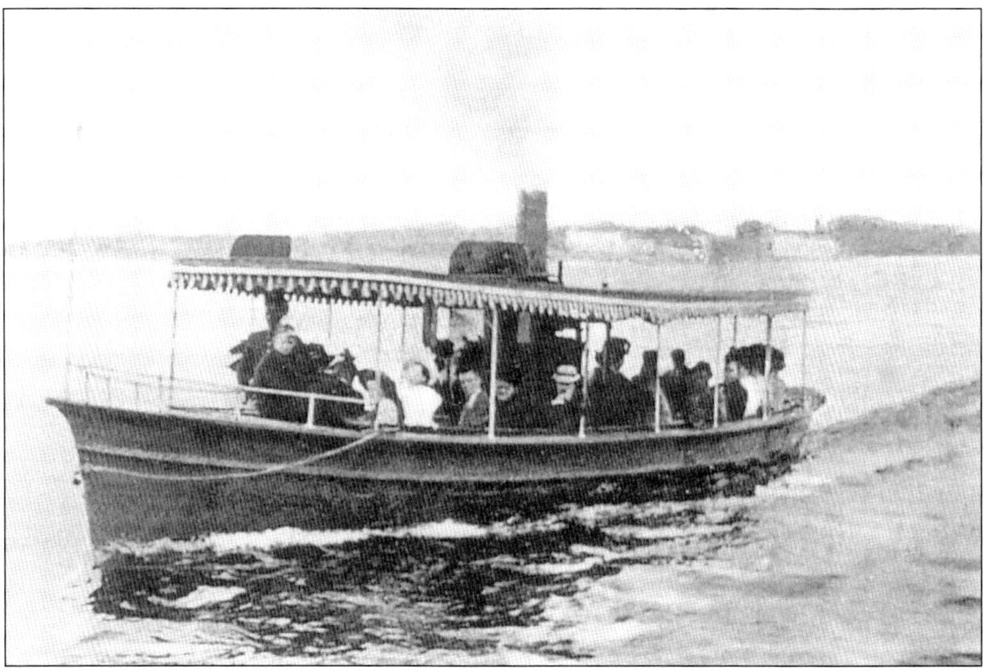

This postcard shows the *Outing*, which joined the fleet of steamers on the lake in 1906. Built in Geneva, Ohio, it was only 50 feet in length. It was open to the breezes of Conneaut Lake but had curtains that could be let down during inclement weather. It operated until 1927. (CHJ.)

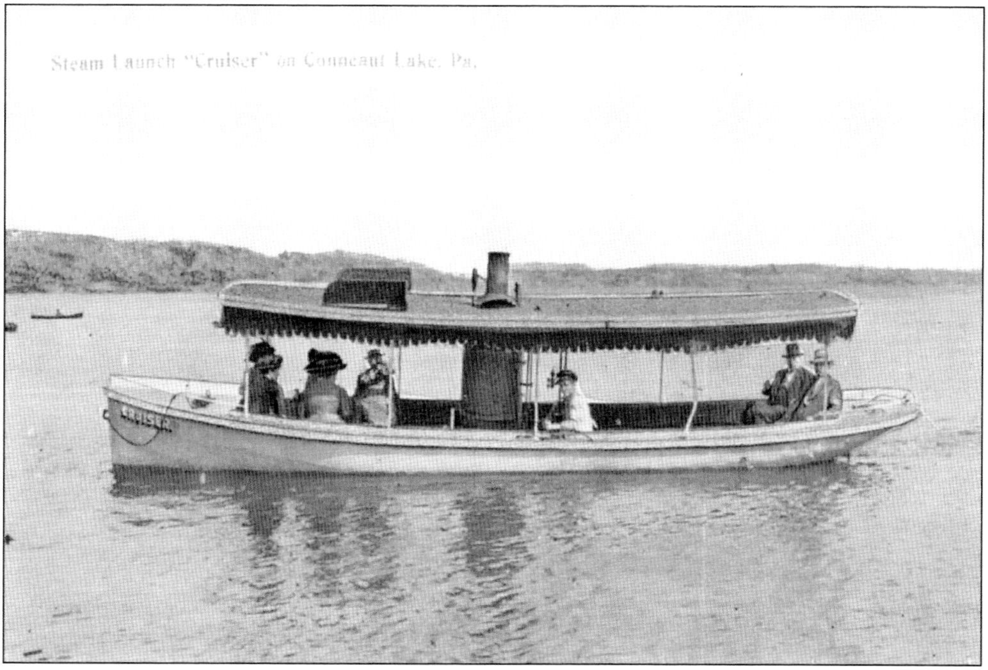

The *Cruiser*, pictured in this early-1900s postcard, was one of the smallest boats on the lake. According to Don Hilton, it often ran "clean-up duty" for larger steamers, meaning it helped pick up passengers between regularly scheduled runs. It was unique because a stern tiller, instead of a wheel, was used for steering. (LFC.)

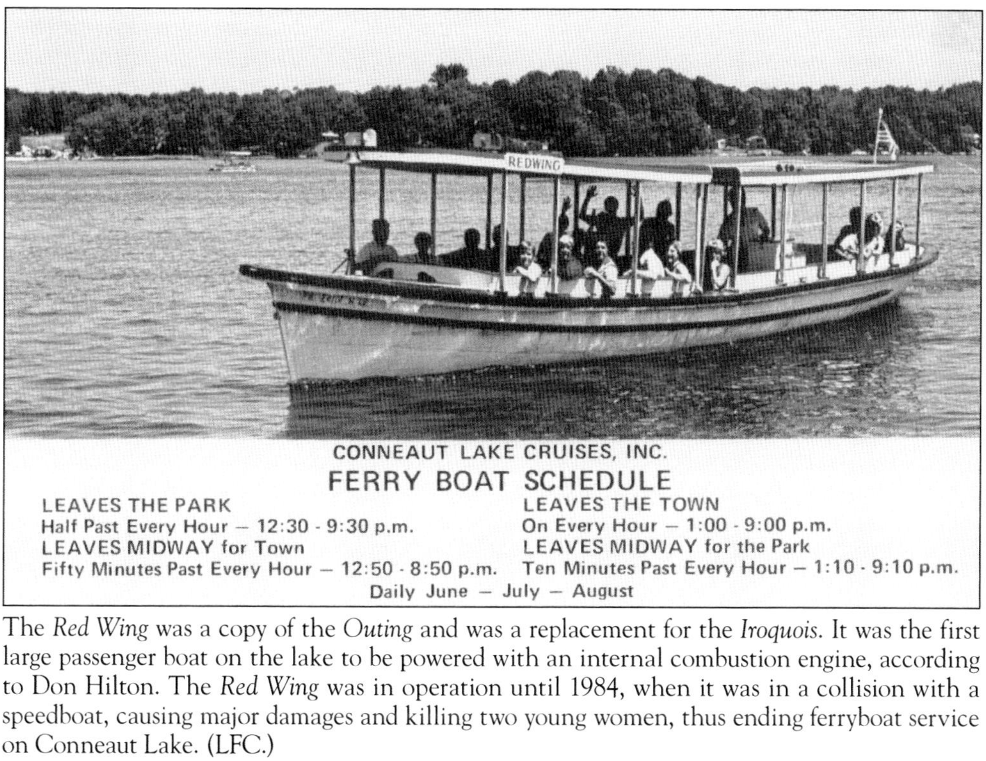

The *Red Wing* was a copy of the *Outing* and was a replacement for the *Iroquois*. It was the first large passenger boat on the lake to be powered with an internal combustion engine, according to Don Hilton. The *Red Wing* was in operation until 1984, when it was in a collision with a speedboat, causing major damages and killing two young women, thus ending ferryboat service on Conneaut Lake. (LFC.)

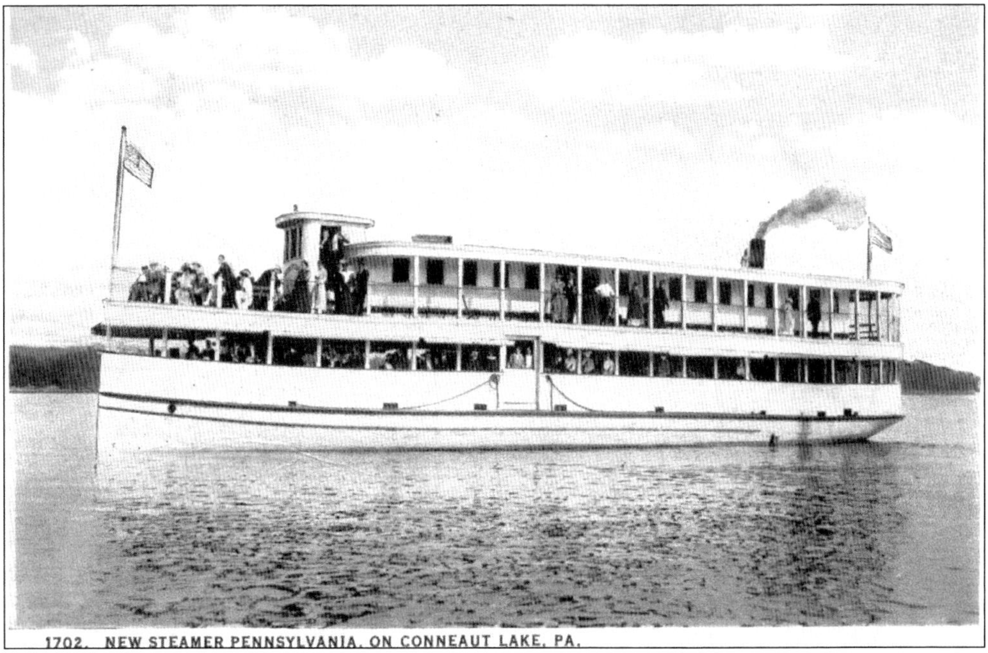

In 1916, the *Pennsylvania* was introduced to Conneaut Lake. It was 102 feet long and had two decks. The lower deck was devoted almost entirely to a dance floor, where people danced to the big band sound as the boat traveled across the lake. It could carry 500 passengers and was built by local men.

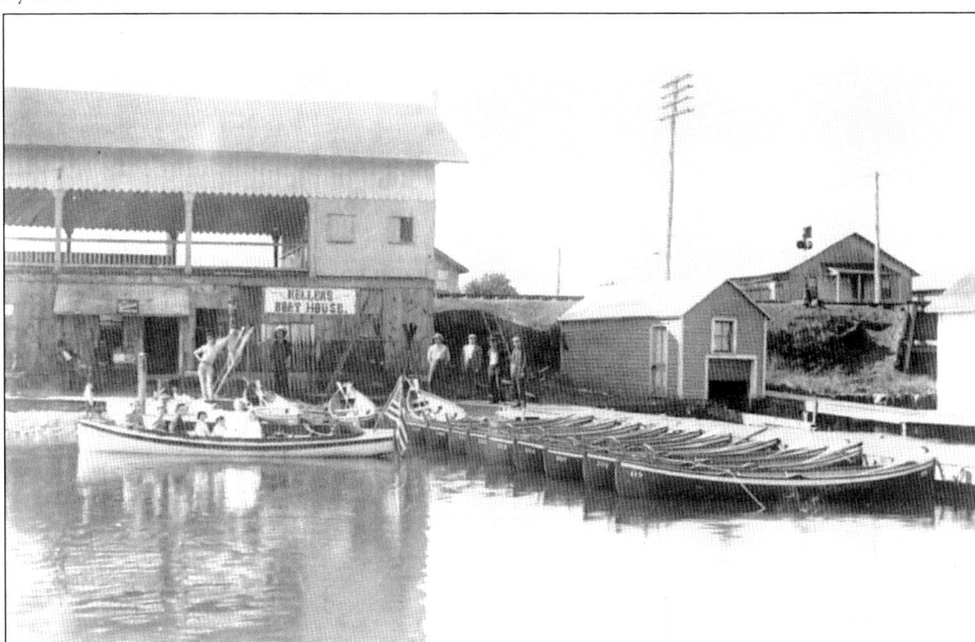

Keller's Boat House, shown in this c. 1915 photograph, was located in Conneaut Lake town and offered boats for rent. In addition to renting boats, owner Wallace Keller also built boats and was one of the owners of the steamer *Conneaut*. He sold the livery to Frank Reimann in the 1920s, as reported in *Sailing through Time*. (LFC.)

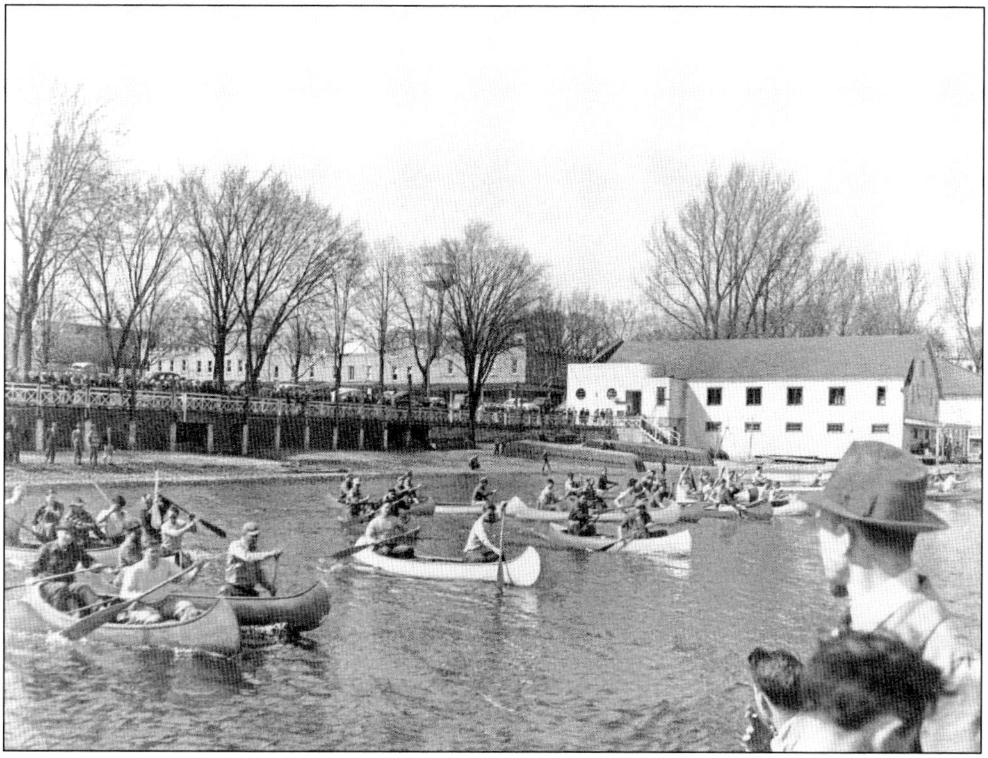

A canoe race from Conneaut Lake to Pittsburgh was part of Crawford County's 1950 sesquicentennial celebration. Canoeists from all areas joined the race. More than 20 teams of two men each competed. Winners were Dr. Robert Moyers and Robert Hixon. (HLF.)

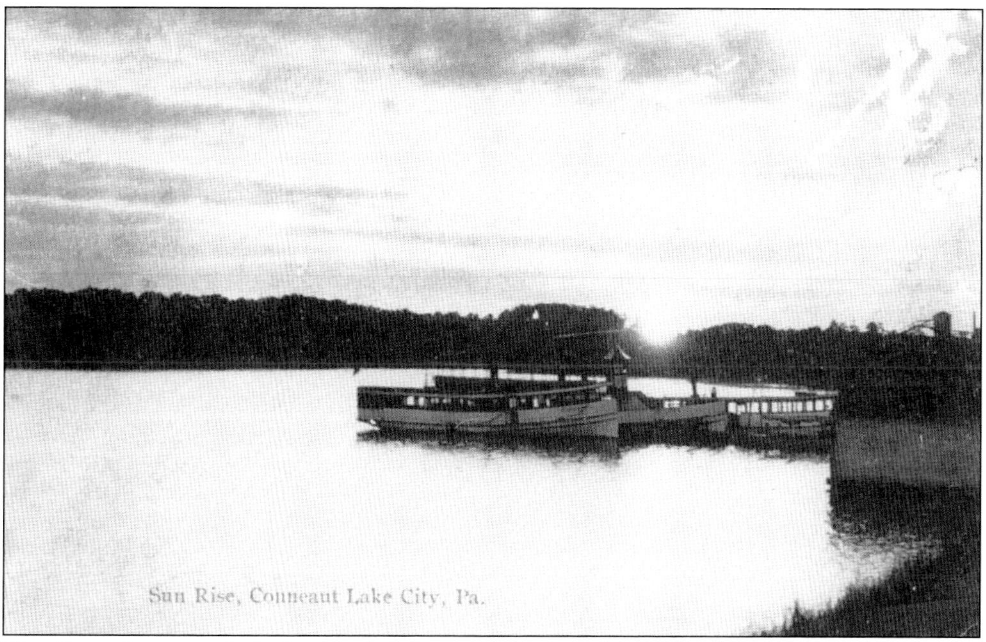

"Sun Rise, Conneaut Lake," reads the caption on this 1919 postcard, showing the beauty of the lake and the natural surroundings with the boats waiting at the docks.

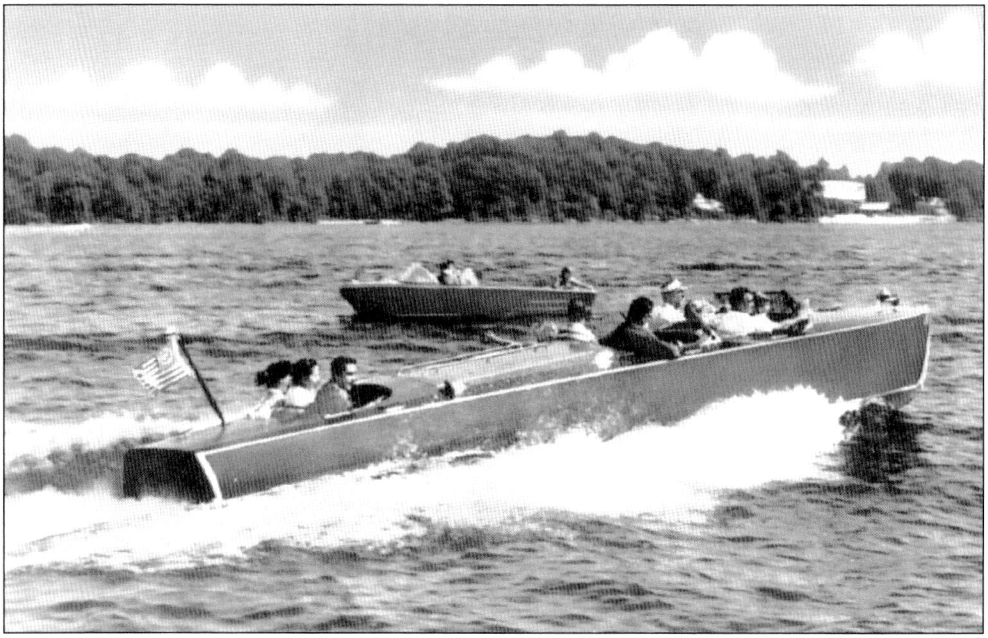

Miss Conneaut, owned by Conneaut Lake Navigation Company, was considered one of the most popular speedboats of its era. Ronald Harned drove *Miss Conneaut I* and *Miss Conneaut II* in the summer of 1950, offering boat rides to tourists at times when boats were very expensive. Reports are six boats were named Miss Conneaut before the boats were sold in 1967. (PHM.)

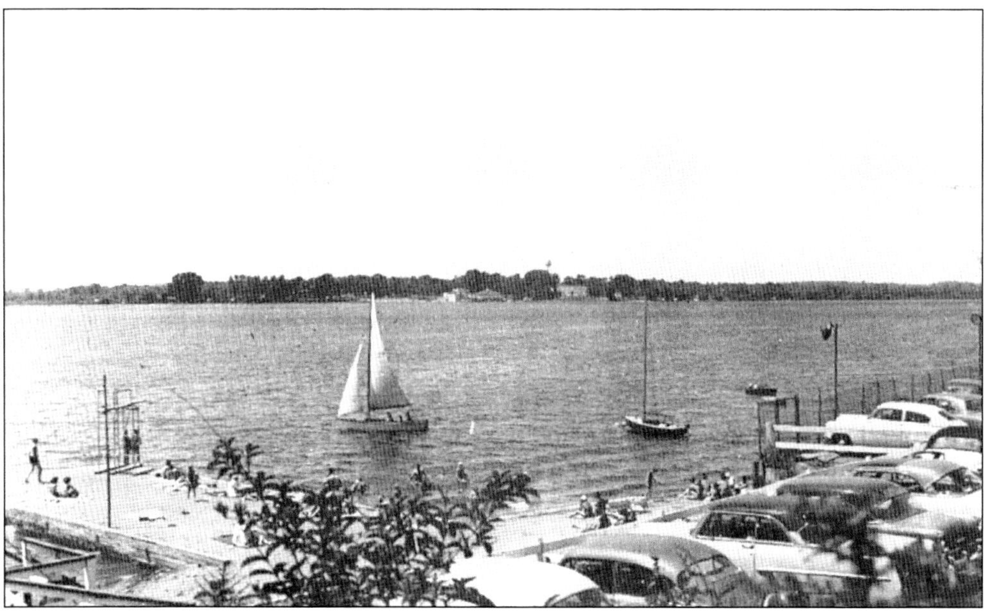

This undated photograph shows the tranquility of a sailboat ride on Conneaut Lake. (PHM.)

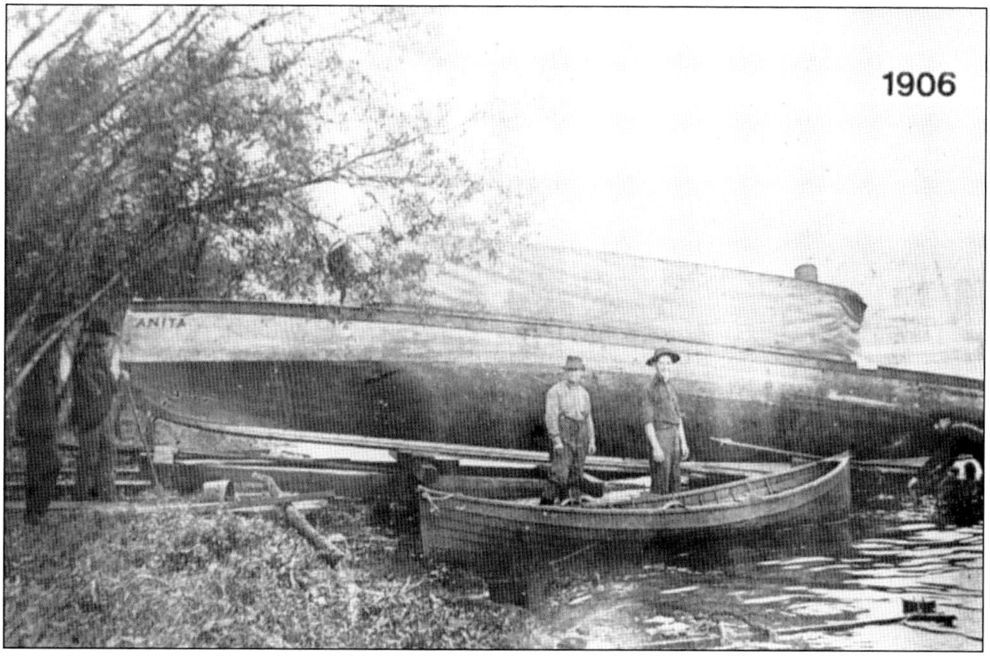

This boat played a major role in Conneaut Lake's history. After buying land adjacent to the lake, Conneaut Lake Ice Co. said it owned the lake and implemented an access fee. Two Pittsburgh men challenged that and put *Anita* on the lake in 1906. It was seized, and the men sued. The Pennsylvania Supreme Court ruled the lake was public property and so no fee could be charged.

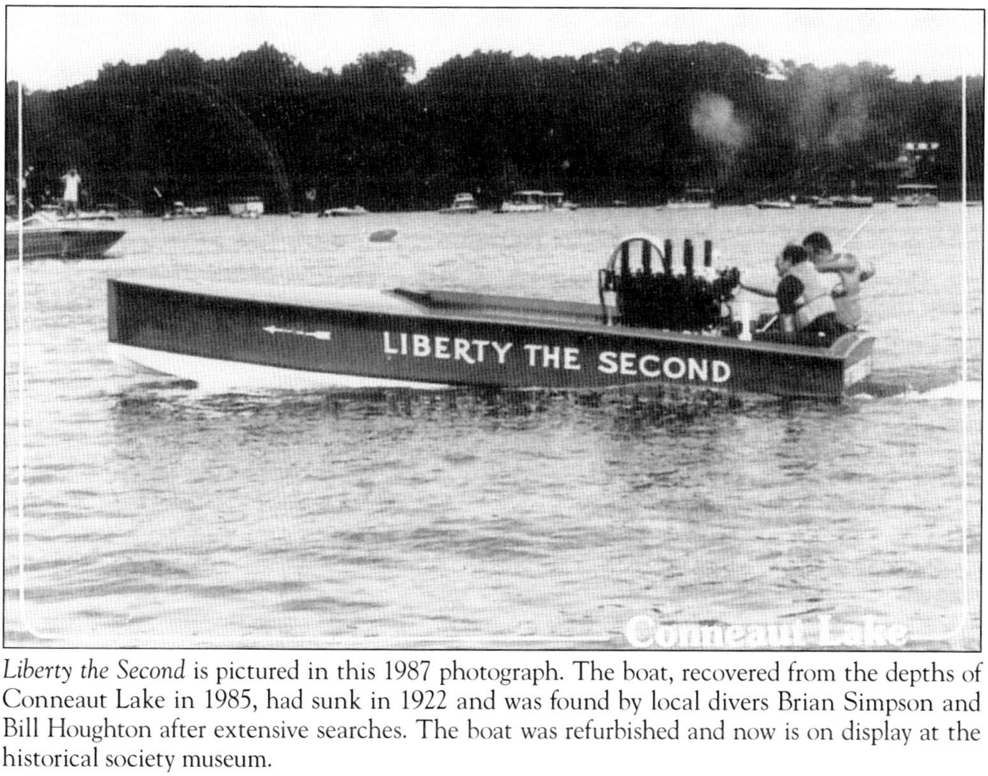

Liberty the Second is pictured in this 1987 photograph. The boat, recovered from the depths of Conneaut Lake in 1985, had sunk in 1922 and was found by local divers Brian Simpson and Bill Houghton after extensive searches. The boat was refurbished and now is on display at the historical society museum.

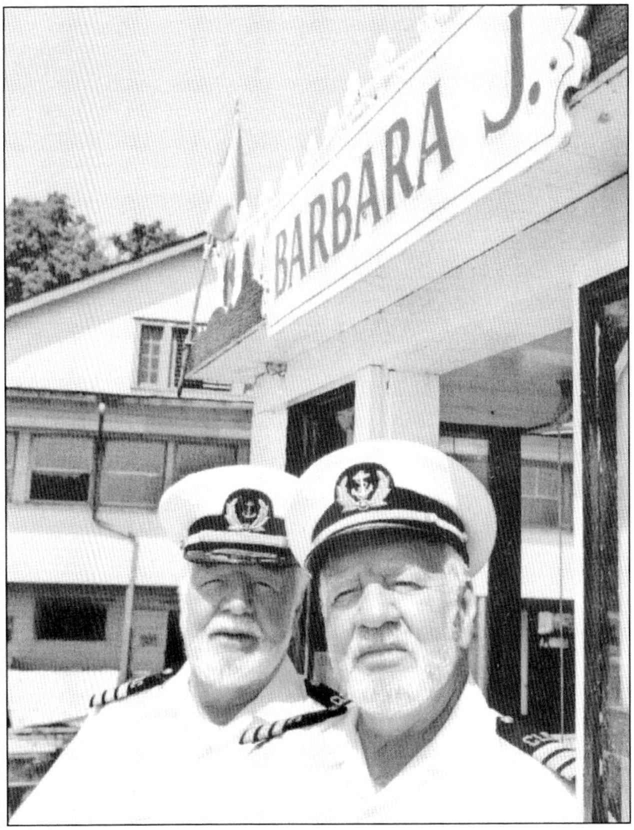

The Hilton twins, Bert and Bill, captains on the *Barbara J.*, pose with the popular paddleboat, which offered rides around Conneaut Lake for tourists and others. The twins, who once rented boats from a livery on the east side, gave talks to acquaint passengers with the history of Conneaut Lake. Decked out in uniforms of boat captains, the men with white beards provided a memorable ride.

The majestic *Barbara J.* made its debut on Conneaut Lake in 1972. Purchased by Lloyd Holland of Conneaut Lake Cruises, it was named in honor of his wife. After the Hollands died in 2000, the boat was purchased by area businessmen. It and the *Kaylee Belle* are the only two passenger boats operating in 2012. It holds 90 passengers and is currently available for charter.

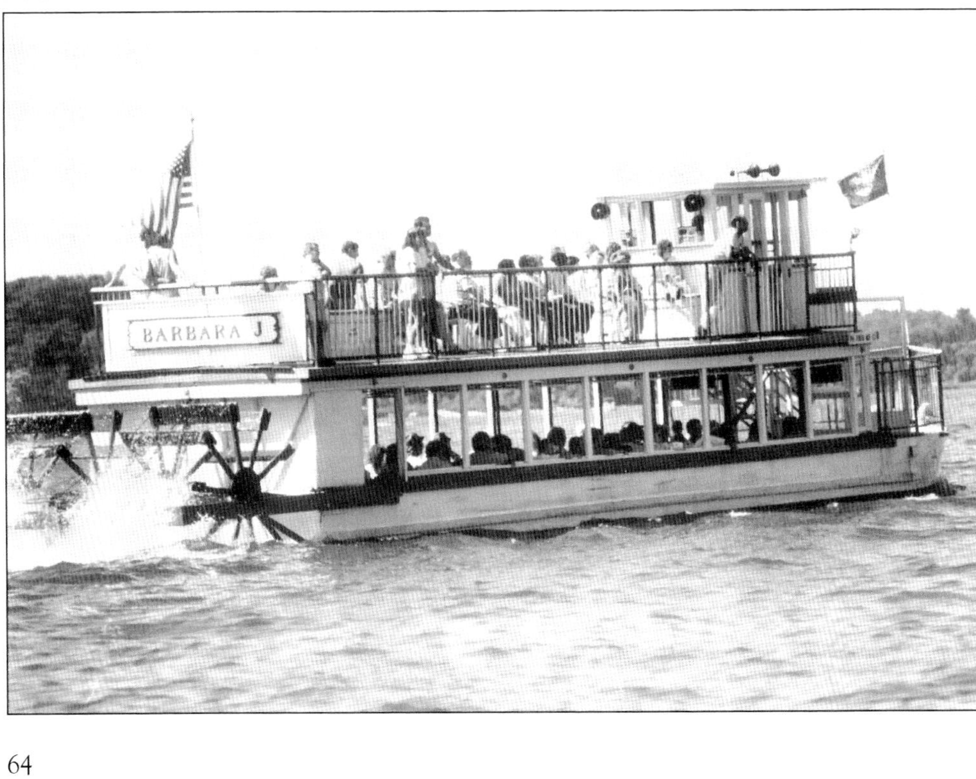

Five

PEOPLE

All communities have one thing that sets them apart from other communities—their people.

Conneaut Lake is no exception. This book shows many of the friendships that have lasted for decades. Photographs of families dating back to the 1800s show not only the faces of ancestors but also their dress and hairstyles.

The personalities of some of these people are evident in the photographs. Pastimes are also evident, such as playing music. Several photographs of musical groups showed Conneaut Lake residents enjoyed all types of music, from country to big band and even the jazz sounds of the Dixie Doodlers. Fishing was another popular pastime.

This chapter also shows Conneaut Lake homes. Some are small bungalows; others are small cottages. Many homes were purchased by people from big cities, who ended up moving to Conneaut Lake year-round. Many people also moved to Conneaut Lake from nearby Meadville. From the Huidekoper Mansion to the small cottages, the welcome mat was always out.

Local residents also got involved in the political scene. James Shellito of Sadsbury Township suggested a new way for political parties to choose nominees. Thus, the Pennsylvania primary system was born. Four other area men served as Crawford County commissioners, James Beatty and Earl Austin of Summit Township and David Glenn and Sherman Allen of Sadsbury Township.

Woven through this chapter, and the entire book, is pictorial evidence of a community where people worked and played together and where people joined hands and hearts to make their hometown a better place in which to live.

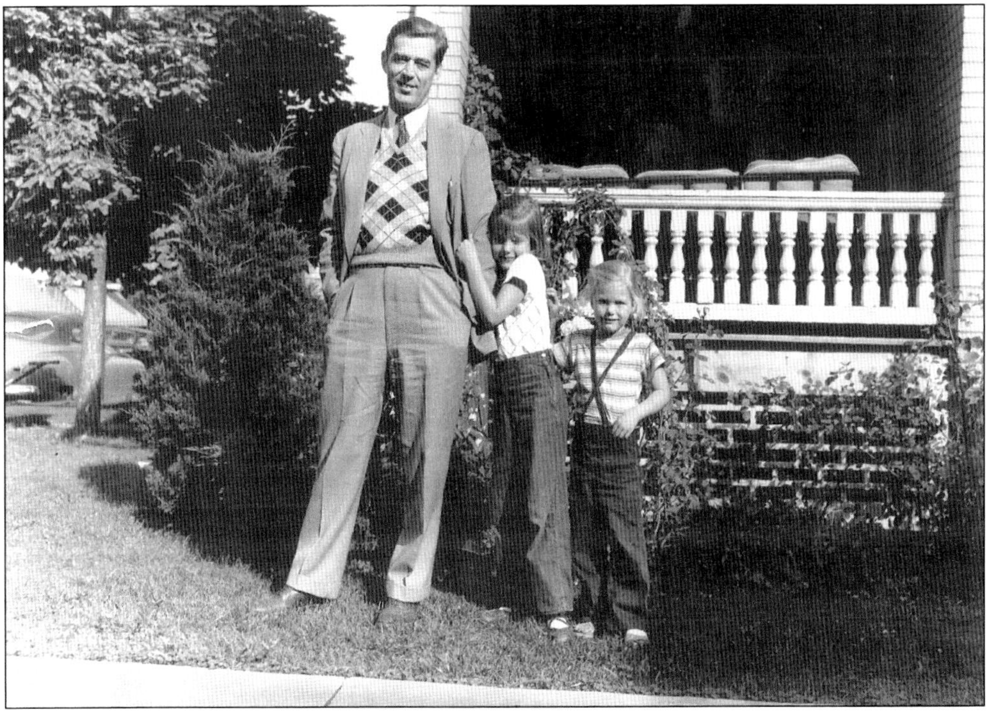

Dr. James Martin, a Conneaut Lake physician for many years, is shown with his two daughters, Bonnie (left) and Nancy. The town honored him when he retired.

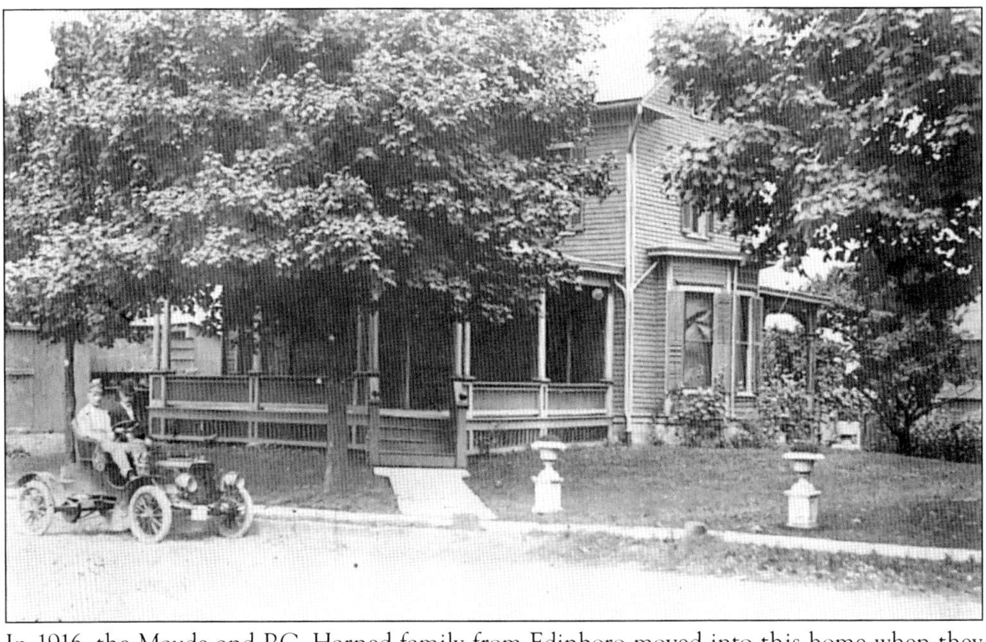

In 1916, the Maude and P.C. Harned family from Edinboro moved into this home when they bought the mill from the Darrow family. When Charles Darrow died, his widow wanted her four girls to attend Edinboro Normal School, so she traded homes with the Harneds. The girls and mother of the Harned family rode the train while father and the four boys moved the furniture by bobsled. The house burned in 1920. (PHM.)

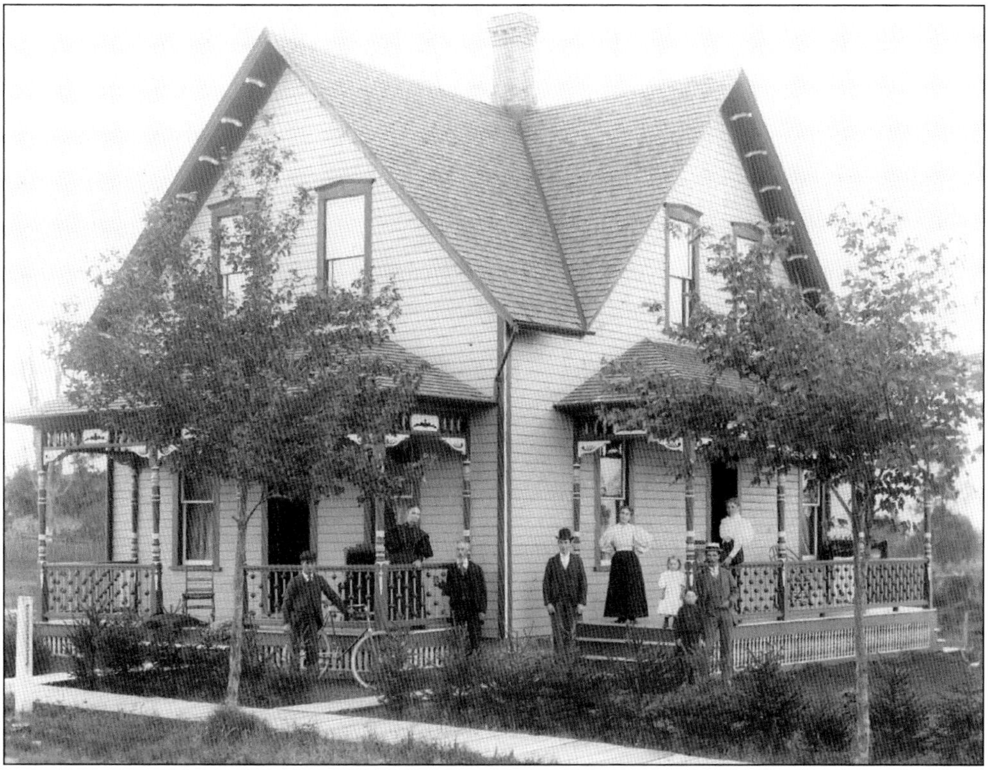

When James and Eliza Moss moved to Evansburg in 1888, they purchased this house and adjoining lot for $150. Built in 1860, the building served as the local school until 1886. Family members in this early-1900s photograph are, from left to right, Ted, Eliza, James, Edward, Verona, Julia, Ralph, Fred, and Lillian. The house sits on the northeast corner of Water and Fifth Streets. (AM.)

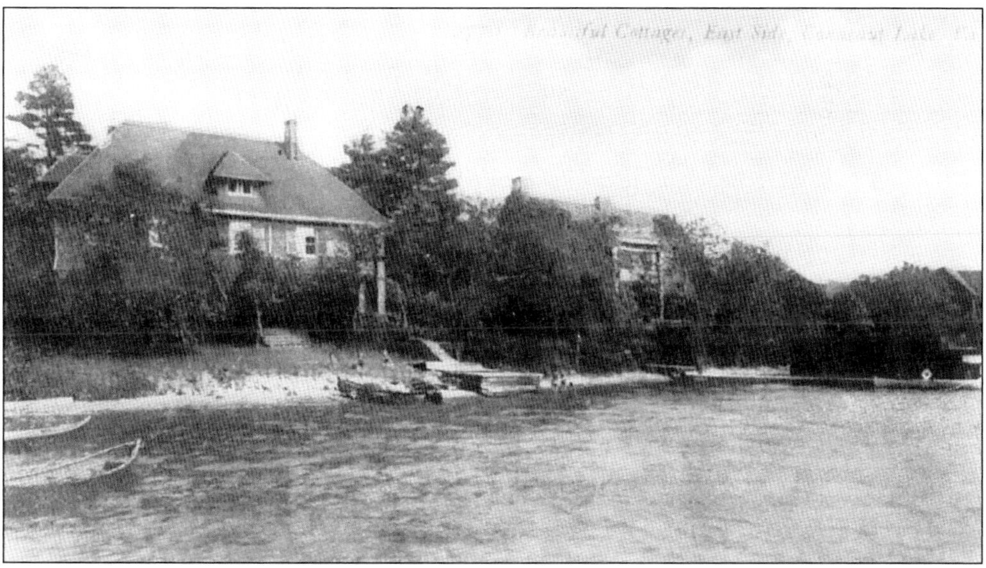

This 1913 postcard shows one of the many beautiful cottages on the east side of Conneaut Lake. Families from Pittsburgh or Cleveland owned many cottages as a summer homes. Many of those families have since moved to Conneaut Lake to live. (LFC.)

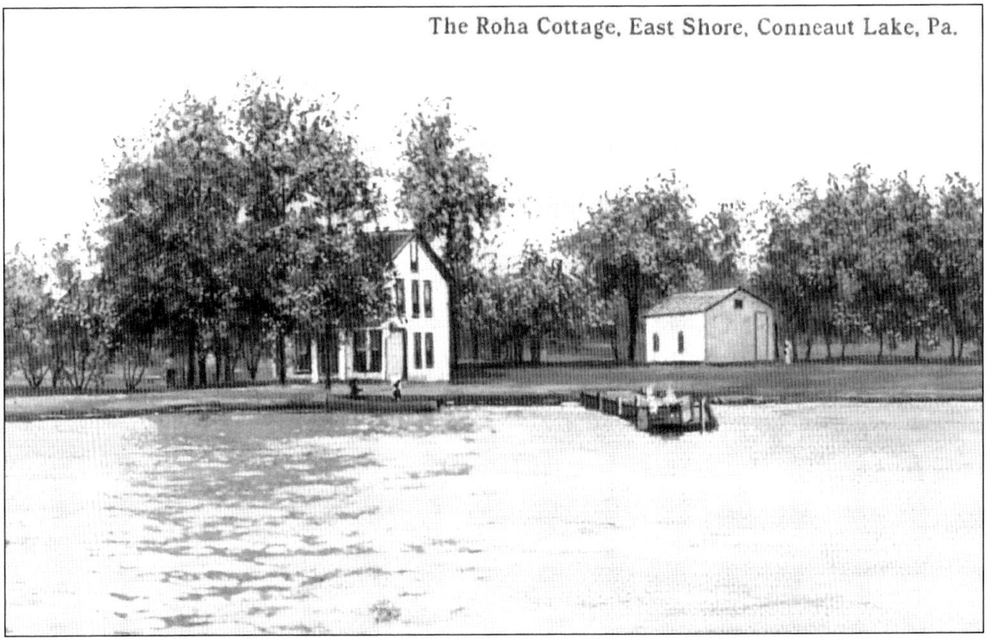

The Roha Cottage on the east shore of Conneaut Lake gives an example of what many cottages looked like in the early 1900s. J.C. Roha was proprietor of the Eastside Inn. The cottage had its own dock for easy access to Conneaut Lake. (PHM.)

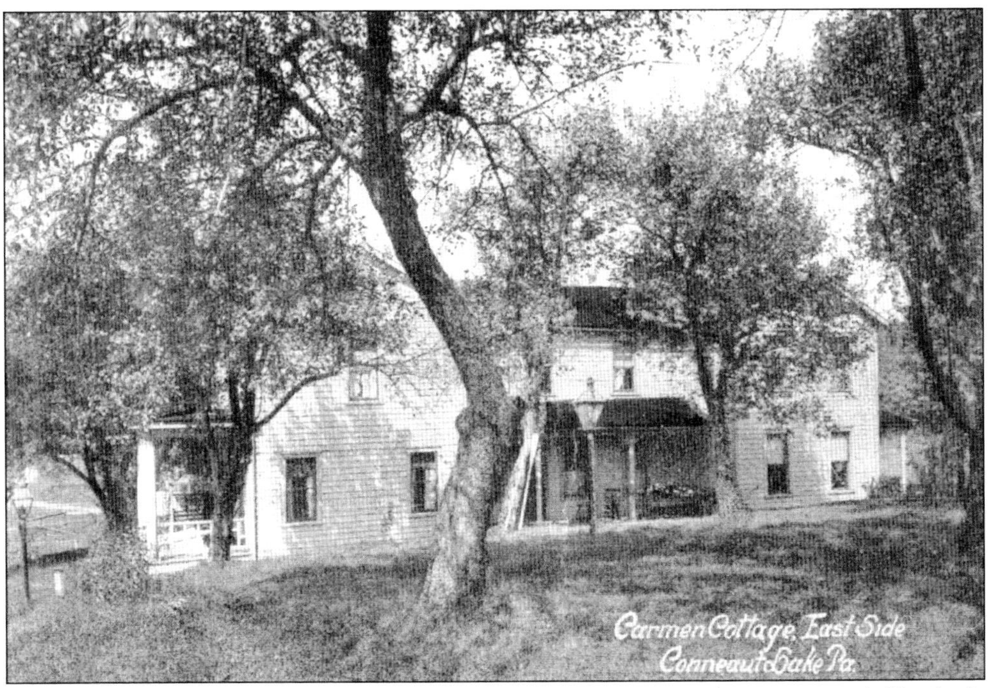

The Carmen Cottage on the east side of Conneaut Lake is a two-story house surrounded by shade trees. It was located near the Iroquois Club. (BH.)

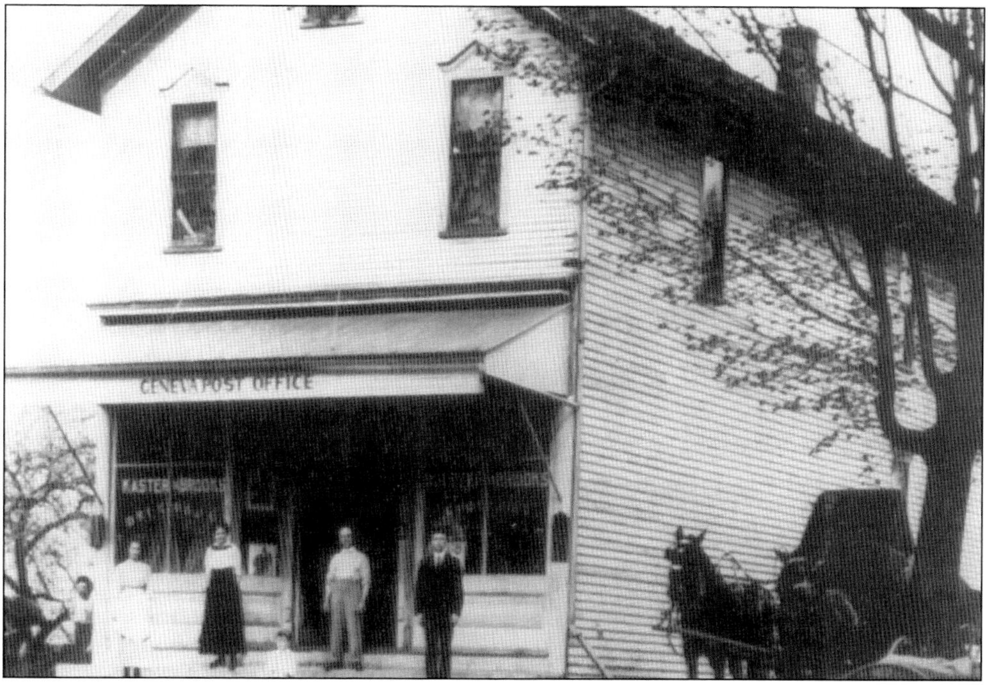

This postcard features a building that was once the post office at Geneva. Fred A. Brooks, one of the owners, was postmaster from 1897 to 1920, at which time the post office was moved to Main Street. It also housed a general store and later a grange hall and community hall. Since 1960, the porch has served as a place for children to wait to board the school bus. (GA.)

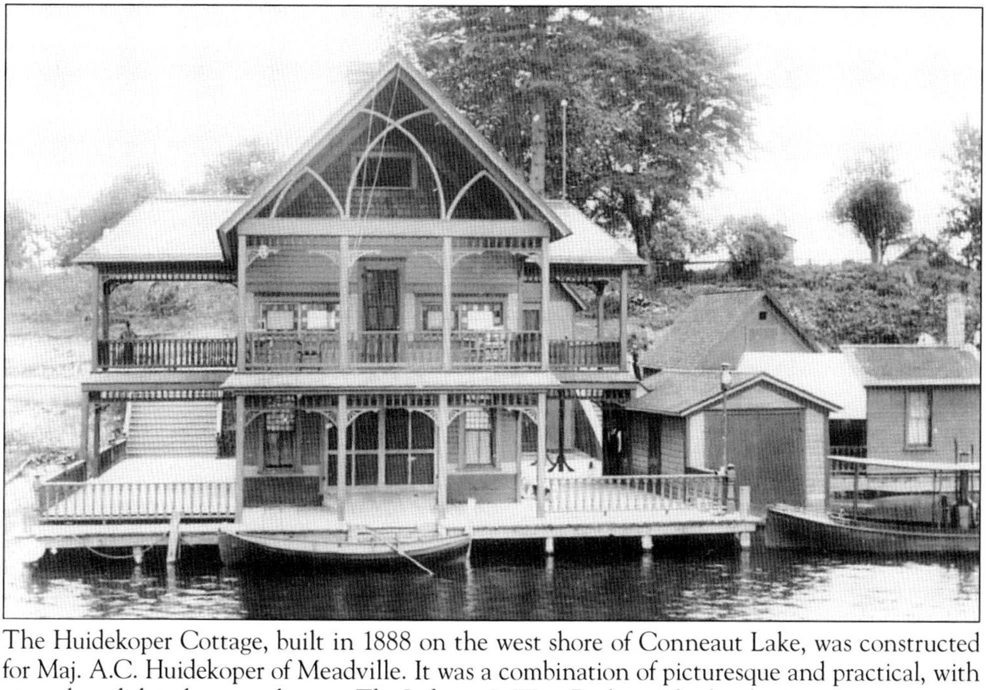

The Huidekoper Cottage, built in 1888 on the west shore of Conneaut Lake, was constructed for Maj. A.C. Huidekoper of Meadville. It was a combination of picturesque and practical, with gingerbread details, according to *The Lake as It Was.* Built on the bank, it was supported by piles. (LFC.)

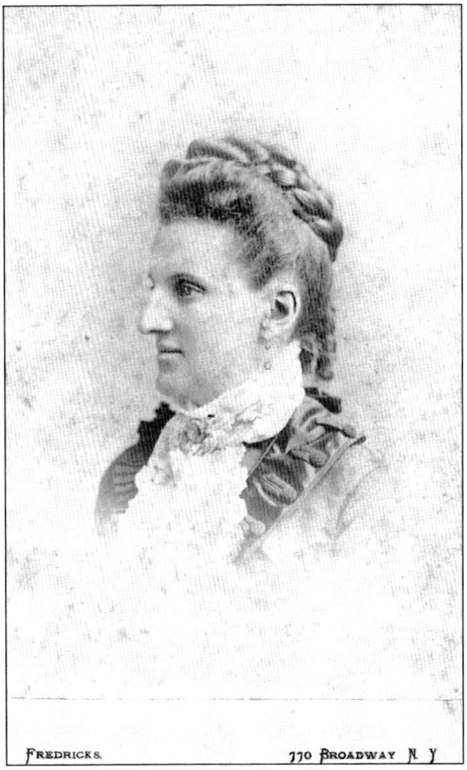

Fannie Huidekoper, wife of A.C. Huidekoper, is seen in this 1880 portrait. She loved to fish, and Fred Moss built a boat specifically to accommodate her. The Huidekopers had a mansion on the bank and operated a horse stock barn on Aldenia Drive. The mansion is still at that location.

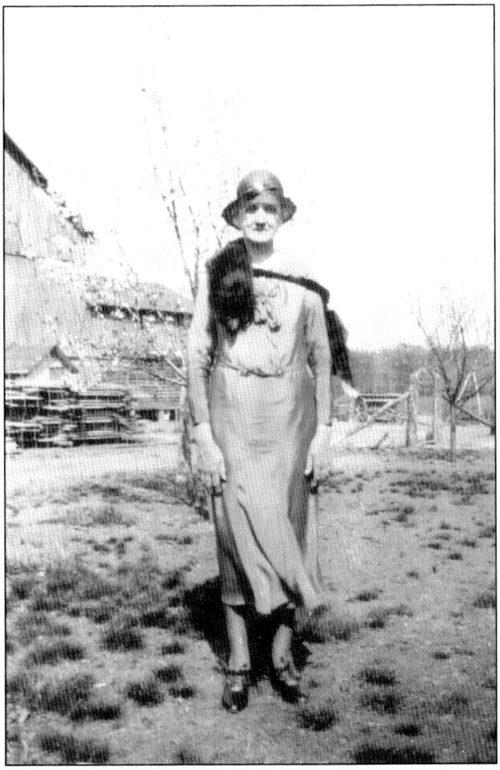

Elsie McCormick Mushrush of the Geneva area was an accomplished songwriter and pianist. She wrote classical and nonclassical songs, including many waltzes with titles associated with the Conneaut Lake area. One example was the "Exposition Park Waltz." She was known nationwide for her work.

The Luty Cottage, located on the east side of Conneaut Lake, was purchased by the Bronson Luty family of Pittsburgh in 1911, after the family had spent summers at the lake for several years. Pictured here are family members and their dog. The original cottage burned in 1922 and was rebuilt in 1923. Bronson and Anne Luty made that cottage their permanent home in 1972. (LFC.)

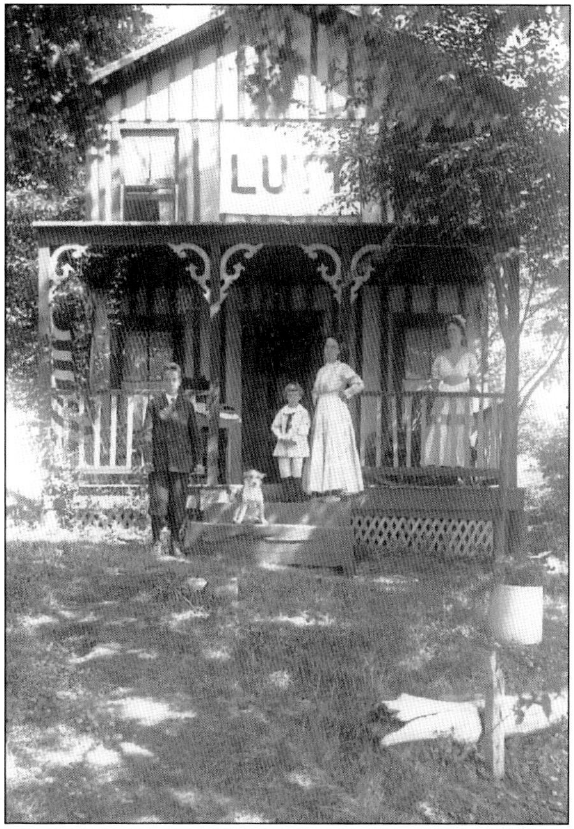

The interior of the Luty Cottage was cozy, with a wicker rocking chair in front of the fireplace and pennants on the walls. (LFC.)

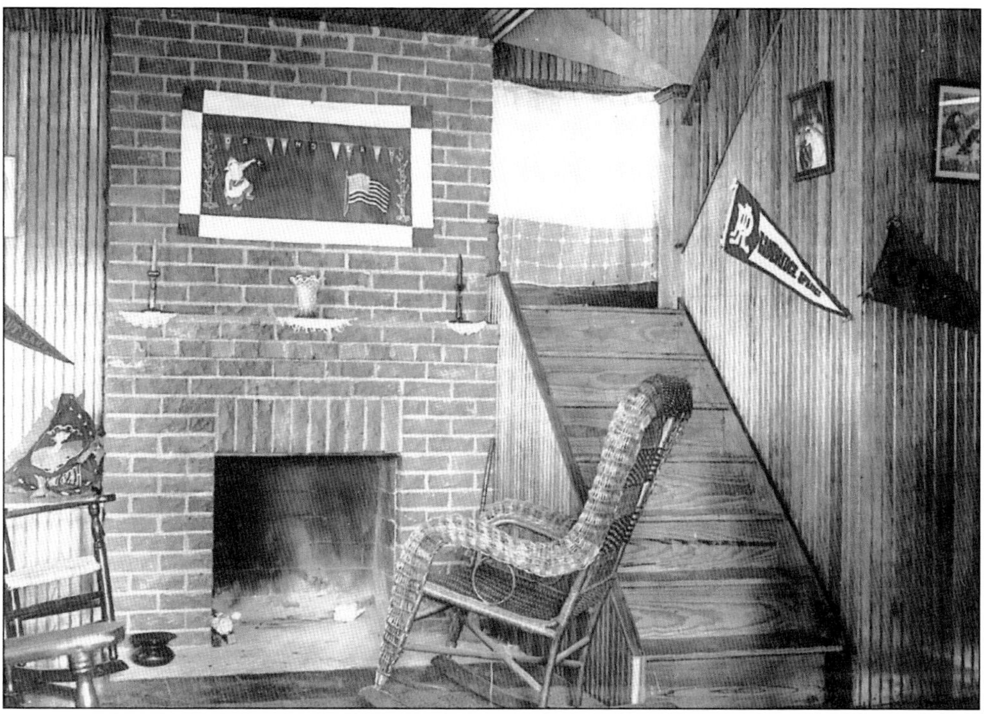

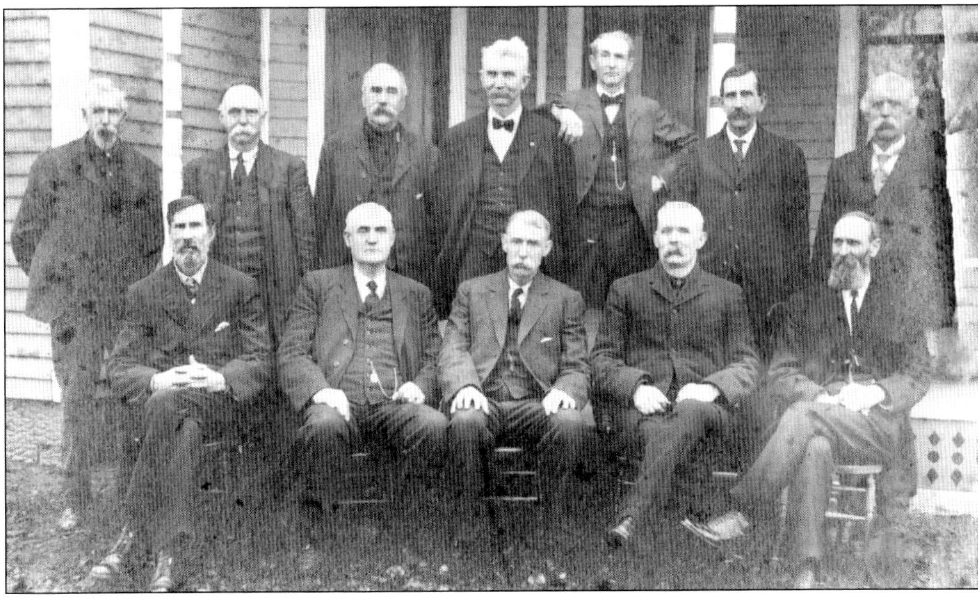

Lifelong neighbors and schoolmates are pictured in 1912. None of the 12 ever smoked or drank and never had a cross word with one another. From left to right are (sitting) William Andrews, Joseph W. "Wink" Adsit, Harvey Andrews, Frank H. Adsit, and Edward Adsit; (standing) Henry See, Harvey Adsit, Abram Adsit, Fred Adsit, George DeArment, Albert Adsit, and Asbury See.

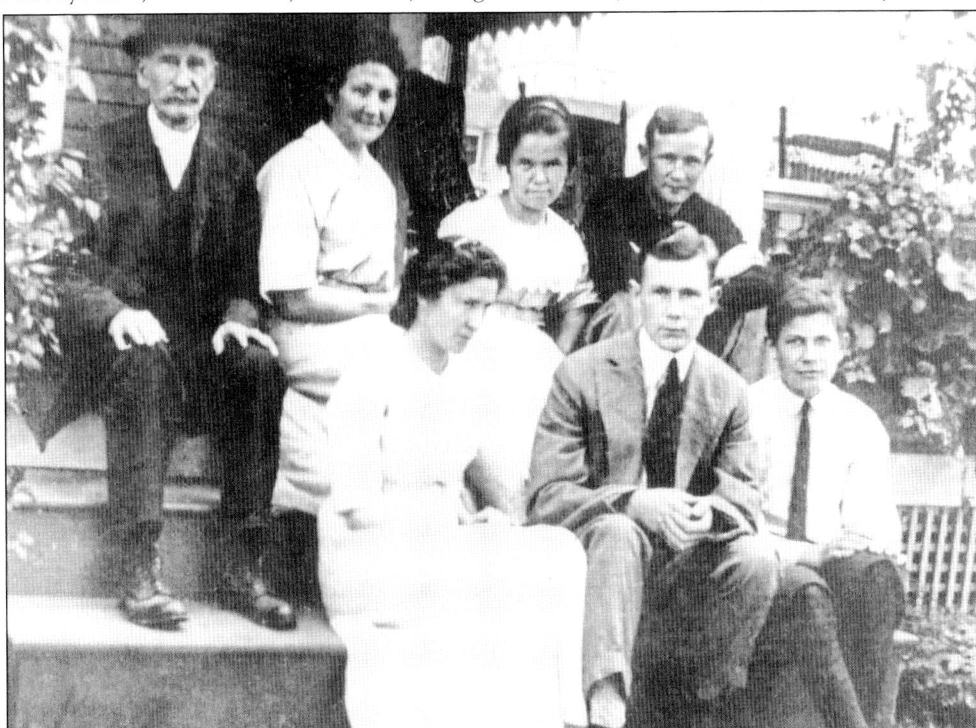

The Ralston family of Conneaut Lake poses in 1915. From left to right are (first row) Maye, Ray, and Paul Ralston; (second row) Wilson Minnis Ralston, Elsie DeArment Ralston, Hazel Ralston and Carl Ralston. The Ralstons were very active in community events in early Conneaut Lake.

Phyllis Martin, wife of Dr. James Martin, poses with her four children in this photograph. Children are, from left to right, Bonnie, Nancy, James Jr., and William. Dr. James Martin was the town physician for decades, with an office in downtown Conneaut Lake. He was honored at a retirement party given by the community. (PM.)

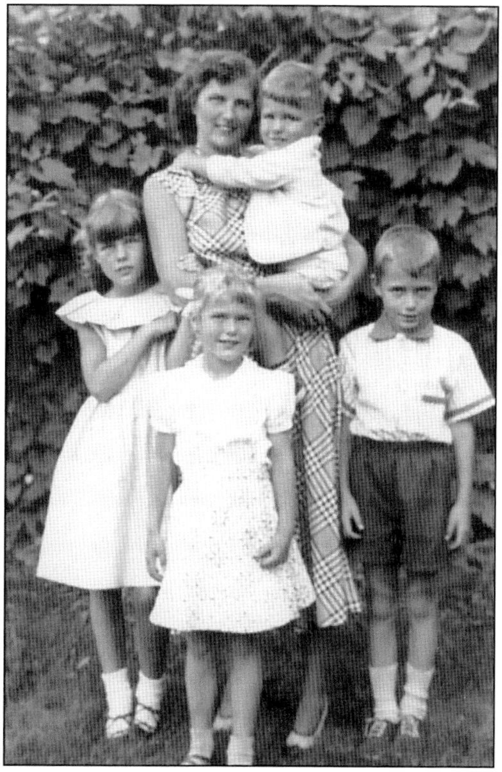

The McGuire family, developers of Oakland Beach and the Oakland Beach Hotel, pose for a family portrait. The McGuires started the Oakland Beach development in 1879, which expanded to include a hotel, bathing beach, mini-park, and more. (LFC.)

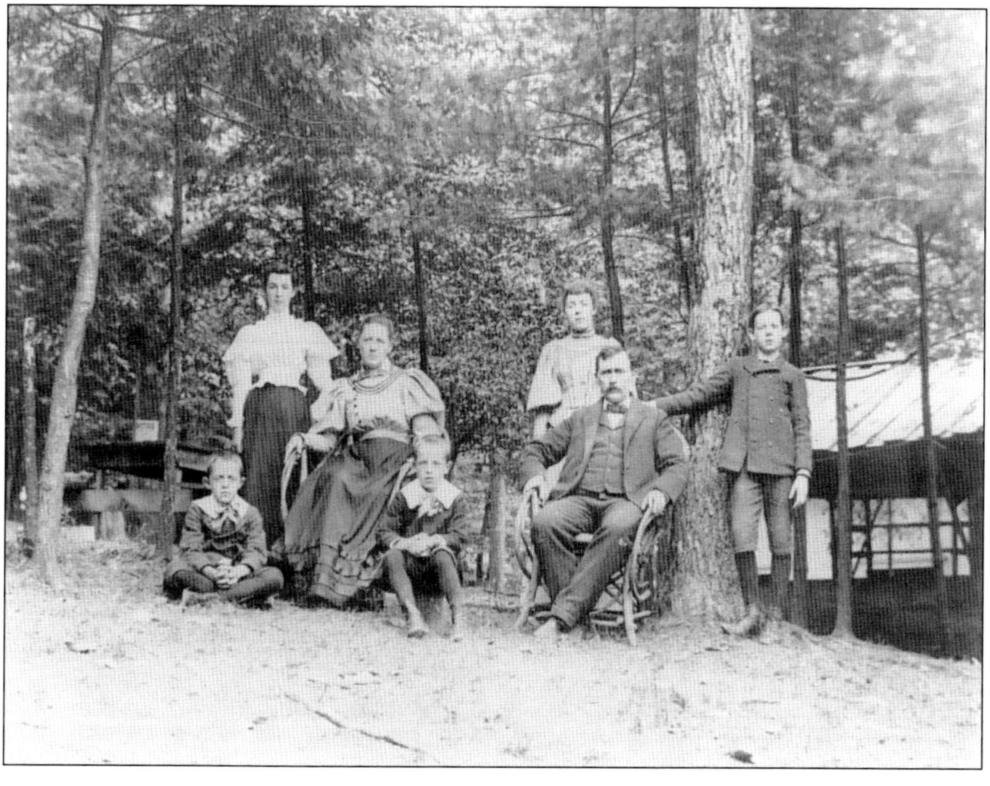

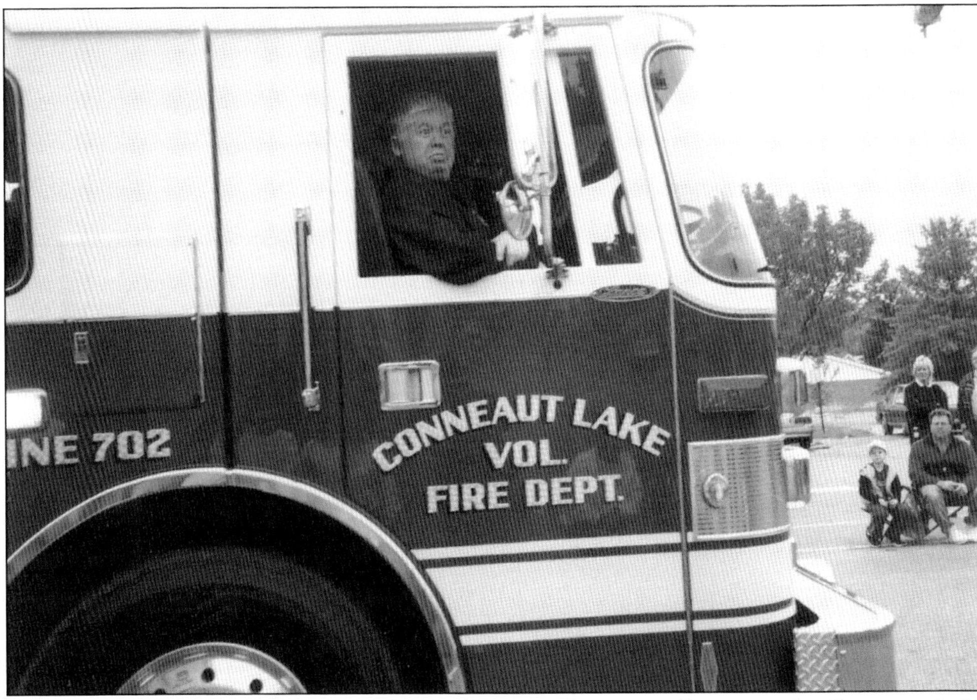

Ron "Butch" Millard, a Conneaut Lake resident, was the guest of honor in the Conneaut Lake Fall Pumpkin Fest Parade as he rides in the fire truck. Although mentally challenged, Millard was accepted by the town and involved in many activities throughout his life.

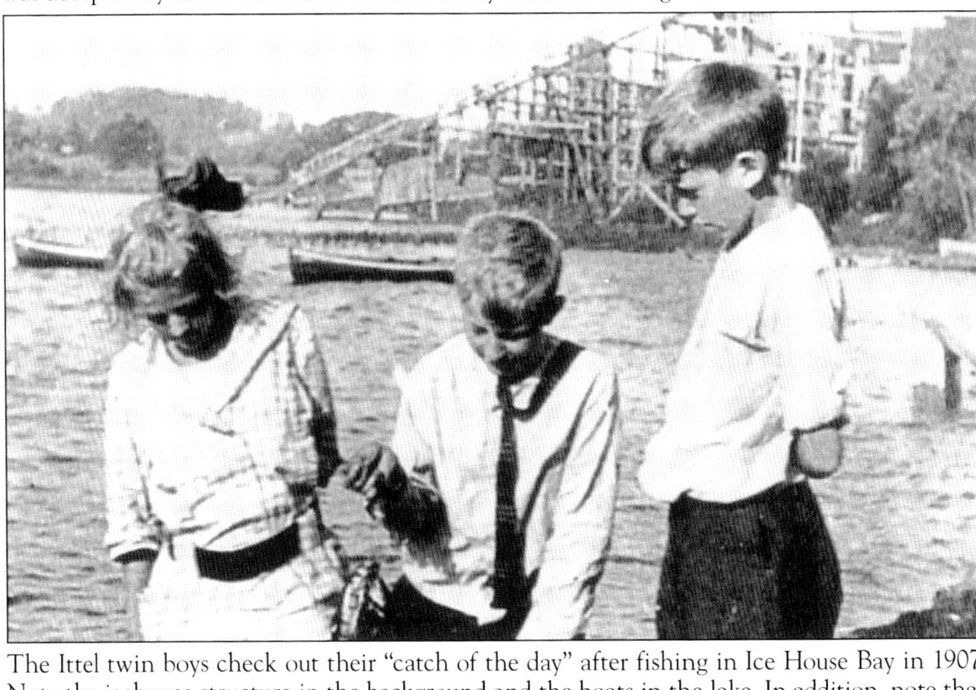

The Ittel twin boys check out their "catch of the day" after fishing in Ice House Bay in 1907. Note the icehouse structure in the background and the boats in the lake. In addition, note that the fishing attire worn by Frank Ittel included a tie. At right is William "Bill" Ittel, who became a dentist and a prominent Conneaut Lake resident. The girl is unidentified. (CHJ.)

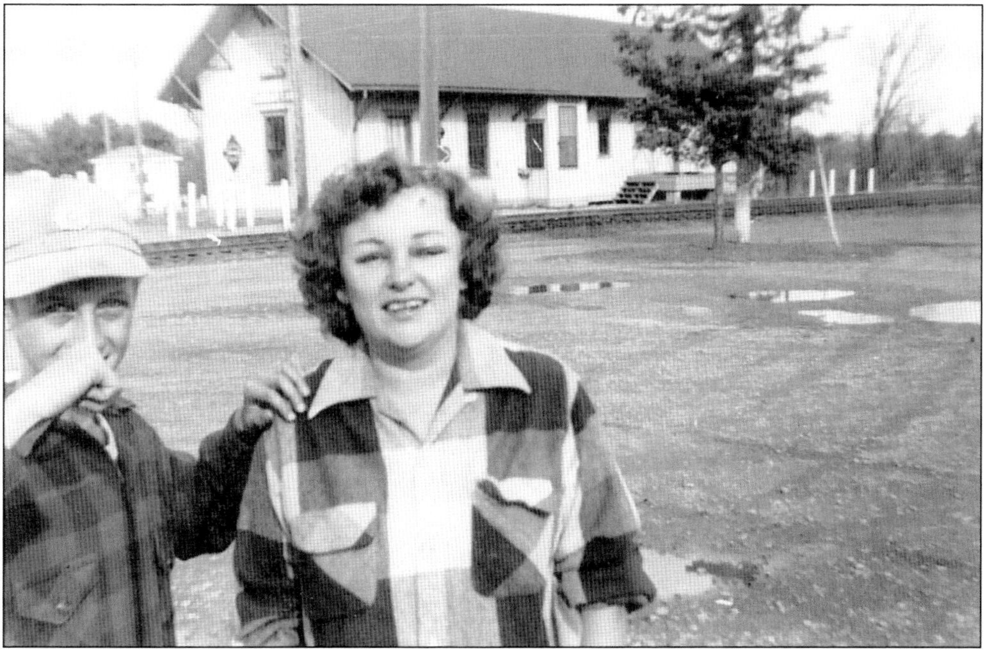

Jim Heffern and his mother, Arlene Heffern, are seen in this 1950s photograph, taken on the south end of town at the Conneaut Lake Railroad Station. The Hefferns have been longtime residents of Conneaut Lake.

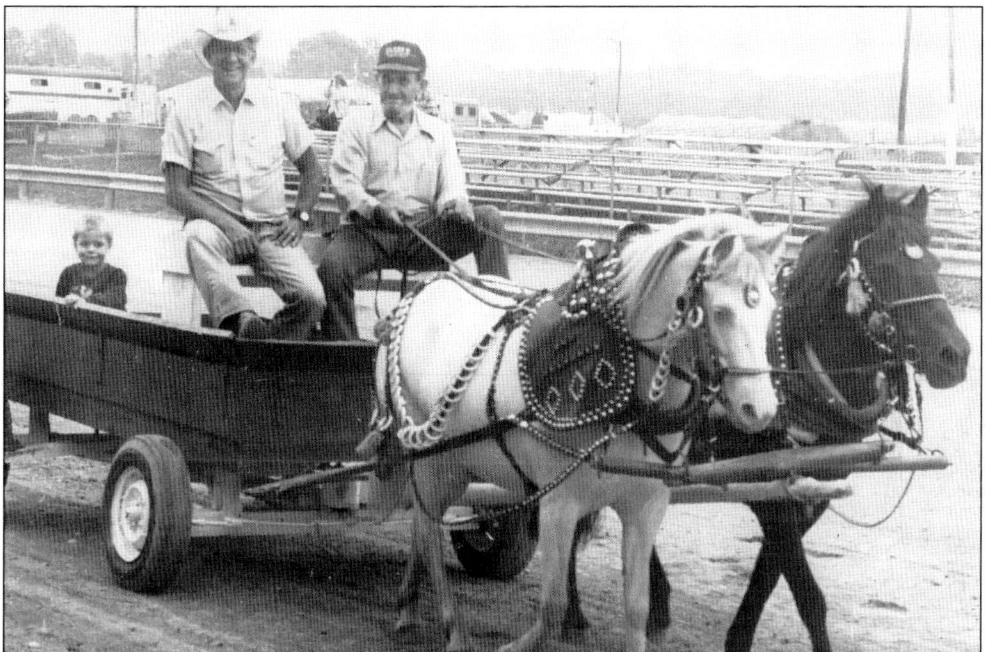

Larry Groger, on the left, formerly of Conneaut Lake, is riding in a horse-drawn wagon at the 1992 Crawford County Fair at Meadville, with his grandson Matt Wilson in the back of the wagon. Until his health did not allow him to participate, Groger spent the week at the fair every year competing in events in the horse department. (MT.)

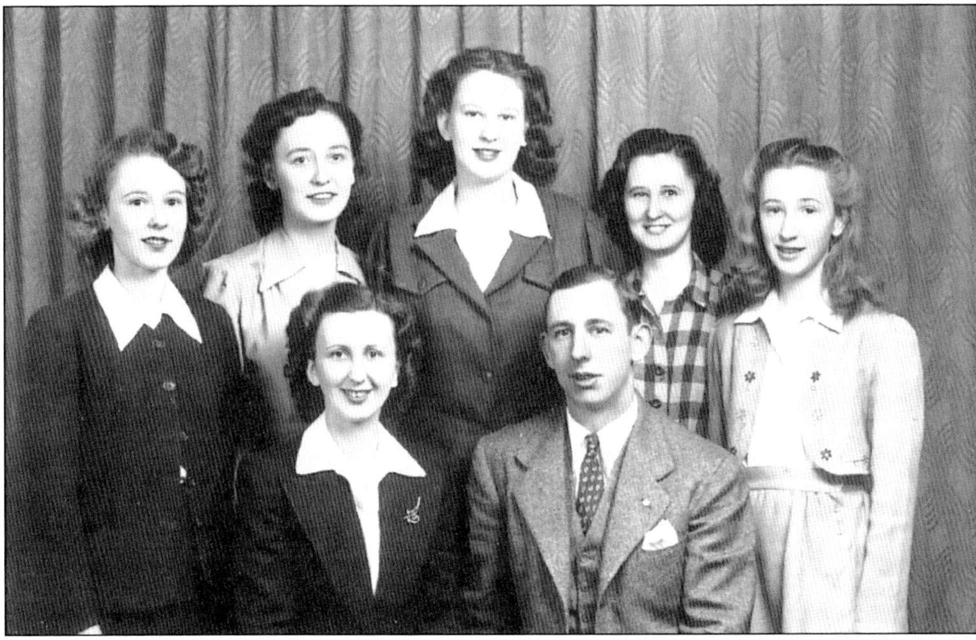

The Stilley siblings pose in this 1947 photograph. From left to right are (first row) Zella and Dick; (second row) Betty, Virginia, Lena, Ann, and Ella. The Stilleys have been a longtime leading family in the community, participating in many community organizations. (BS.)

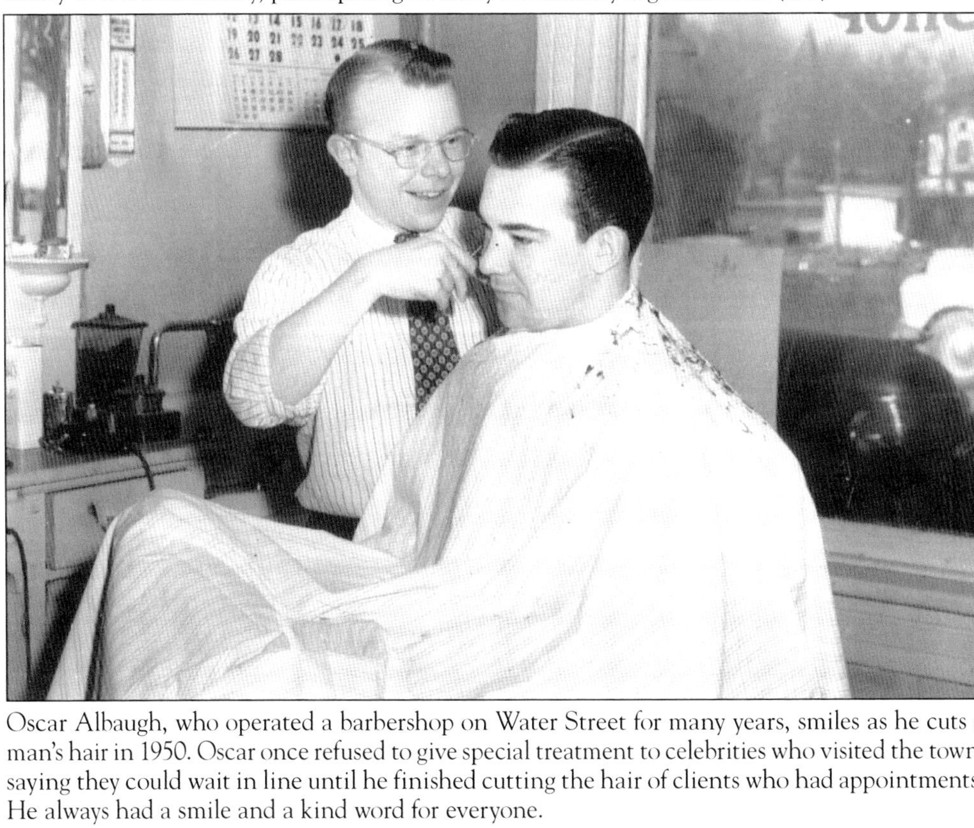

Oscar Albaugh, who operated a barbershop on Water Street for many years, smiles as he cuts a man's hair in 1950. Oscar once refused to give special treatment to celebrities who visited the town, saying they could wait in line until he finished cutting the hair of clients who had appointments. He always had a smile and a kind word for everyone.

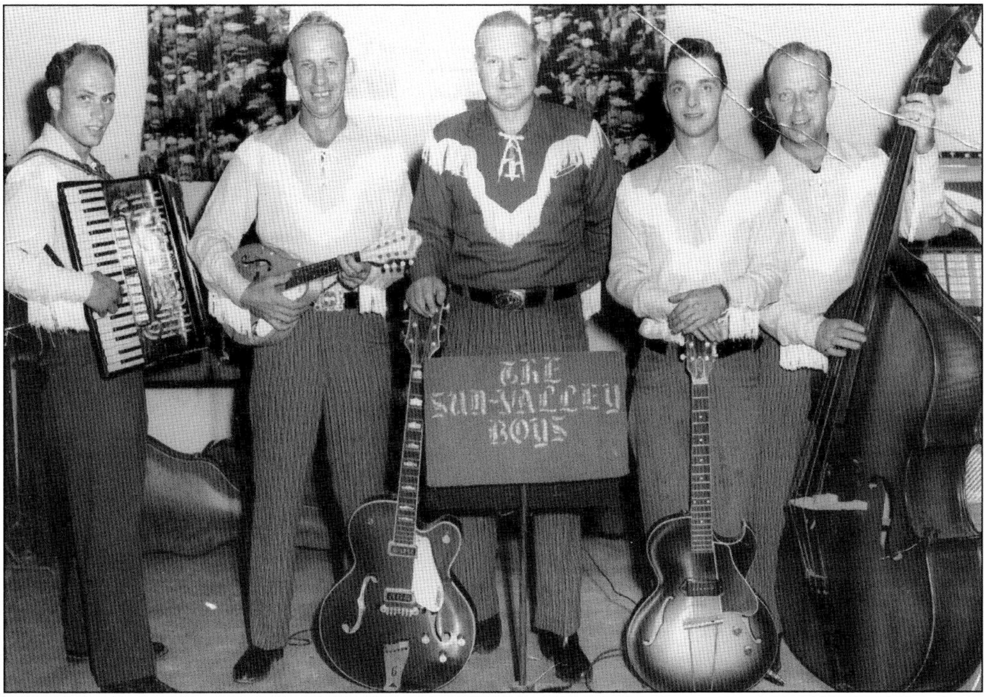

The five members of the Sun Valley Boys are, from left to right, unidentified accordion player, Larry Groger, Chet Roberts, Roy Blackburn, and unidentified bass player. In the 1950s (when it is believed this photograph was taken), band members all dressed alike. Country music was popular in the Conneaut Lake area at that time.

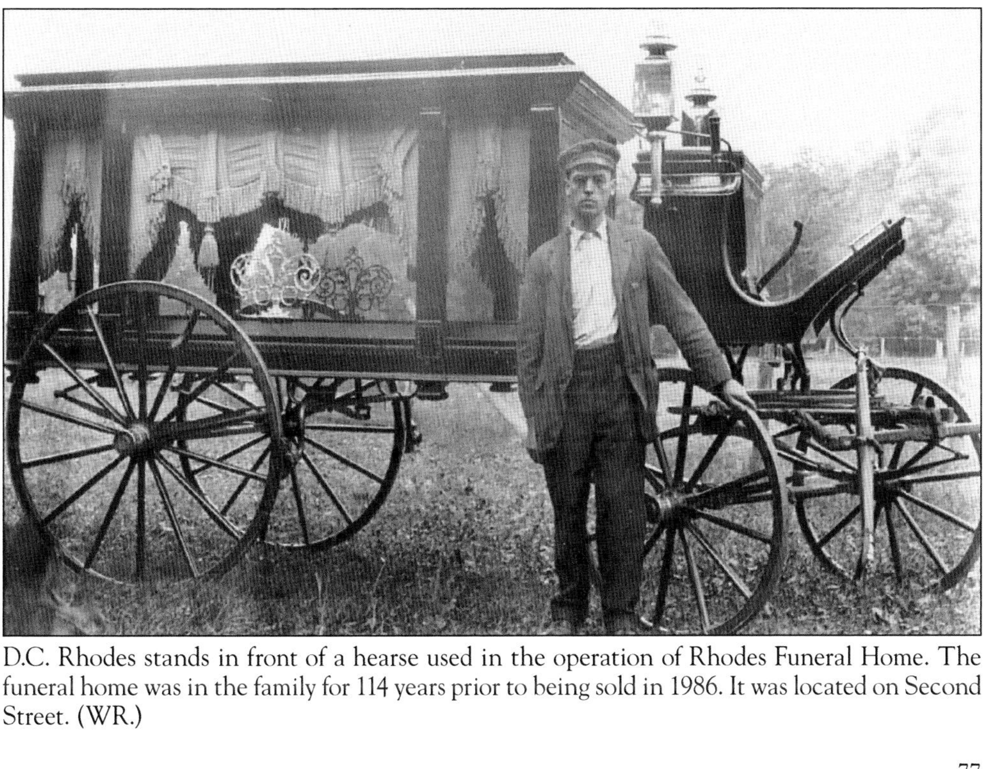
D.C. Rhodes stands in front of a hearse used in the operation of Rhodes Funeral Home. The funeral home was in the family for 114 years prior to being sold in 1986. It was located on Second Street. (WR.)

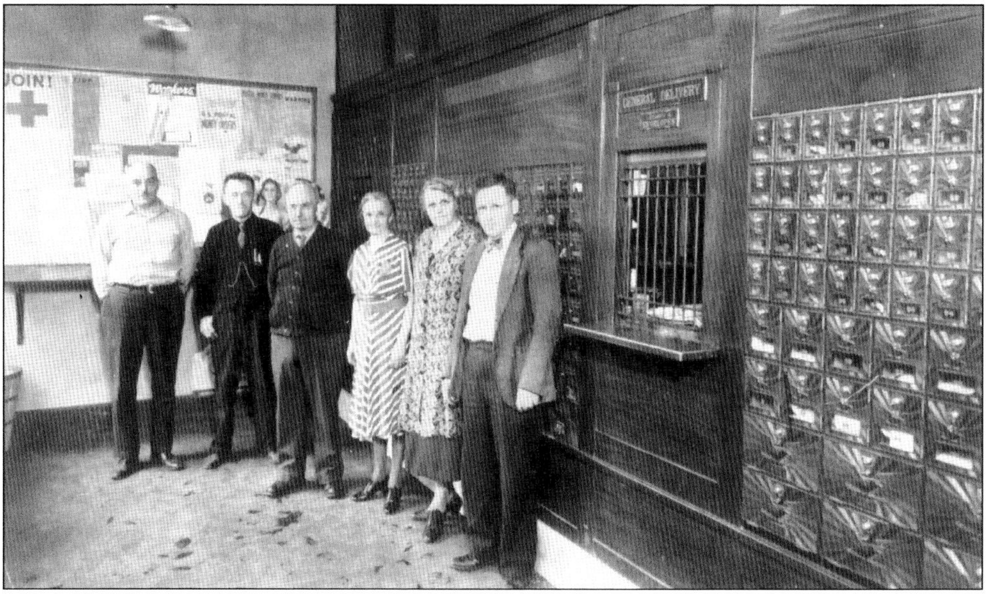

Six US Post Office employees are photographed in this picture from the 1930s. From left to right are Charles W. Olson, carrier for Route No. 2; J. Irving Cleveland, carrier for Route No. 1; Frame Shontz, afternoon worker; Margaret Shontz, clerk; Emma Voelger, clerk; and George W. Scott, carrier for Route No. 4.

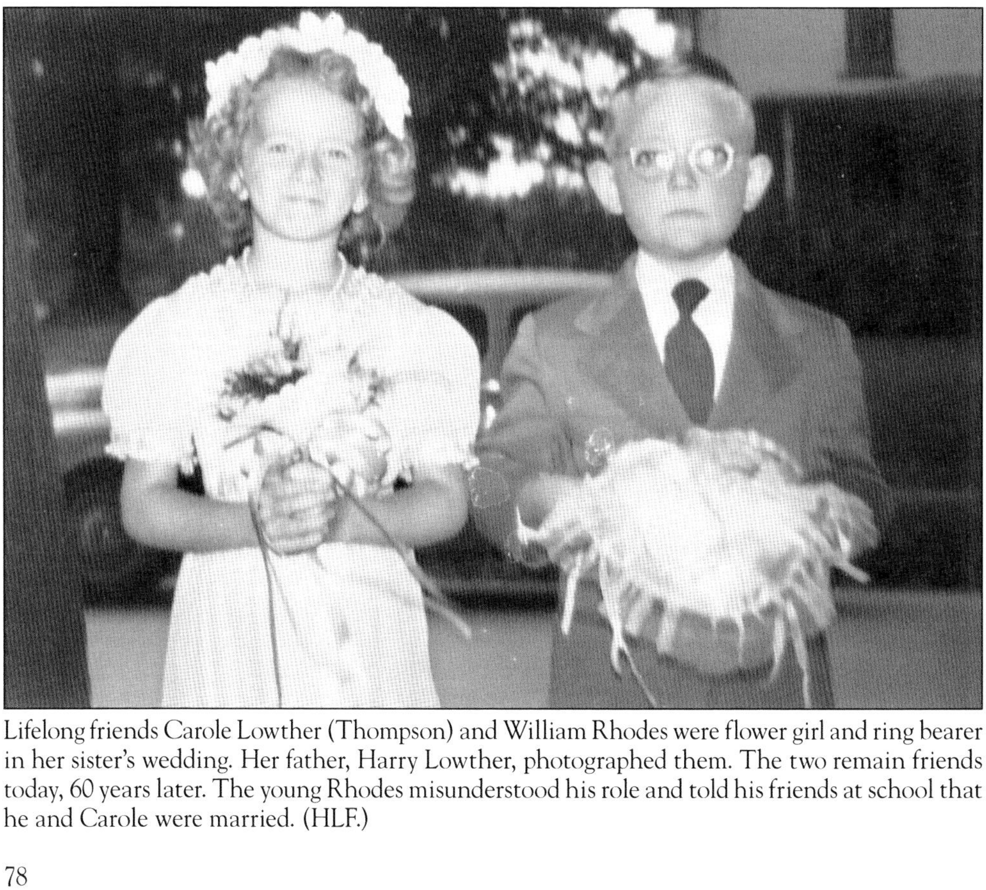

Lifelong friends Carole Lowther (Thompson) and William Rhodes were flower girl and ring bearer in her sister's wedding. Her father, Harry Lowther, photographed them. The two remain friends today, 60 years later. The young Rhodes misunderstood his role and told his friends at school that he and Carole were married. (HLF.)

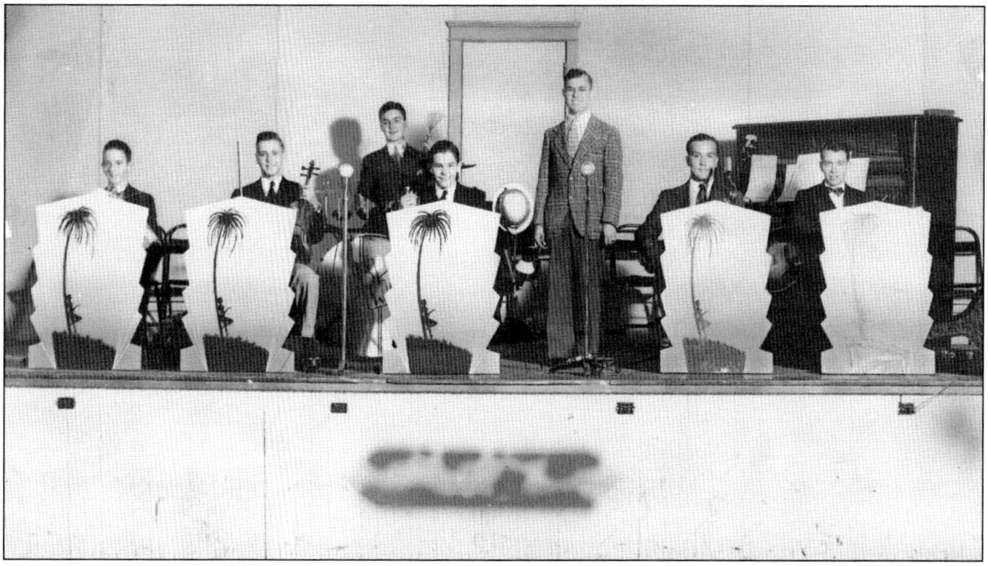

Musical entertainment at the Conneaut Lake Community Hall in 1937 included musicians, from left to right, Charles Hornstein, accordion; Joseph Hornstein, guitar; Bill Wardian, drums; Lyle Petterson, trumpet; Newty Griffith, leader and piano; Paul "Dusty" Rhodes, saxophone; and D. Moody, guitar.

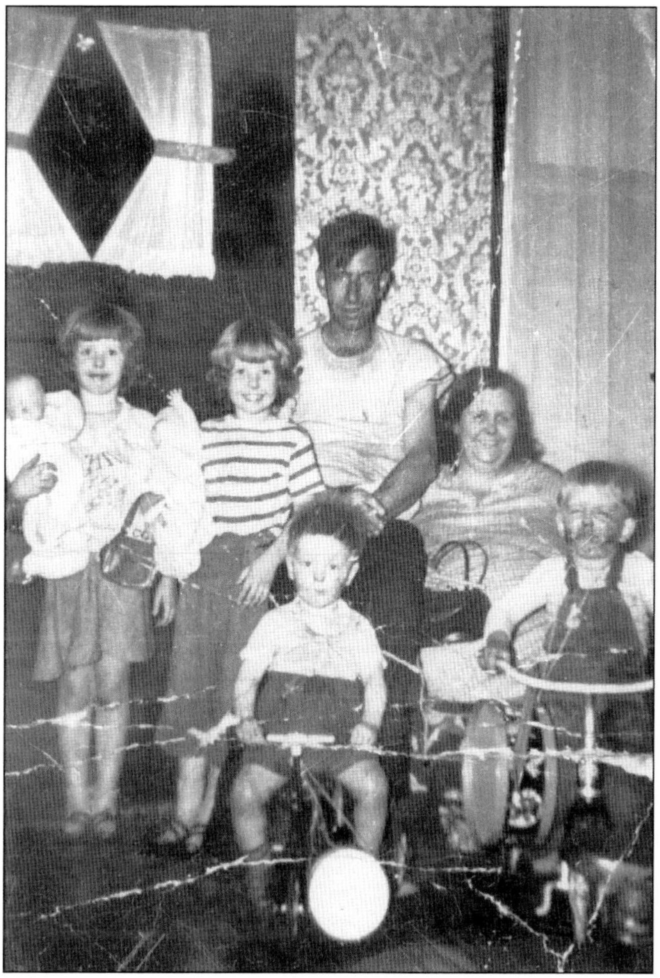

This portrait of the family of Ernest and Virginia "Jimmie" Groger was taken Christmas morning 1952. Faces of the family members are a little dirtier than usual because of problems with the coal stove that morning. The children are, from left to right, twin girls, Jane and Jean, holding their baby dolls, and boys, Chuck and John, sitting on their new bicycles.

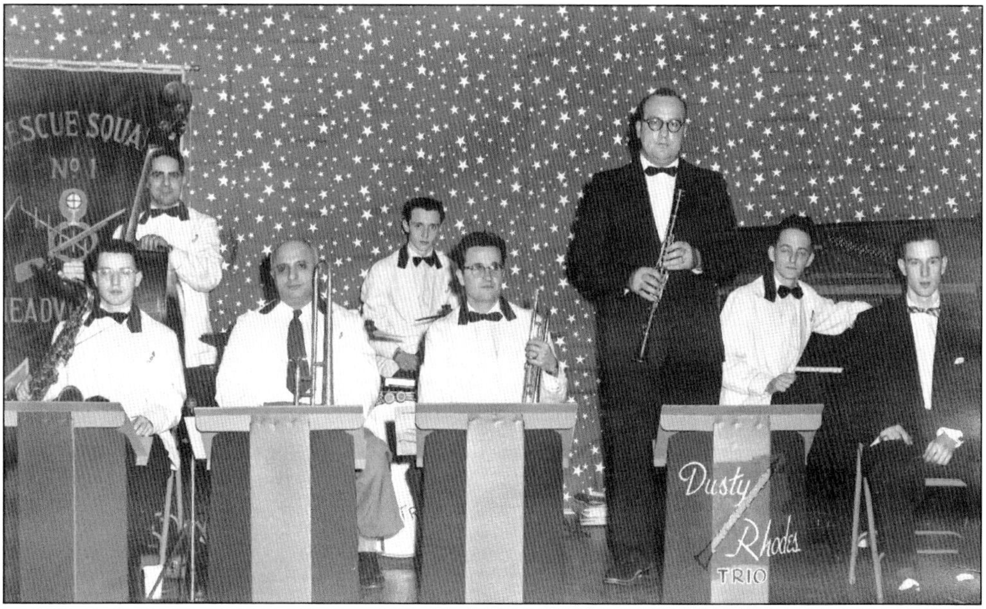

The Dusty Rhodes Trio was eight-members strong the night they played for the Rescue Squad banquet in the 1950s. Musicians are Lance Dowdell, saxophone; Darryl Sheakley, drums; Dusty Rhodes, clarinet; Charles Hornstein, piano; Blaine Houserman, trumpet; and Lew Verrico, bass. The trombonist and singer are unidentified.

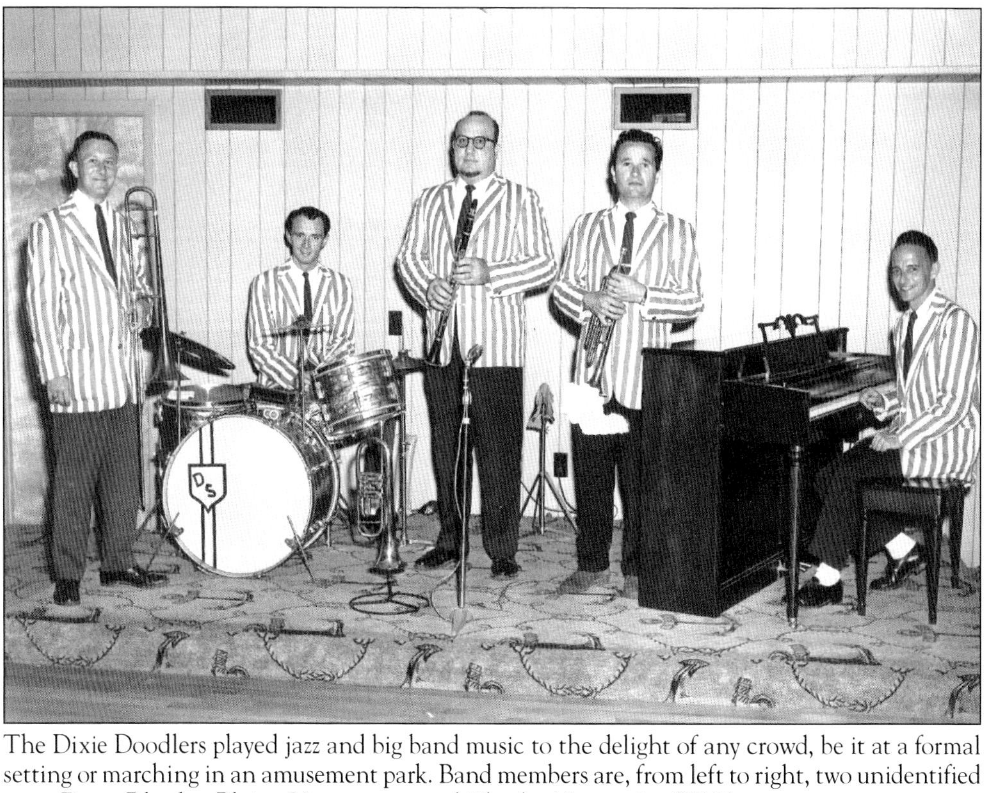

The Dixie Doodlers played jazz and big band music to the delight of any crowd, be it at a formal setting or marching in an amusement park. Band members are, from left to right, two unidentified men, Dusty Rhodes, Blaine Houserman, and Charles Hornstein. (SRP.)

Six

Celebrations

Like any town, Conneaut Lake loves to celebrate, whether it is a personal milestone, a religious observance, or a community-wide event.

From firemen's festivals in early days to Memorial Day observances, the town has always been supportive in cheering at parades and providing events for the community as well as visitors. Memorial Day is traditionally the first big event of the year with a parade down Water Street that ends with a service at Memorial Park where the band plays. Speakers remind those in attendance of the importance of observing the holiday. Military members are honored for their service and remembered for their sacrifices.

A summer boat parade, fireworks, and a live nativity have all been part of community celebrations. The Fall Pumpkin Fest is another annual event, started as a way to extend the tourist season. Winter also has had its share of fun. Events have included snowmobile races, a snowball pageant, and ice fishing.

For the centennial celebration in 1958, a pageant was a big highlight, and men were strongly encouraged to grow beards or other facial hair. Men and women alike wore clothing from the 1858 era. It was a week of Kangaroo Courts, events for children, and a gala pageant with dozens of participants. A queen was chosen to reign over the event, including a huge parade.

Fifty years later, the event to celebrate 150 years of life in Conneaut Lake included a community picnic, community worship service, crowning of a queen, and a large parade. A time capsule included everything from coins and pictures to newspapers reflecting what life was like in 2008. The final event was a Sesquicentennial Stroll, led by Mayor Tim Kaider and his wife, Pat, who were joined by "strollers" from all ages. Conneaut Lake also had an official bicentennial celebration marking the 200th birthday of the nation. Memorial trees were planted, and a parade was held.

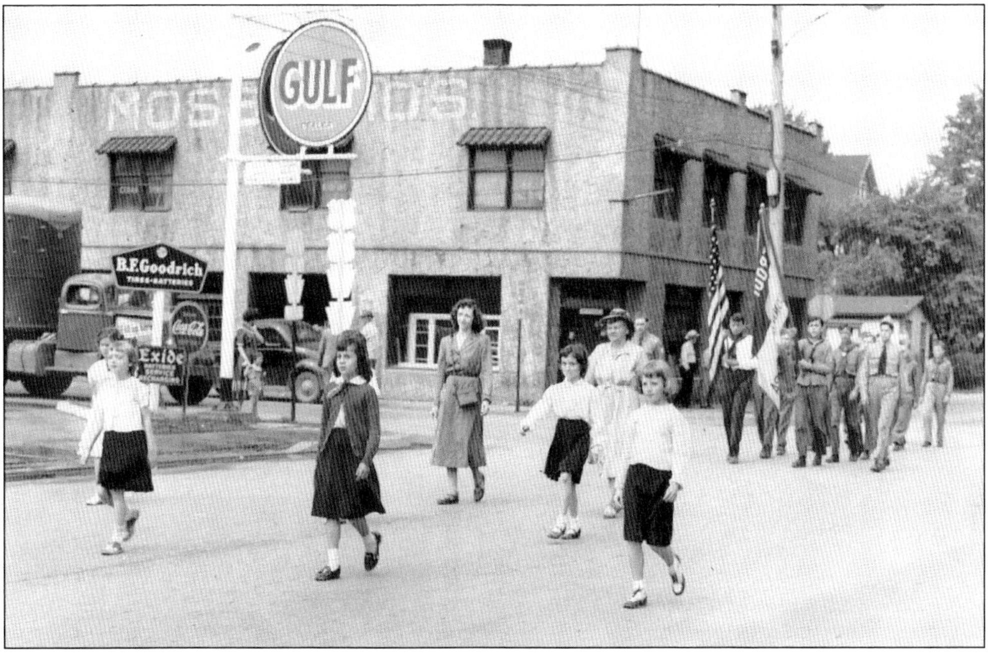

Girl Scouts and Boy Scouts join the Memorial Day Parade in 1951, saluting those whose sacrifices gave us our freedoms. The parade route traditionally went from Sixth Street down Water Street and dispersed at Memorial Park, where others joined parade participants for an annual ceremony marking the sacrifices made by our military.

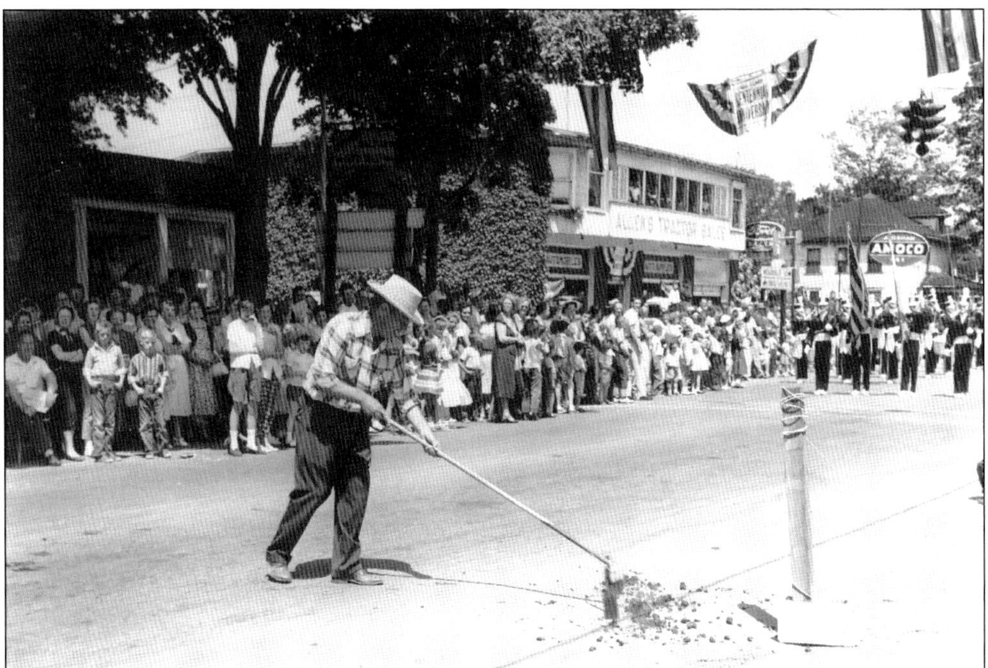

At the 1958 Centennial Parade, Ralph Moss, one of the leading citizens in town, was sweeping aside horse manure before another parade unit came by. It was always a designated chore for someone to be the "manure sweeper" to keep the rest of the parade participants' shoes clean.

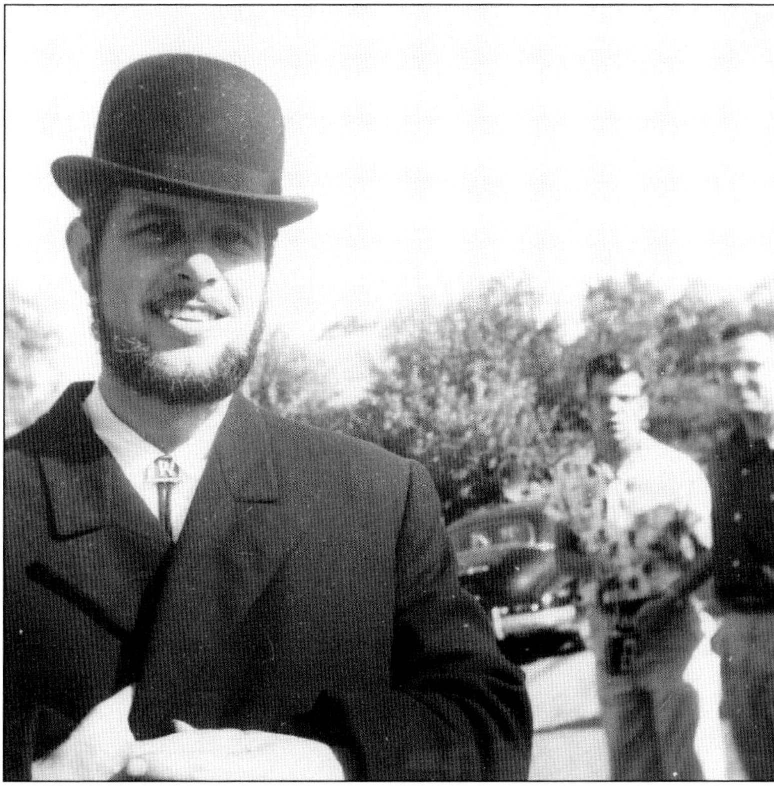

Dick Williams was one of the volunteer firemen from Greenwood Volunteer Fire Department when he wore the derby hat and a long black coat to participate in the 1958 Centennial Parade, which included many volunteer fire departments, horses, marching units, bands, and of course, the queens. Older people from town were honored during the event.

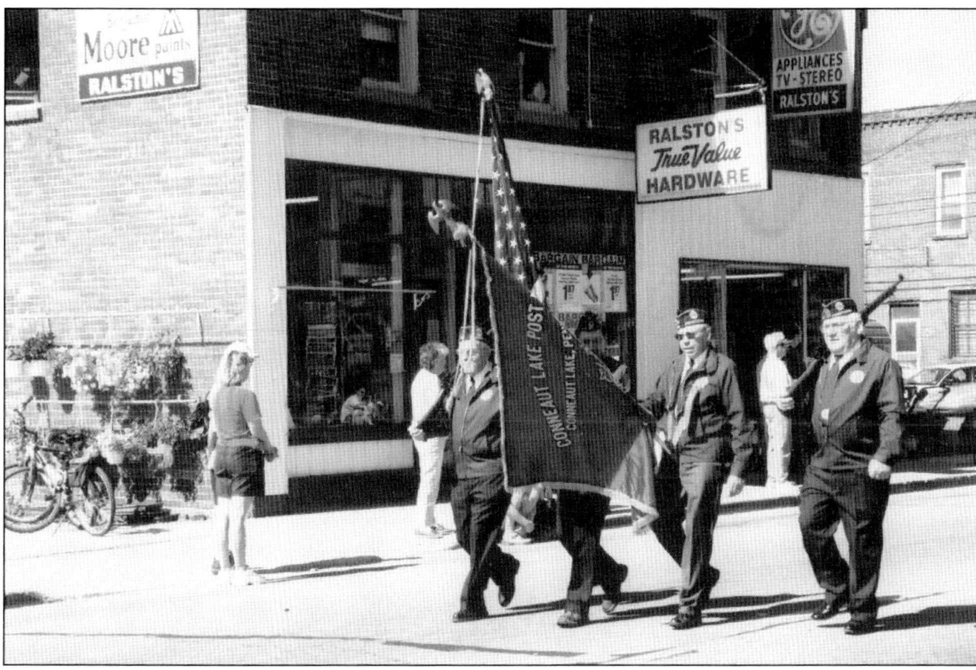

A color guard from Conneaut Lake American Legion Post No. 587 leads the Memorial Day Parade. The color guard also participated in raising the flag and placing flowers at the monument in Memorial Park during the ceremony that followed. (DE.)

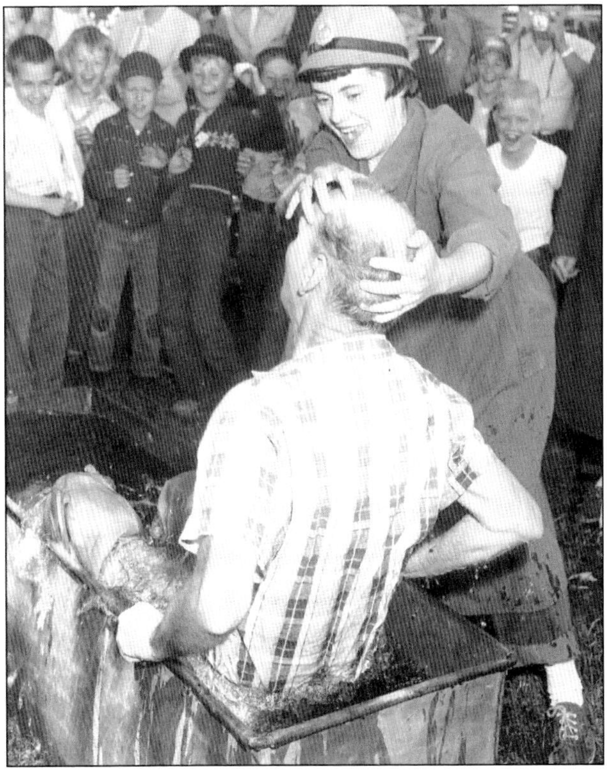

Conneaut Lake barber Emerson Burtner is dunked by "lady cop" Joyce Burchfield at the Kangaroo Court in 1958. Burtner was paying a penalty for a centennial rules infraction with a trip to the dunking tank as youngsters gather around to watch and laugh at the antics. (HLF.)

Seen in an old car driven by members of the Brothers of the Brush for the 1958 Centennial Parade, some of the area's oldest citizens were special guests. Another Brother of the Brush with the long black coat and tall hat preceded the car, charming the many onlookers. (HLF.)

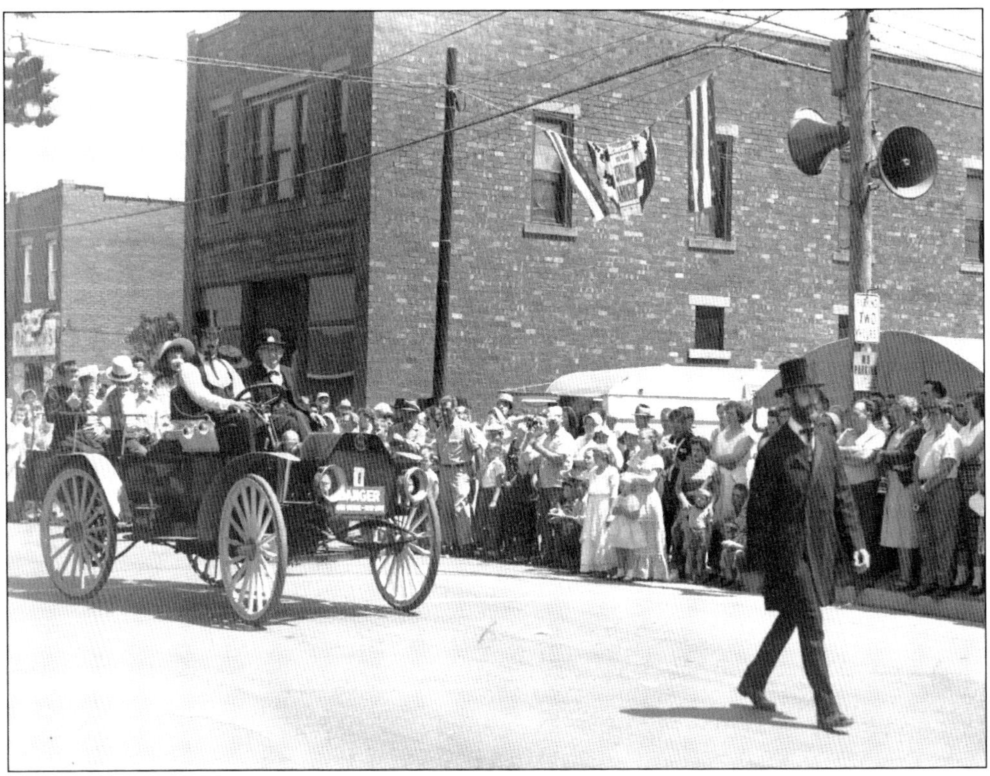

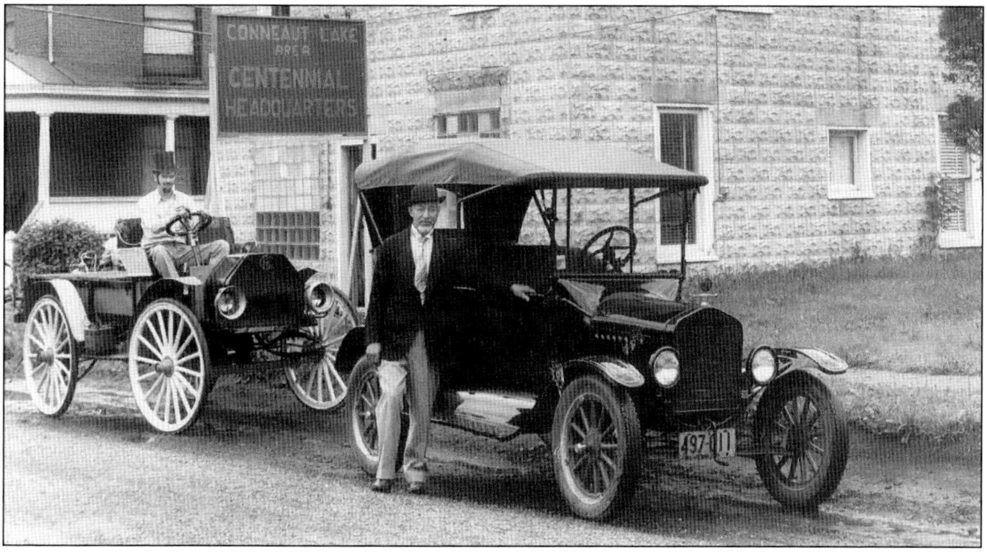

Walter Lasch Sr., one of the borough's oldest citizens and a leading businessman, poses beside an old Model T in front of the Conneaut Lake Area Centennial Headquarters before the huge parade started in 1958. This photograph also includes a Brother of the Brush in another antique vehicle. (HLF.)

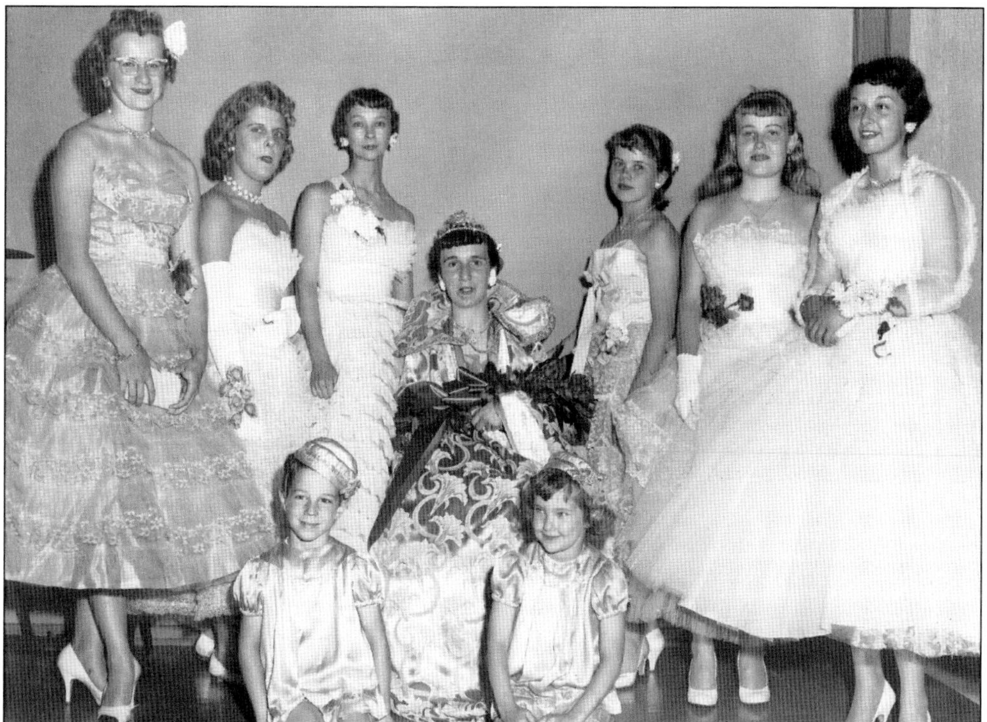

Conneaut Lake Centennial queen Lucilla "Lucy" Copeland holds her bouquet of roses while posing with her court at the coronation. From left to right are Carole Lowther, Karol Orzepowski, Sandra Kean, Elaine Scott, Nancy Winans, and Mazie Sousa. The pages are, from left to right, Glenn Moss and Rosemary Steadman. (HLF.)

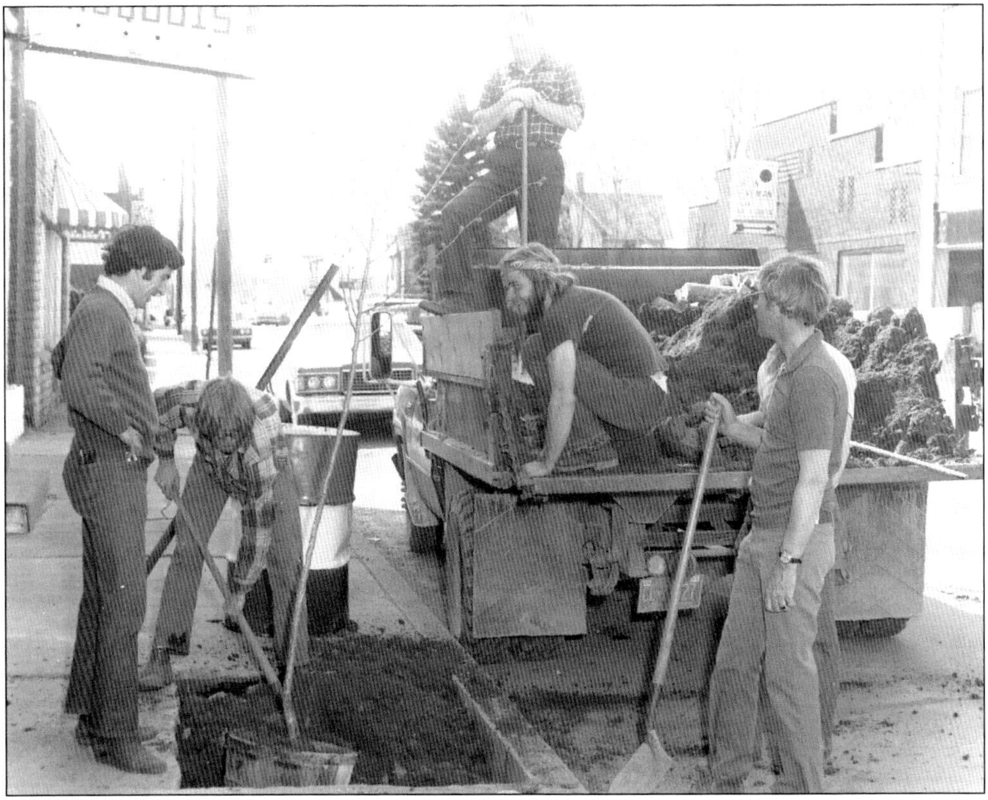

In 1976, Bill Darrin, on the far left, owner of the Plant Place; Dr. Robert Moyers, standing in truck; and Lee Moss, standing with shovel, planted trees on Water Street for the nation's bicentennial. Trees were planted in front of the Hotel Iroquois at the corner of Water and First Streets, but when the hotel burned two years later, the trees had to be replaced. (HLF.)

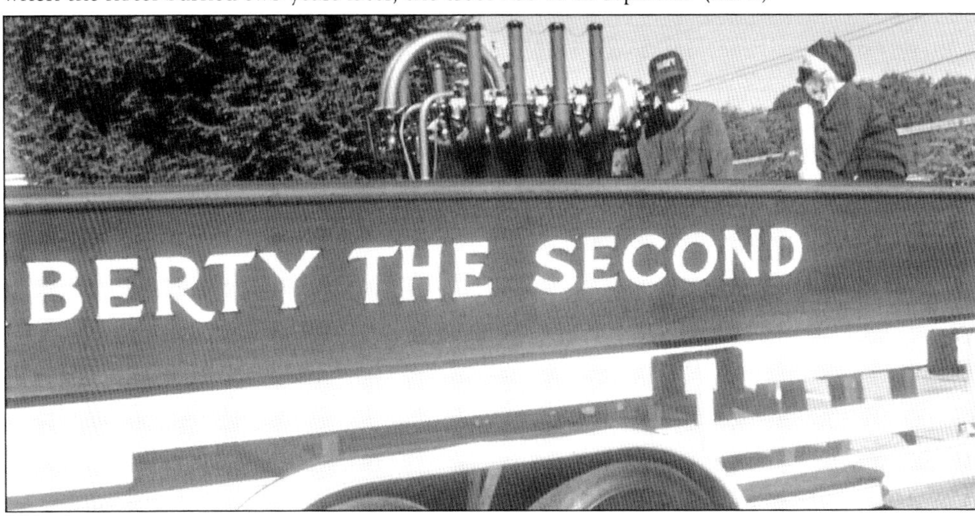

"Keeping History Afloat" was theme of this entry in the 2008 Sesquicentennial Parade. Fred Moss (left) and Kate Hilton, both considered true historians, were seen on *Liberty the Second*. It seemed fitting that Kate Hilton should be on the boat, as she was very involved in the early days of raising funds and working at the museums where the boat was displayed.

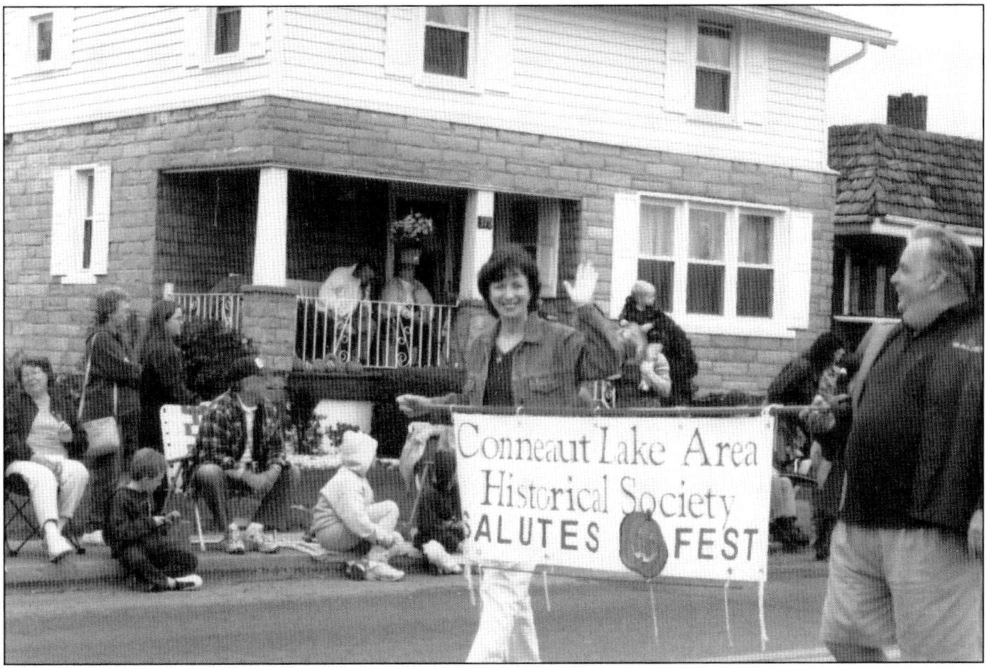

Julia Catalano and Hale Jenkins, charter members of the Conneaut Lake Area Historical Society, carry a banner from the society saluting Fall Pumpkin Fest in this 2005 photograph. The historical society has participated in parades since the society was organized in 1999.

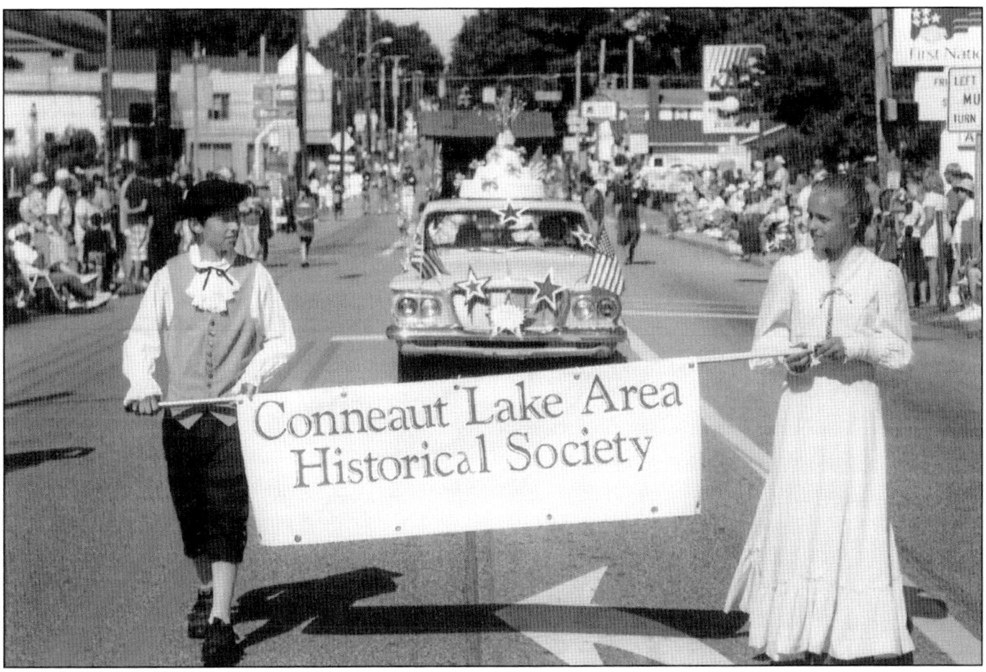

Spencer Boyd and Challen Litwiler carry the banner from CLAHS during the 2008 Sesquicentennial Parade. The parade also included floats, marching units, and the high school bands. Special groups also thrilled the crowd, especially if members threw candy for the children.

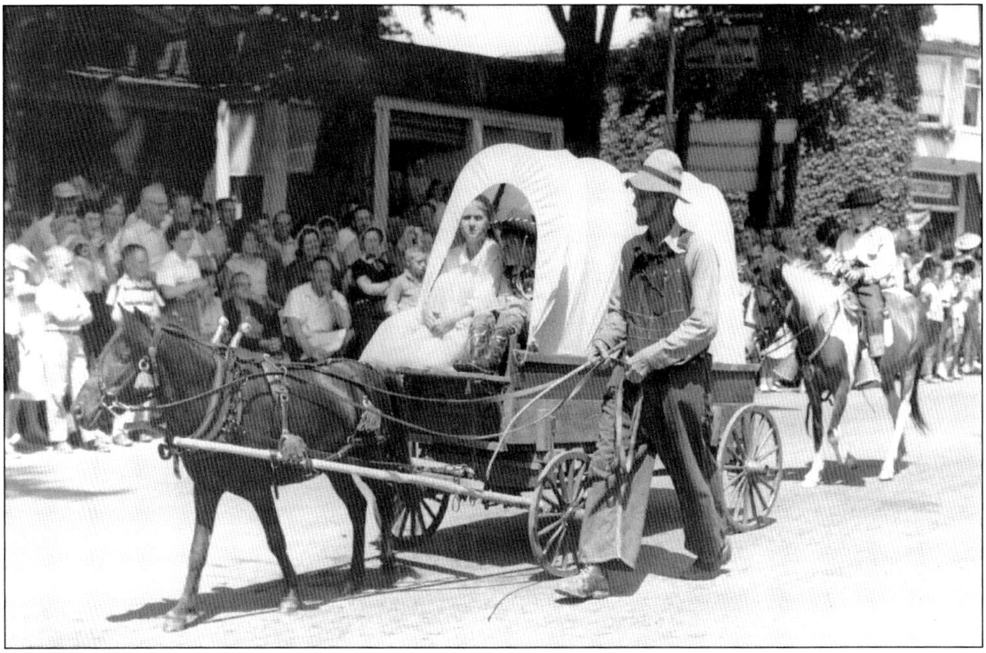

A wagon train, pulled by a mule, was a big hit in the 1958 Centennial Parade. The wagon train included a family dressed in old-time clothes in the coach, accompanied by a farmer-type father, and followed by a horse ridden by another parade participant. (HLF.)

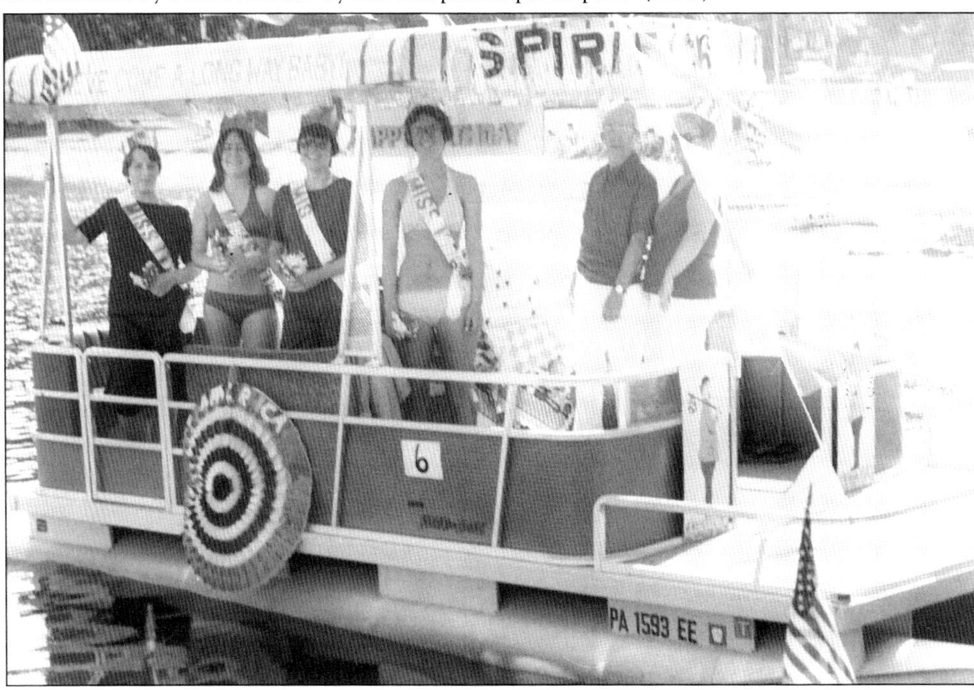

A "Spirit of the Times" theme was featured in this boat, which was among those photographed during an annual boat parade sponsored by Midway Civic Club on July 4, 1976. Boat owners decorate their boats in specific themes designated by the club. A queen and runners-up were among the guests on this boat, which goes around the lake for the parade. (HLF.)

Elsie Ralston, the oldest woman in town during the 1958 centennial celebration, receives a gift from James Kribbs, chairman of the centennial celebration. (HLF.)

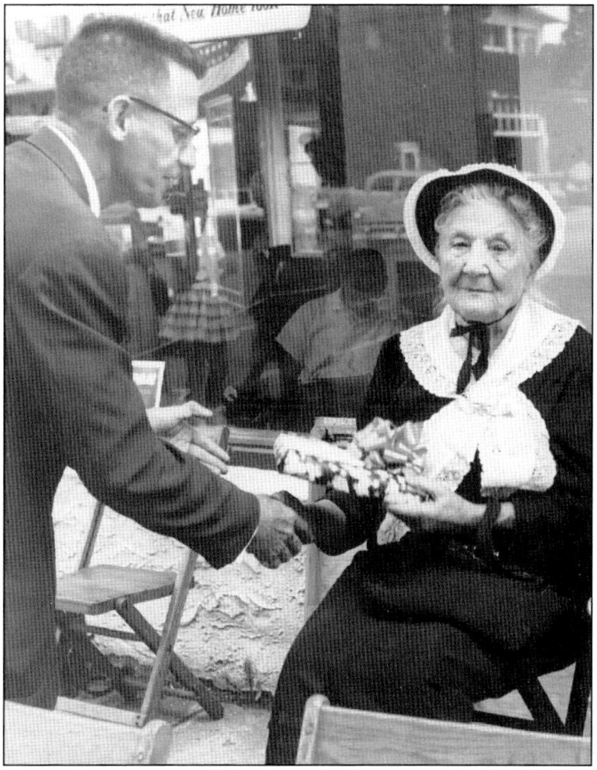

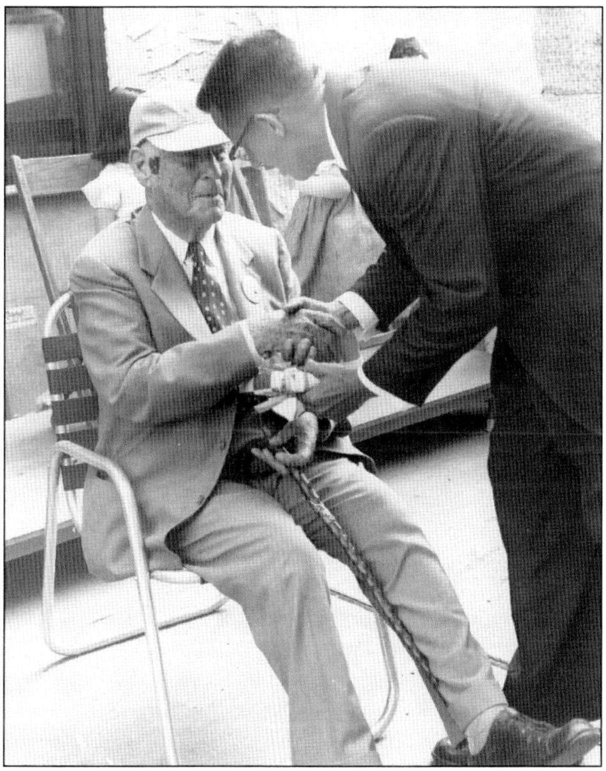

Fred Moss, the oldest man in Conneaut Lake town, is pictured after the 1958 Centennial Parade, receiving a gift and congratulations from James Kribbs, chairman of the centennial celebration. The parade honored some of the oldest area citizens, giving them special recognition.

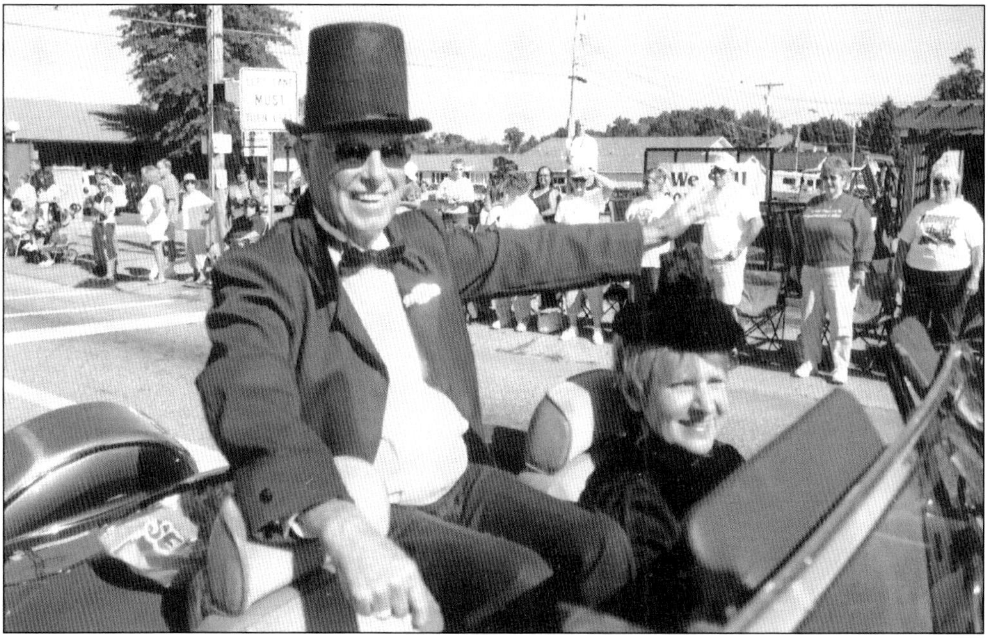

Dick Williams, grand marshal of the 2008 Conneaut Lake Sesquicentennial Parade, and his wife, Jan, wave to the crowd. The couple provided convertibles for queens in the various community parades for decades.

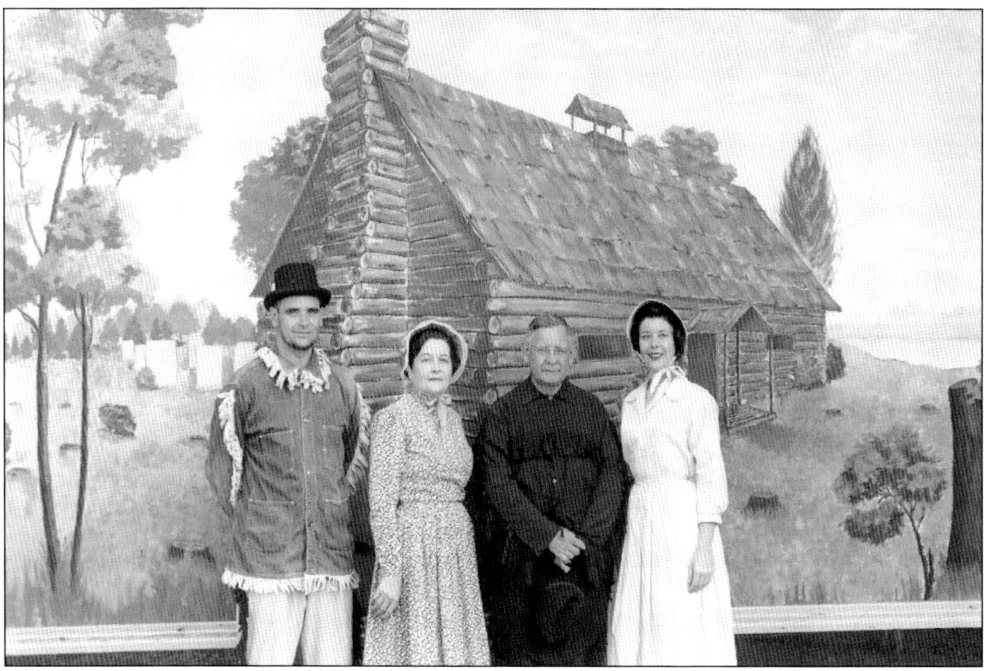

The Rutherford family, dressed in period clothing for Conneaut Lake's Centennial Celebration in 1958, pose before a painting by Lee and Ann Moss of the log church. From left to right are George Rutherford Jr., his mother, Hazel Rutherford; his father, the Rev. George Rutherford; and his sister, Edith Rutherford Johnson. Reverend Rutherford was pastor of the Presbyterian church for decades, and the family was very active in community organizations for decades. (HLF.)

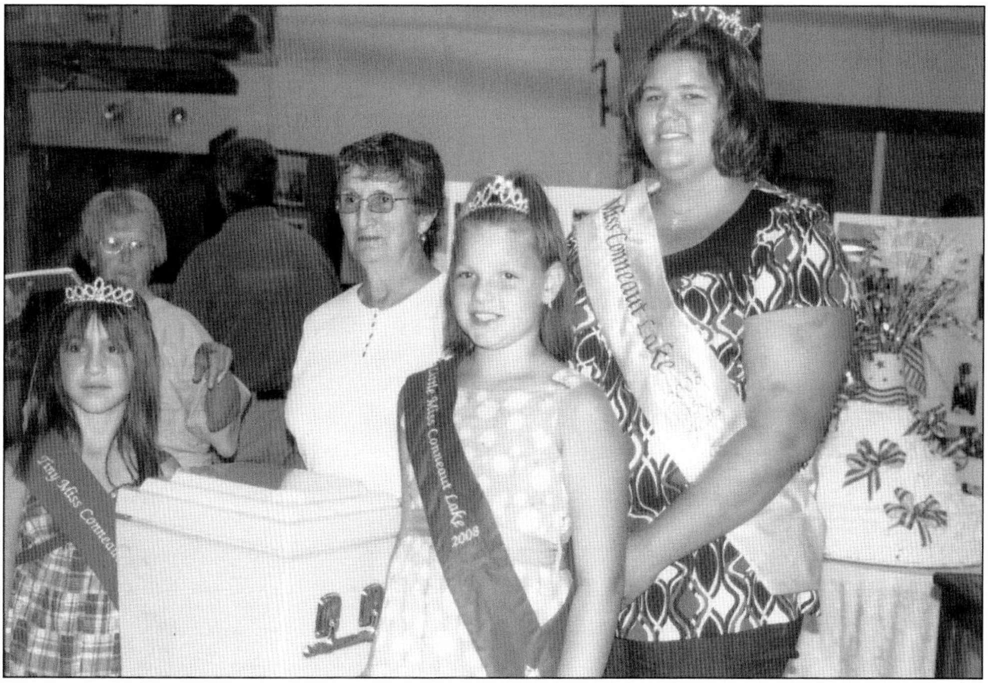

The sesquicentennial queens help fill a time capsule at the conclusion of the 2008 event at the historical society museum. From left to right are Tiny Miss Elizabeth Vittorio; Lucy Copeland Pisani, the 1958 centennial queen; Little Miss Sesquicentennial Paige Coon; and Senior Miss Sesquicentennial Sasha Foust.

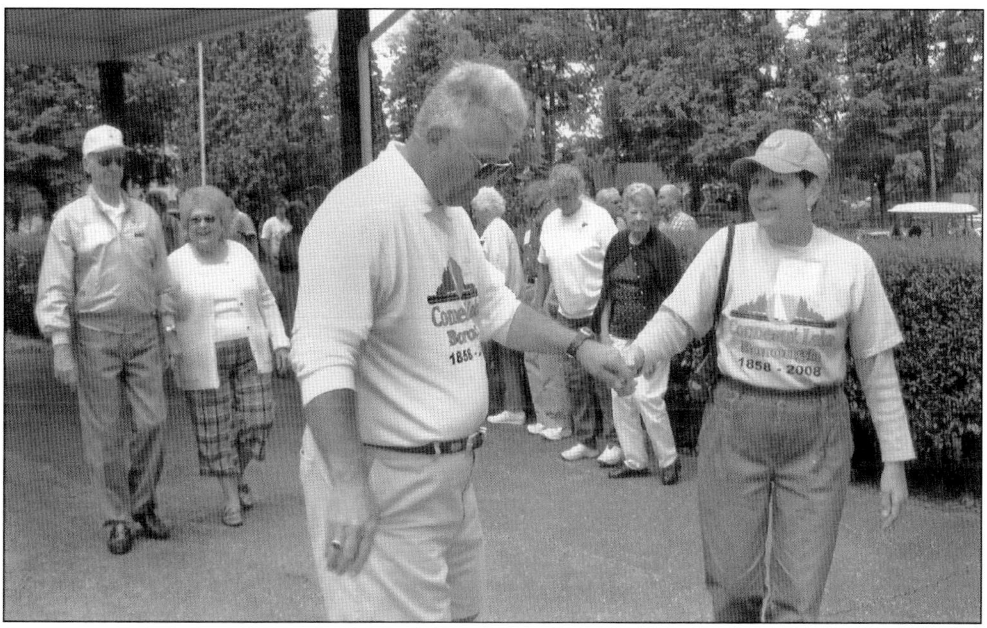

Conneaut Lake mayor Tim Kaider and his wife, Pat, do the Sesquicentennial Stroll at the conclusion of the sesquicentennial celebration, figuratively leading celebrants from the past to the future. People of all ages participated in the event. The final event was held at Hotel Conneaut, Conneaut Lake Park.

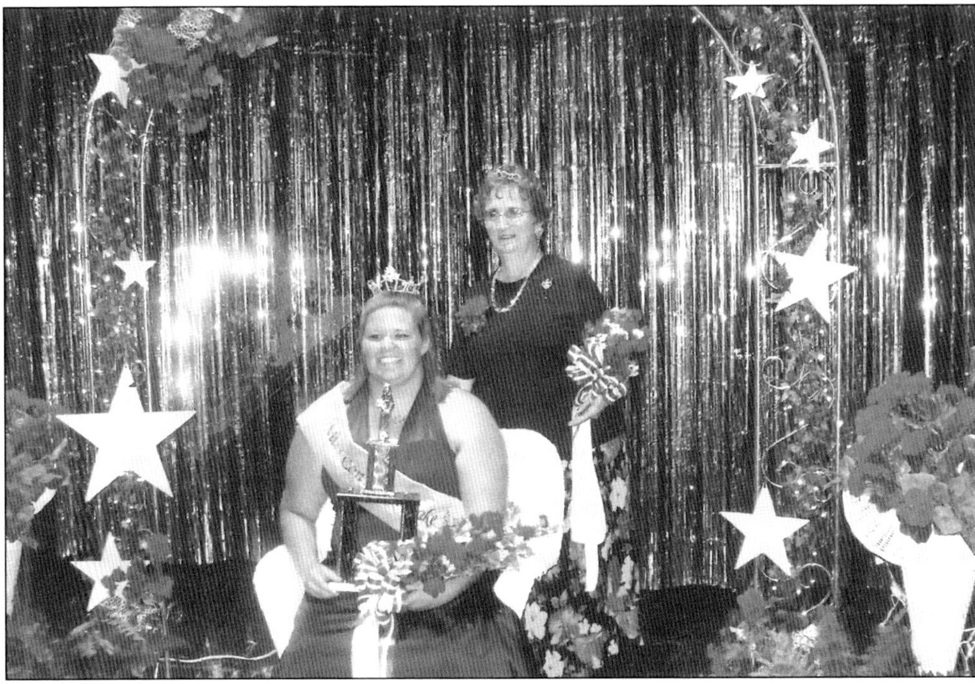

Fifty years after being crowned, Conneaut Lake Centennial queen Lucilla Copeland Pisani still had one more honor. Lucilla is shown in this photograph with the 2008 sesquicentennial queen, Sasha Foust, following the official announcement and crowning of the town's new ambassador. The queen's pageant marked the opening of the sesquicentennial celebration. Sasha was one of several queens crowned that day.

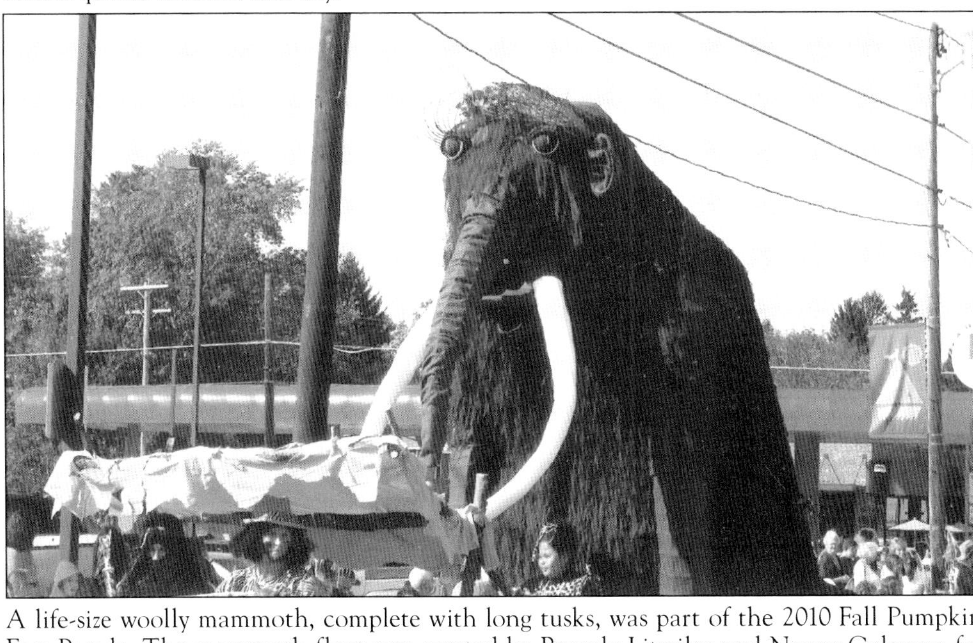

A life-size woolly mammoth, complete with long tusks, was part of the 2010 Fall Pumpkin Fest Parade. The mammoth float was created by Beverly Litwiler and Nancy Coleman for CLAHS. Woolly mammoth bones that are more than 10,000 years old are on display at the historical society museum.

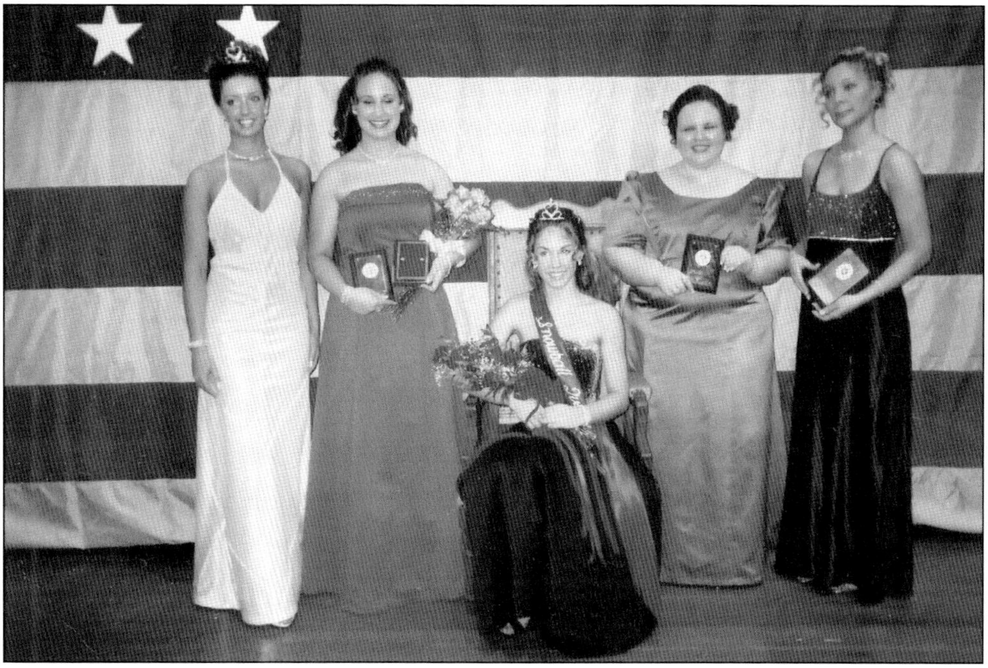

Crowned by the 2001 queen, Jana Wielobob, on the far left, Kiwanis Club's 2002 Snowball Festival queen Kelsey Stanton, seated, is joined by members of her court, first runner-up Danielle Hewston, second to the left; second runner-up Jessica Middleton; and Miss Congeniality Mardonna Schlock, far right. Kiwanis Club started the pageant in 1973 as part of the annual festival.

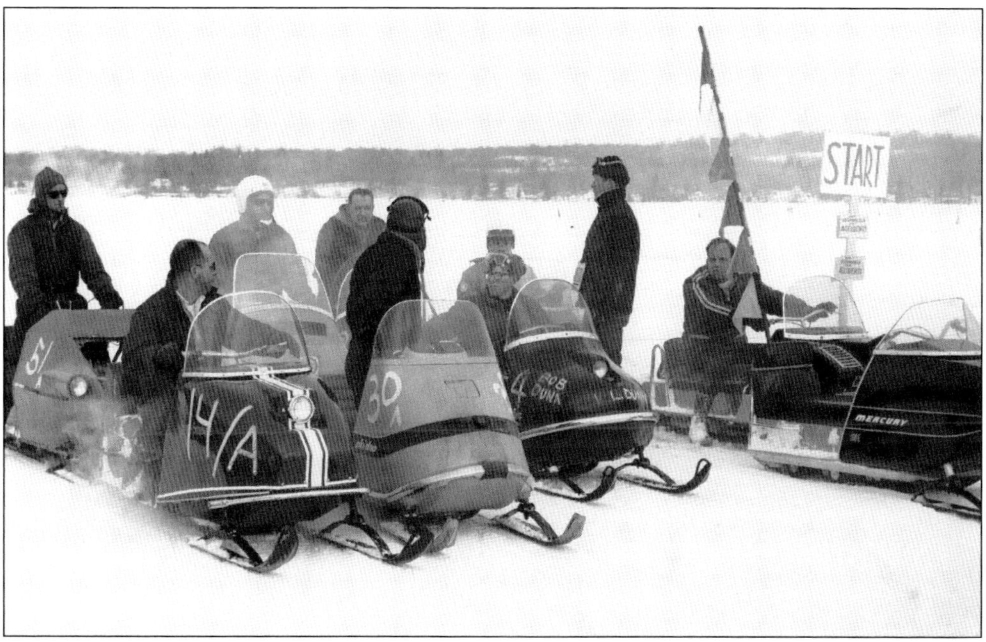

Snowmobile racers line up to begin a race on the frozen ice of Conneaut Lake. The 1968 event was a joint effort by local officials to hold a winter festival where people could compete for trophies and the community could cheer the participants to victory. Audley Hays won the race. Although a popular event, insurance liability issues ended the contest a few years later. (HLF.)

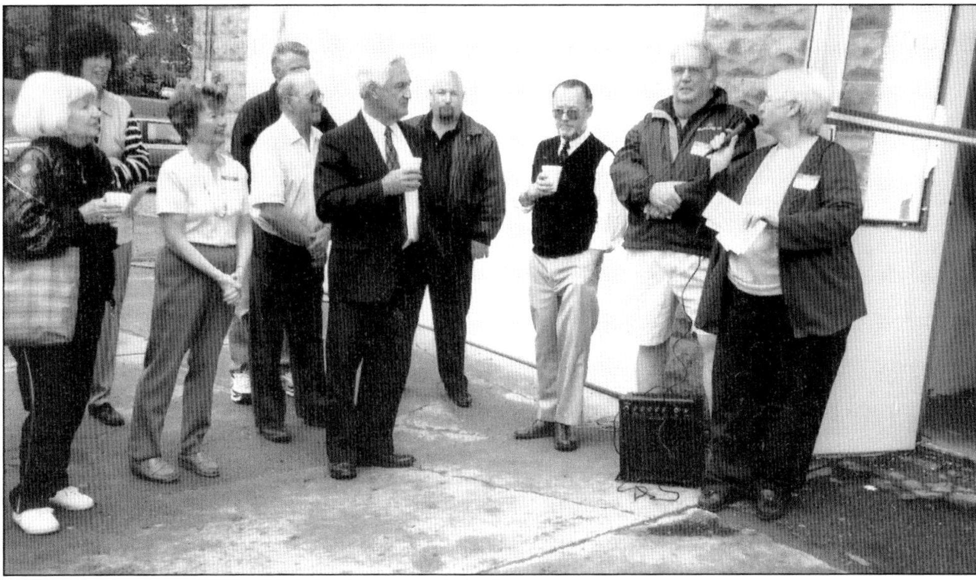

State and local officials join Conneaut Lake Area Historical Society's dedication ceremony, marking the opening of the historical society museum in 2003. State senator Robert Robbins, center, secured a state grant for renovations of the old community hall. Council president Dick Holabaugh joined society members for the celebration.

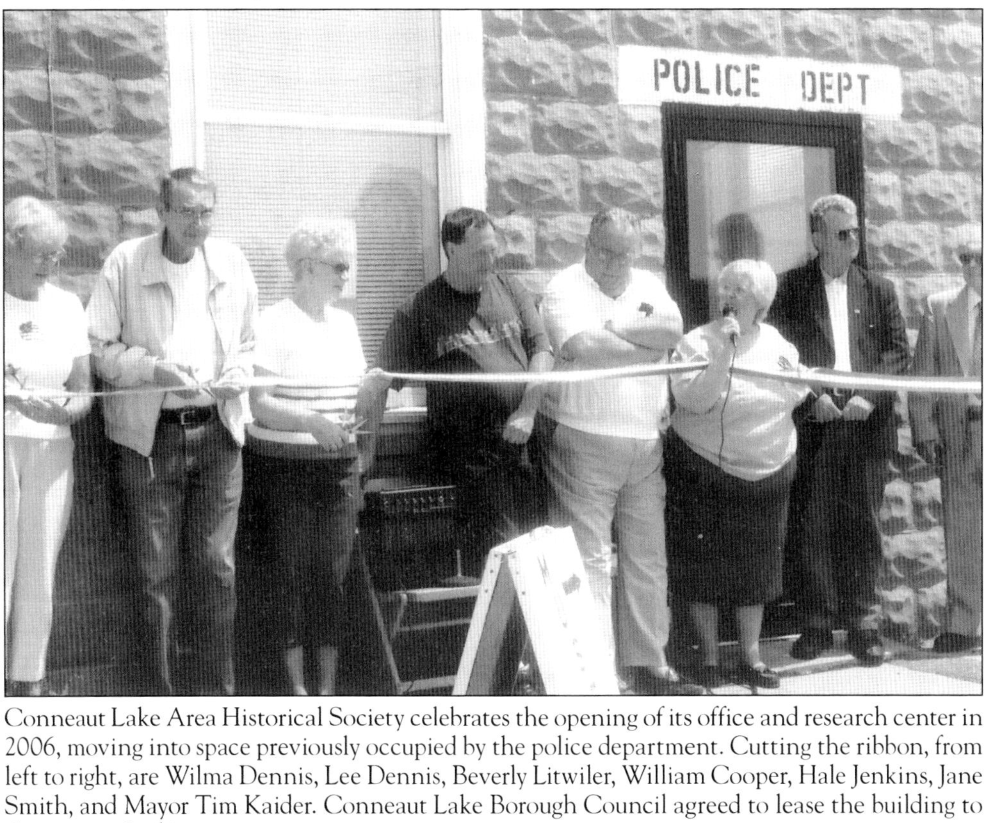

Conneaut Lake Area Historical Society celebrates the opening of its office and research center in 2006, moving into space previously occupied by the police department. Cutting the ribbon, from left to right, are Wilma Dennis, Lee Dennis, Beverly Litwiler, William Cooper, Hale Jenkins, Jane Smith, and Mayor Tim Kaider. Conneaut Lake Borough Council agreed to lease the building to the society for $1 a year.

Seven

Community Organizations

The people of a community make it unique, and when those people work together in an organized fashion, the community prospers. This chapter shows some of those organizations and the people involved, as they work to make their town a better place in which to live. Organizations range from Boy and Girl Scouts to school, church, service organizations, military, cemetery associations, library board, garden clubs, and a historical society.

There are some groups that are specific to the area, founded by people who saw a need and answered it. For example, many people joined forces to plan and construct R Playground on Fireman's Beach in 1993. Another group of women meets weekly to make quilts, which are then donated to area residents. Another special organization in Conneaut Lake is the Samaritans, formed in 1982 after a child died of malnutrition. Determined that never happens again, the Samaritans was formed to assist needy families.

Conneaut Lake Pride also is specific to the area. Its goal is to help keep the borough clean, free of litter, and beautiful, planting flowers in the community. Other associations take care of cemeteries, including Lakeview Cemetery Association. In nearby Geneva, trustees of the Geneva Memorial Cemetery Association assumed ownership and responsibility for that cemetery in 1945. In 1988, the former Methodist church was transferred to the association to be used as a funeral chapel. It also is used as the base for annual community picnics.

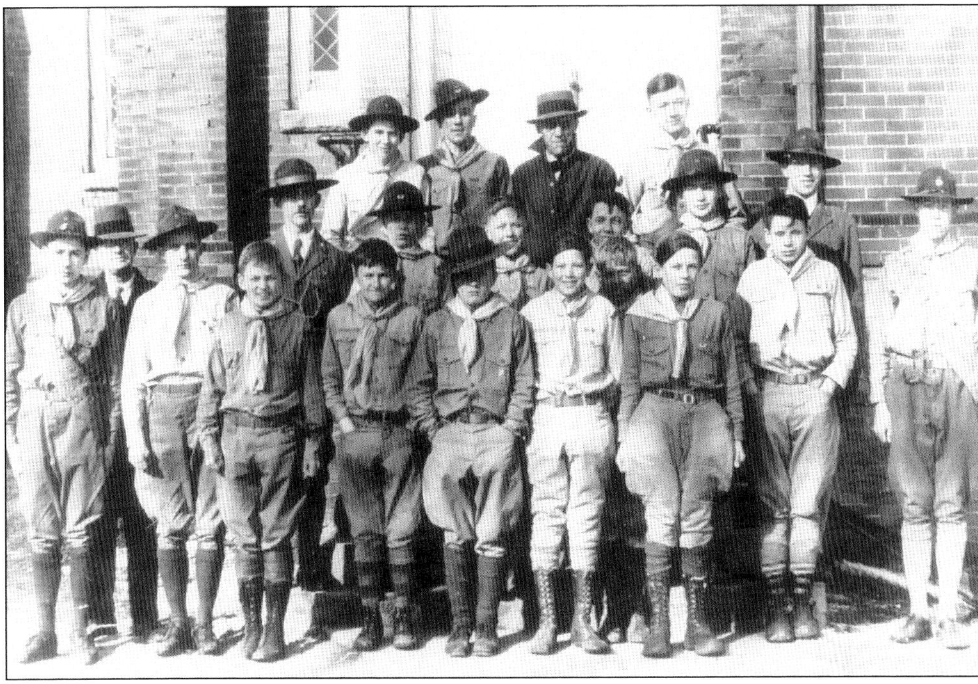

A new Boy Scout troop, sponsored by the trustees of the Presbyterian church, was formed in 1923 in Conneaut Lake. P.C. Harned, Frame Shontz, and Fred Moss were troop committee trustees. Troop membership totaled 15. Geoge C. Cobler was elected scoutmaster. The first members of the troop are pictured here. Uniforms have changed since 1923, but the scout purpose remains the same.

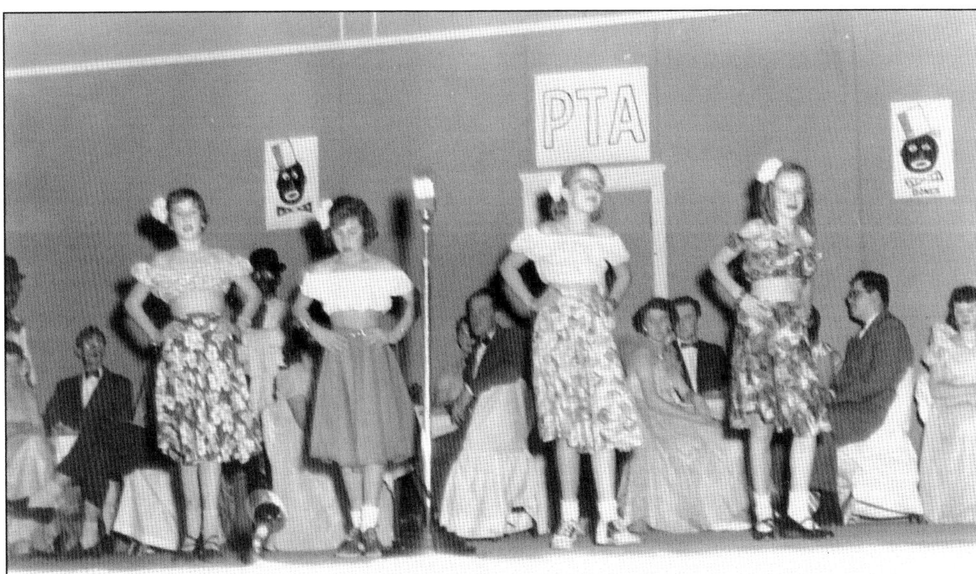

Young girls perform a skit in this show sponsored by Conneaut Lake Kiwanis Club in the mid-1950s. In the photograph, from left to right, are Janet Cooley, Scarlett Conrad, Elaine Scott, and Carole Lowther. The event was held at the Conneaut Lake Community Hall, now home to the historical society museum. (HLF.)

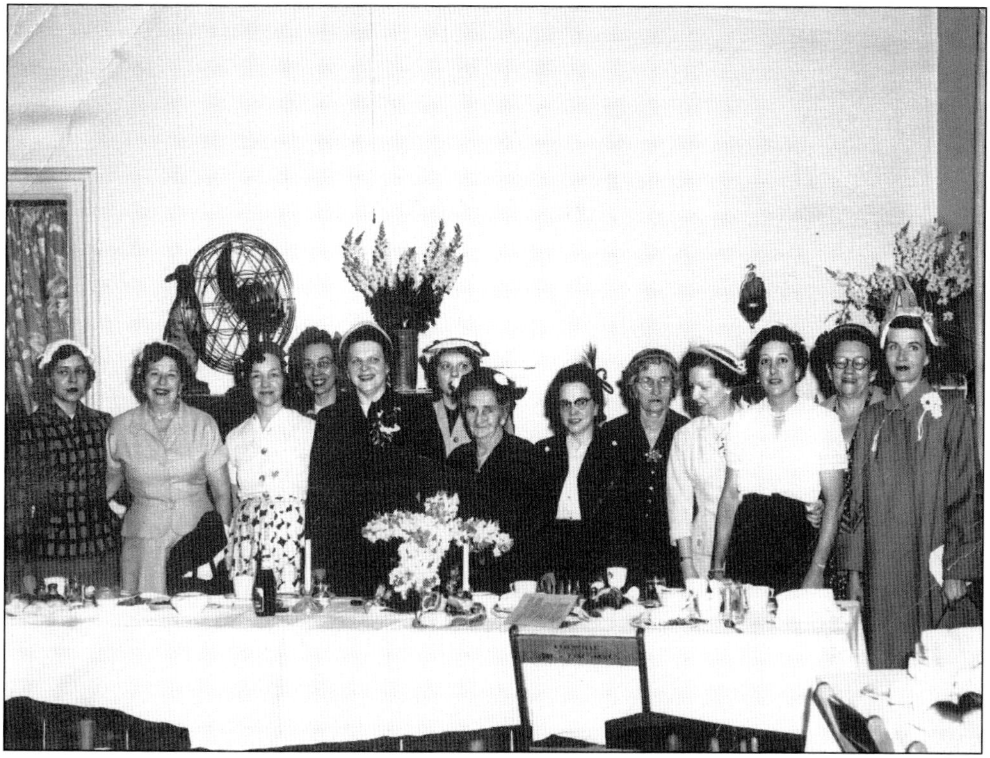

Members of the Rosary and Altar Society of Our Queen of the Americas Roman Catholic Church pose for a photograph following a dinner meeting. The society also was involved in nonchurch-related activities. At one time, society members wrote to actor Clark Gable to inquire about purchasing a tombstone for his mother, buried in a nearby Catholic cemetery. (Photograph by Blood's Studio.)

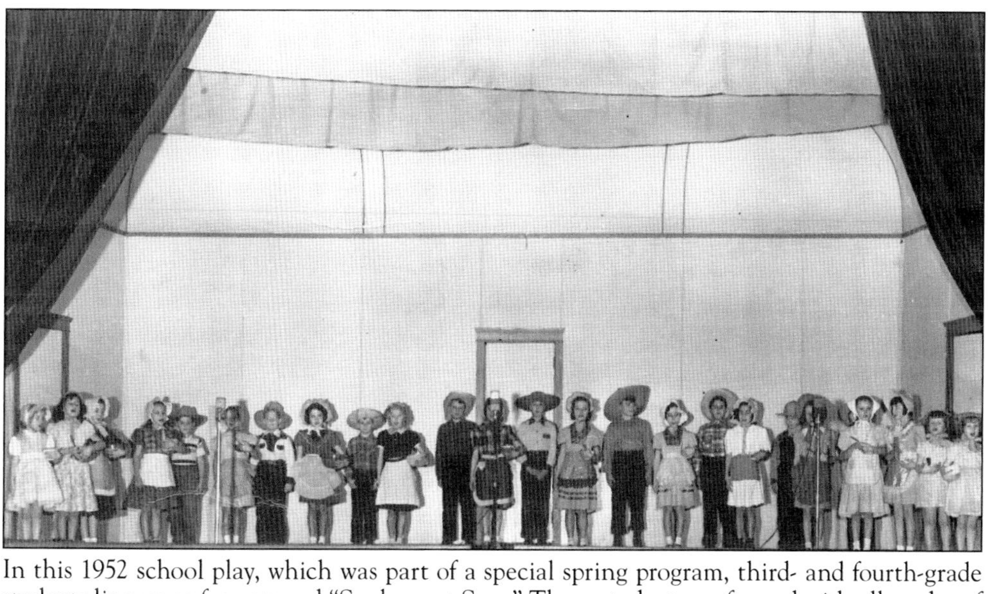

In this 1952 school play, which was part of a special spring program, third- and fourth-grade students line up as farmers and "Sunbonnet Sues." These students performed with all grades of Conneaut Lake Elementary School. (HLF.)

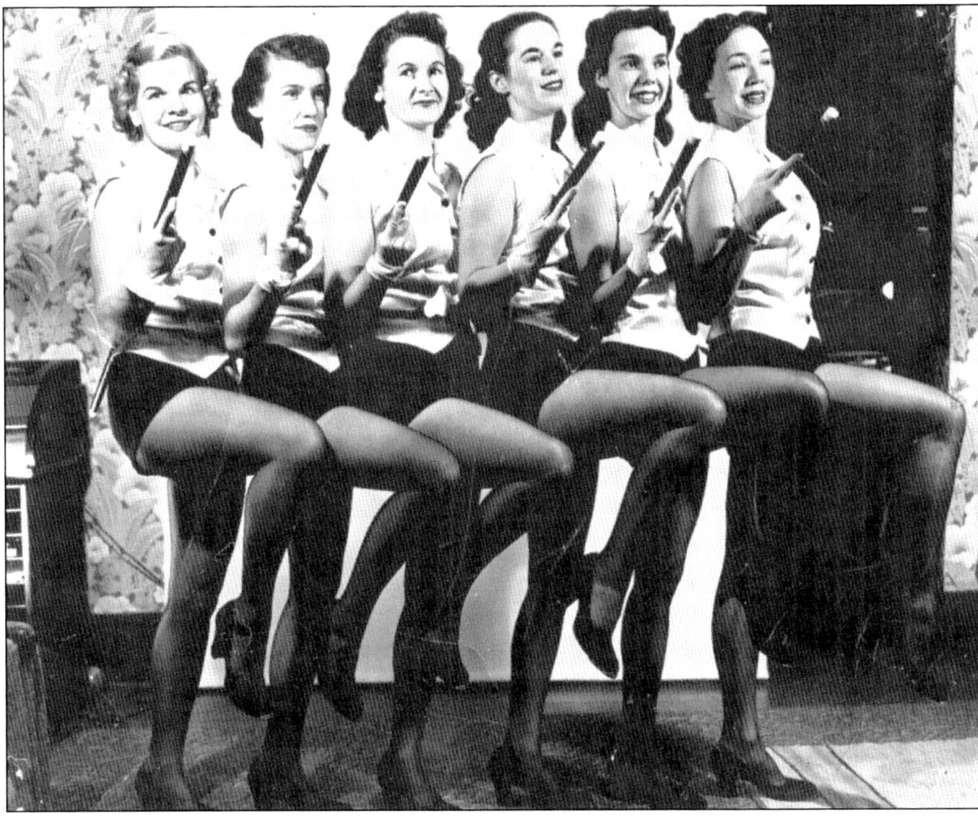

Women from Conneaut Lake, none of whom were professional dancers, took the stage in the 1950s to dance in a Conneaut Lake Kiwanis Club show. They donned tights and white blouses to support the Kiwanians and the community. From left to right are Gloria Brown, Janet Travaglini, Betty Kribbs, Jackie Houserman, Ann DeWalt, and Joanne Steadman Scaduto.

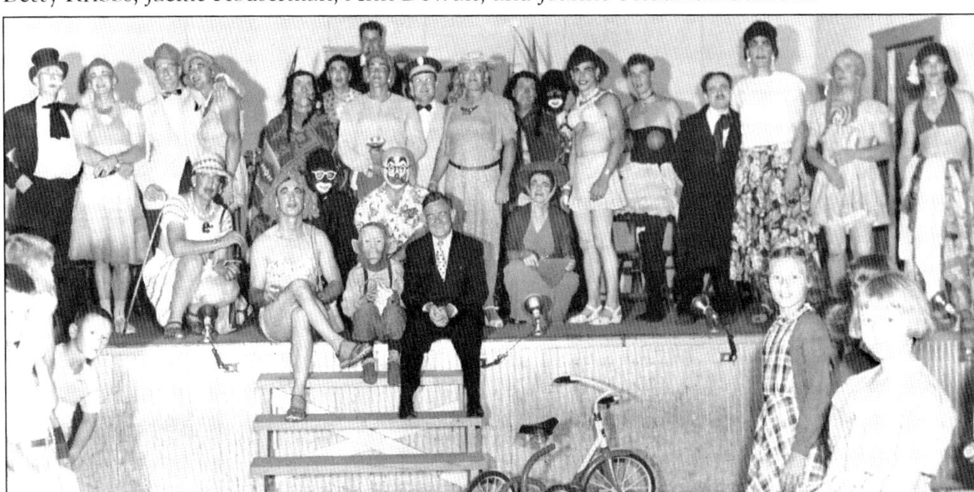

Conneaut Lake residents of all ages and walks of life dress in costume for this fun-filled Kiwanis Club show in the mid-1950s. This photograph shows many of the men dressed in women's clothing as young people watched with amazement.

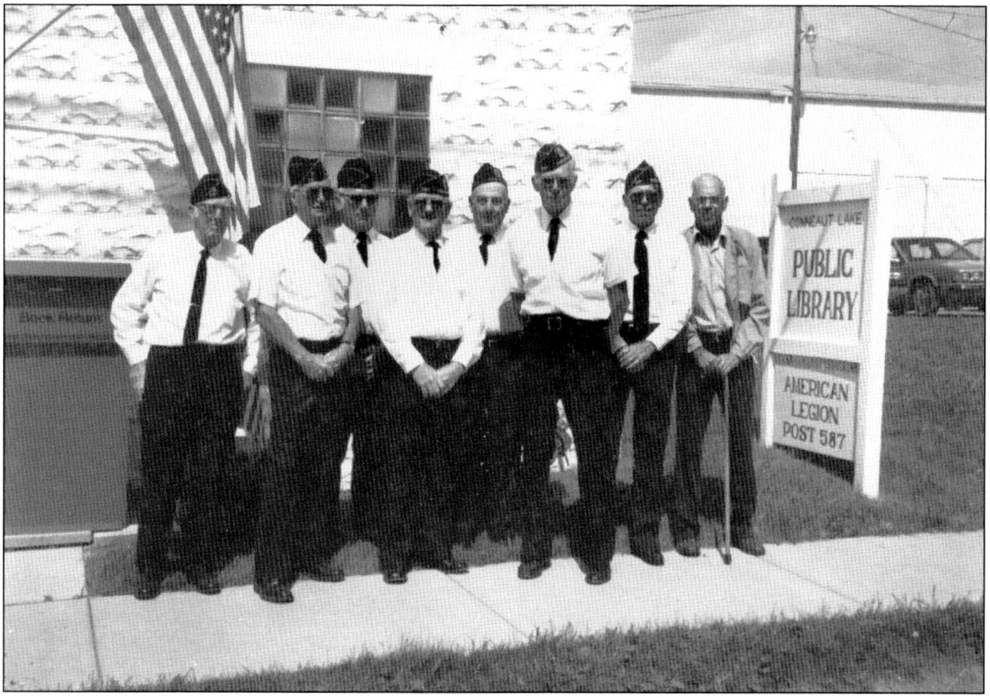

Members of the Conneaut Lake American Legion Post No. 587, founded in 1920, pose in front of the post home. From left to right, members are Jack Hughes, Lyle McGuire, Dan Warner, Dick Moyer, Kent Klink, Ed Hamilton, Arnold Ecklund, and Pap Helbig.

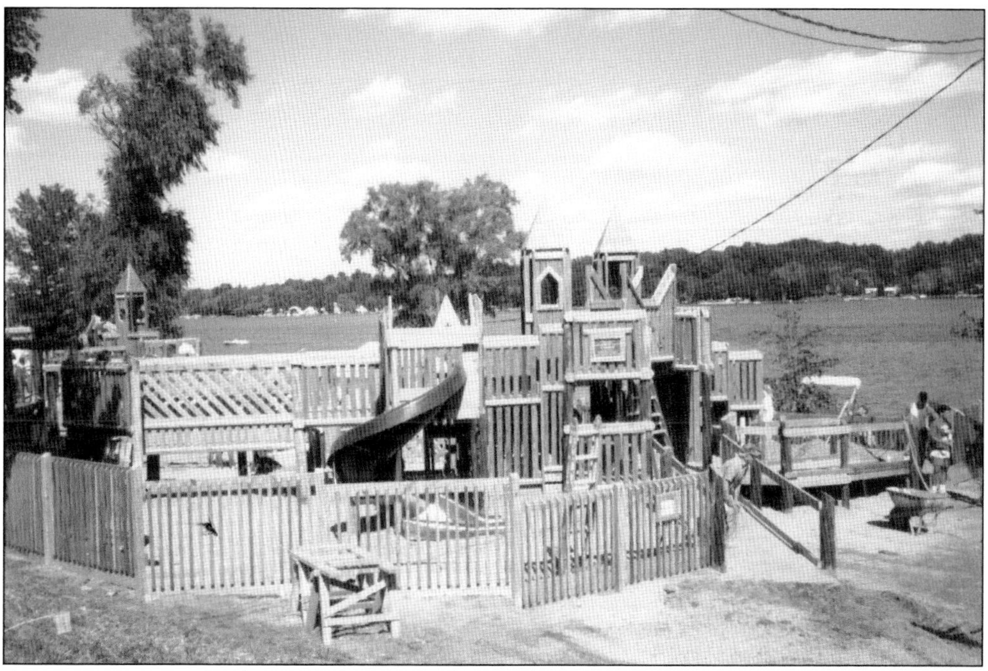
A new community R Playground was unveiled in this 1993 photograph. A group of volunteers worked for months designing and constructing the old-fashioned wooden playground. It was located on Fireman's Beach.

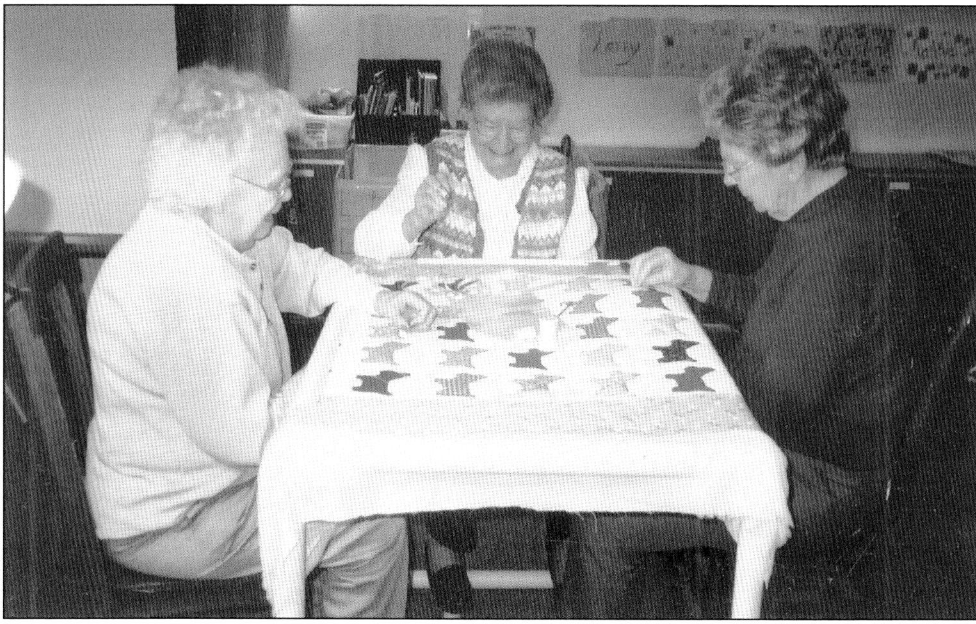

Quilting was a weekly tradition for many women in the community, who gathered to sew the colorful coverings. Once complete, the quilts were donated to help people in the community. From left to right are Kathryn Keppel, Alice Oswald, and Betty Haworth, working on a crib quilt in this 2002 photograph. (DE.)

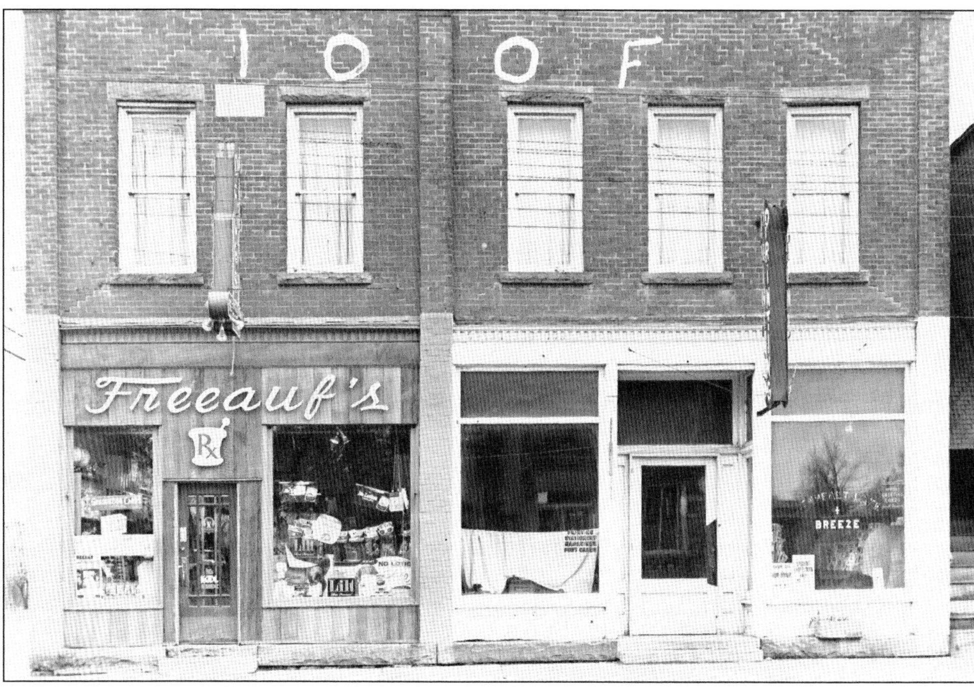

Many organizations have buildings for meetings and special events. The Independent Order of Odd Fellows (IOOF) Building is located on the corner of Water and Second Streets. The Odd Fellows met upstairs, and the space on the first floor was rented by businesses. The Conneaut Lake Lodge of IOOF was founded about 1923. (HLF.)

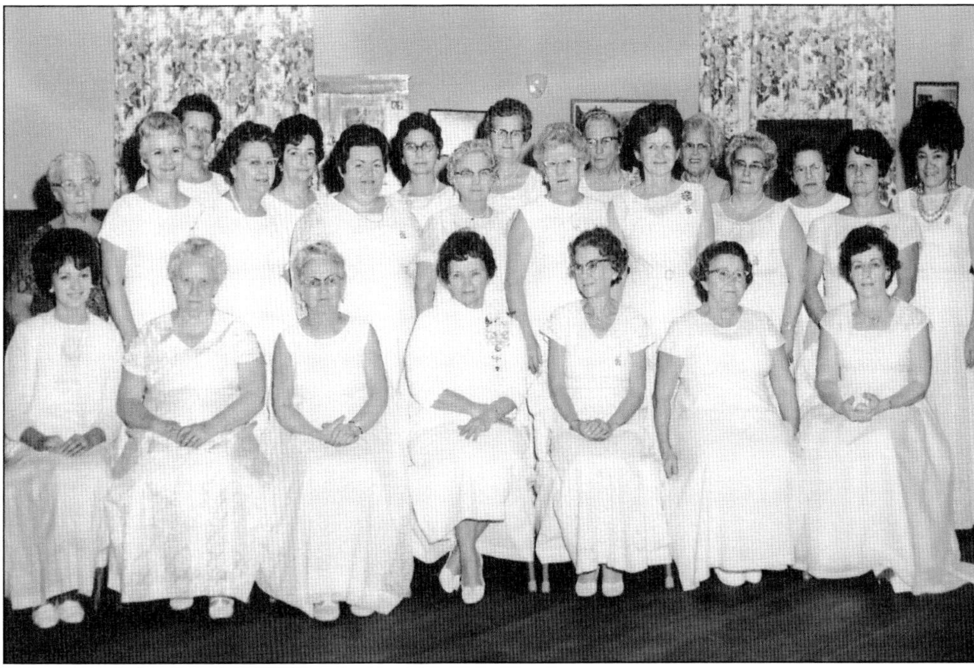

Members of the Rebekah of the Lake Lodge of Conneaut Lake pose for a formal photograph each year with members dressed in the required long white gowns. The Conneaut Lake lodge was formed in 1939 and disbanded in 2002, having served this community for more than 60 years.

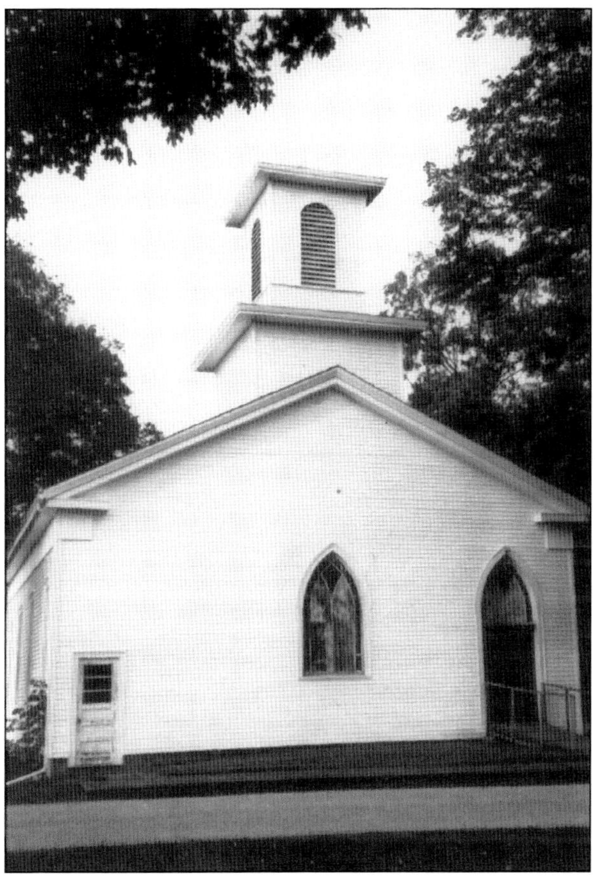

The former Geneva Memorial Church became the home base for the trustees of the Geneva Memorial Cemetery Association in 1988. It was to be used as funeral chapel. It also is used as the base for annual community picnics. The cemetery association has been taking care of the cemetery since 1945.

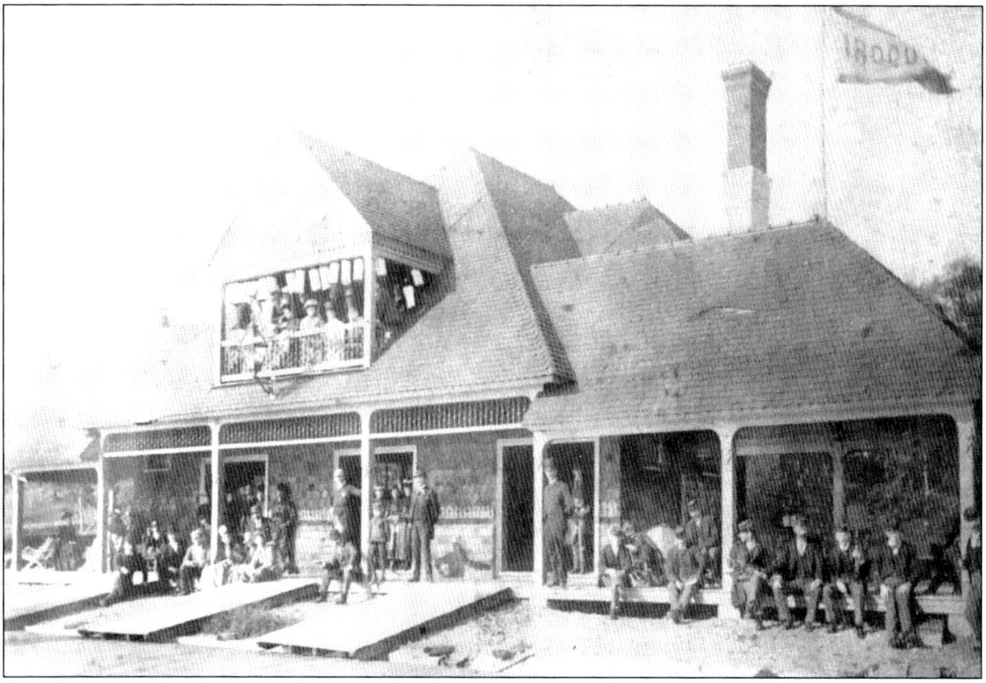

When the Iroquois Hunting and Fishing Club organized in 1887, it chose this structure for its first home. The building was close to the lake, as evident by the boats docked at the lower right corner of the photograph. A 1928 fire destroyed the original Victorian clubhouse, but members built a new one, which still operates in 2012, allowing members to enjoy boating as well as dining facilities. (LFC.)

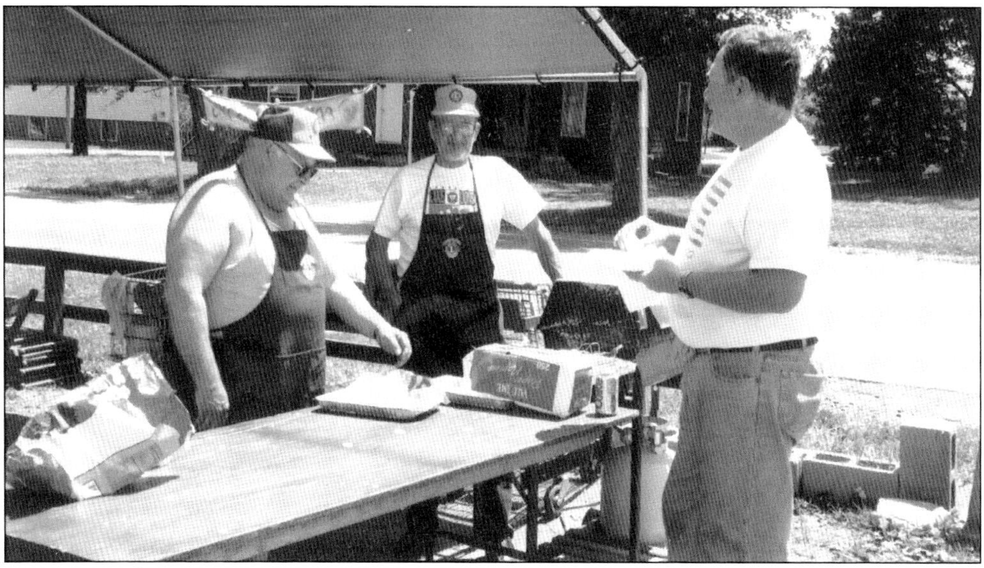

Conneaut Lake Lions Club members wait for customers at their annual chicken barbecue to raise funds to support its mission in this 2001 photograph. One of the main projects of Lions Club worldwide is to assist with people with eyesight issues. On a Sunday morning, those traveling the streets of Conneaut Lake will see a life-size chicken, calling to people to stop and have a nice Sunday dinner.

Eight

SPORTS

Conneaut Lake has lent itself to numerous types of sports, including fishing, hunting, skating, boating, swimming, and skiing. This chapter will show the success of some fishermen, including Lewis Walker, who holds the record for the largest Muskie ever caught in the state of Pennsylvania. A champion skier, barefoot no less, and members of the Conneaut Lake Ski Club will also be seen as they take advantage of the waters of Conneaut Lake. Although some people enjoyed water sports, others took to the links to do some golfing at the Park Golf Course, Oakland Beach Golf Course, or Klinging Hills Golf Course. Still others preferred horseback riding at stables on both the east side of the lake and just outside Conneaut Lake Park.

Perhaps one of the most treasured claims to fame in the sports history of Conneaut Lake are the two state high school champion basketball teams, the boys in 1965 and the girls in 1981. Both teams were coached by the same man, Don Weyel, the only person in the state's history to have coached both a boys' and girls' team to state championships. Conneaut Lake also boasts a state champion wrestler, Bill Kuhn, and a girls' state volleyball champion team. And, local resident Art Hoover coached a number of girls' softball teams to national championship honors.

Nearby Harmonsburg claims two of its own, brothers Darryl and Lynn Jones, for their part in bringing honor to this small community. Darryl played for the New York Yankees. Lynn played for the Detroit Tigers and Kansas City Royals and was a member of the coaching staff for the Marlins and the Boston Red Sox. Lynn won two World Series rings as a player for the Kansas City Royals and as a coach for the Boston Red Sox. Although the area has had many champions, it also has dozens of teams, including little league, soccer, football, and organized school sports teams. All are designed for recreational purposes and for building relationships.

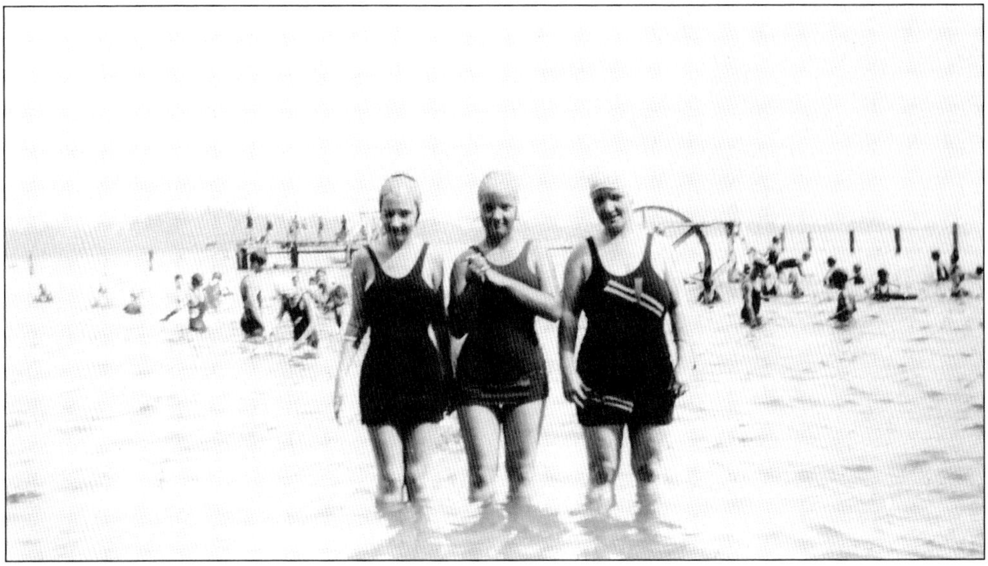

From left to right, Betty, Ruth, and Edna (last names unknown) are bathing and swimming in Conneaut Lake in July 1932. Note the swimsuits provide more coverage than those of 2012.

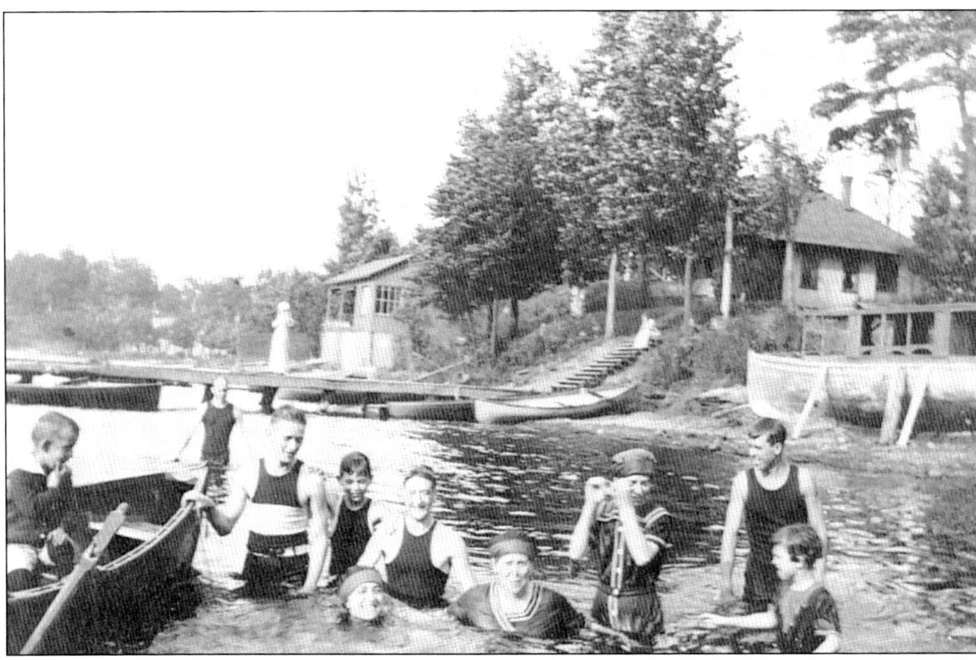

In the 1930s, swimmers and boaters are pictured on the east side of the lake.

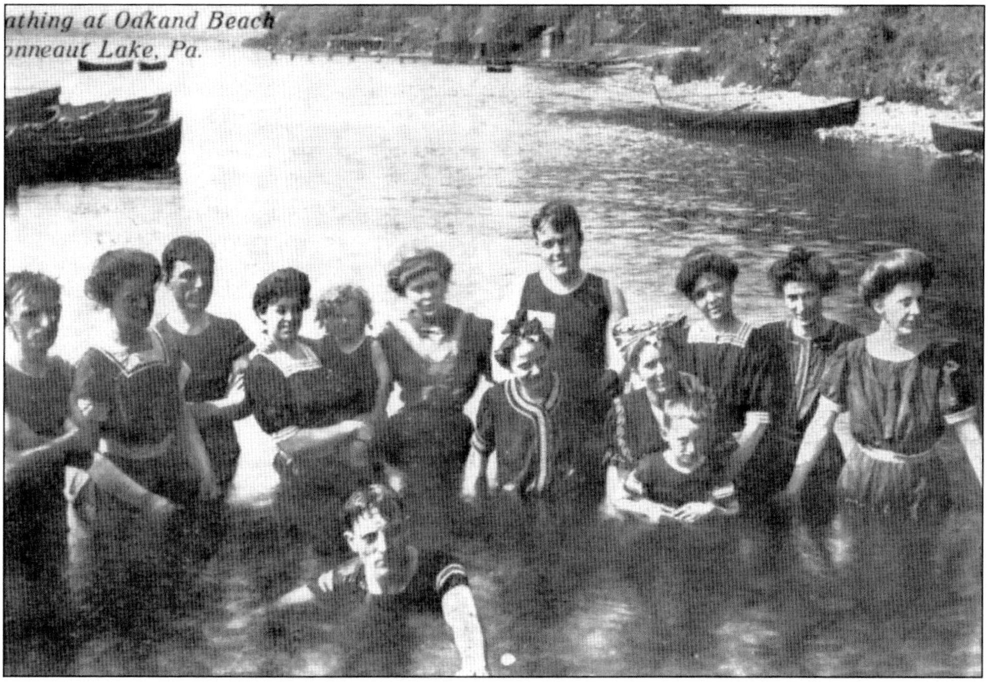

Men, women, and children are photographed standing in the water at Oakland Beach on the east side of Conneaut Lake. (BH.)

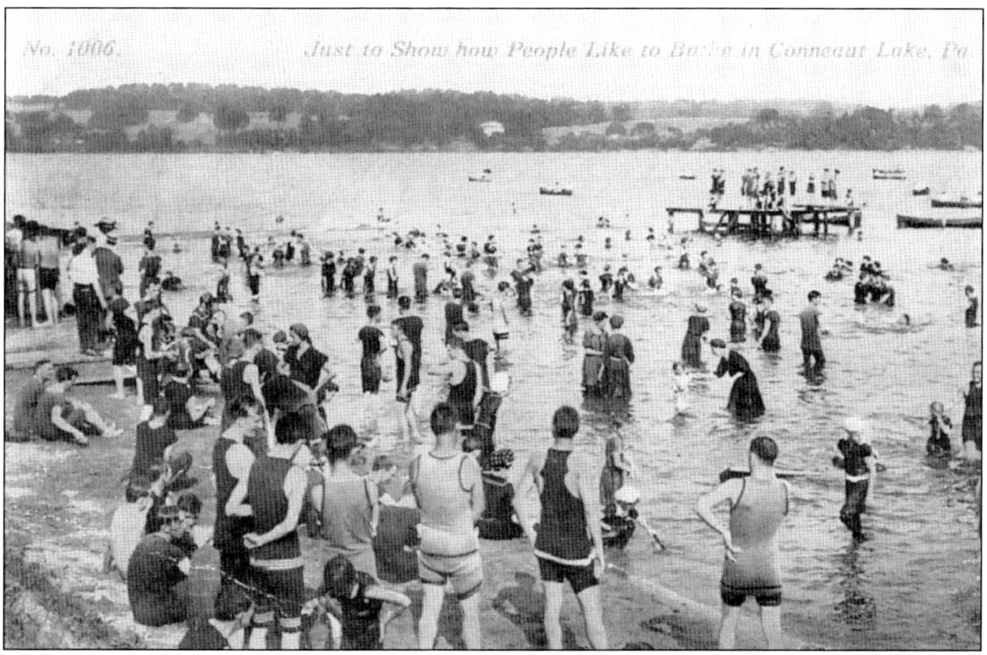

This postcard from the early 1920s was titled "Just to Show how People Like to Bathe in Conneaut Lake." Note the platform in middle of the lake; bathers made big splashes as they landed. (LFC.)

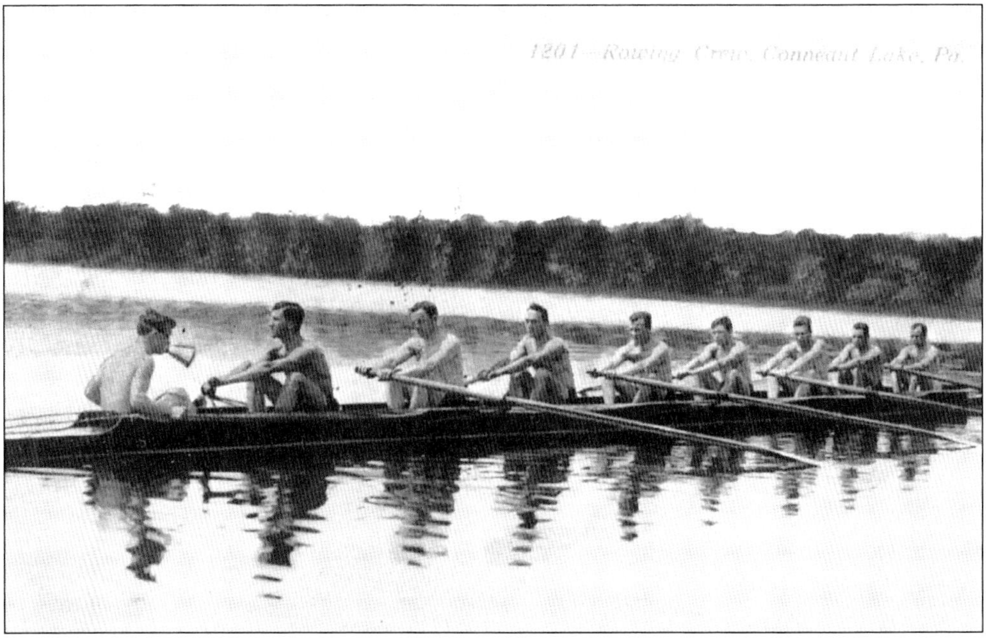

The rowing club of Conneaut Lake is pictured here. They competed in various events on Conneaut Lake during the summer, which was when the lake was full of people enjoying all types of sports, including boating and swimming. (HS.)

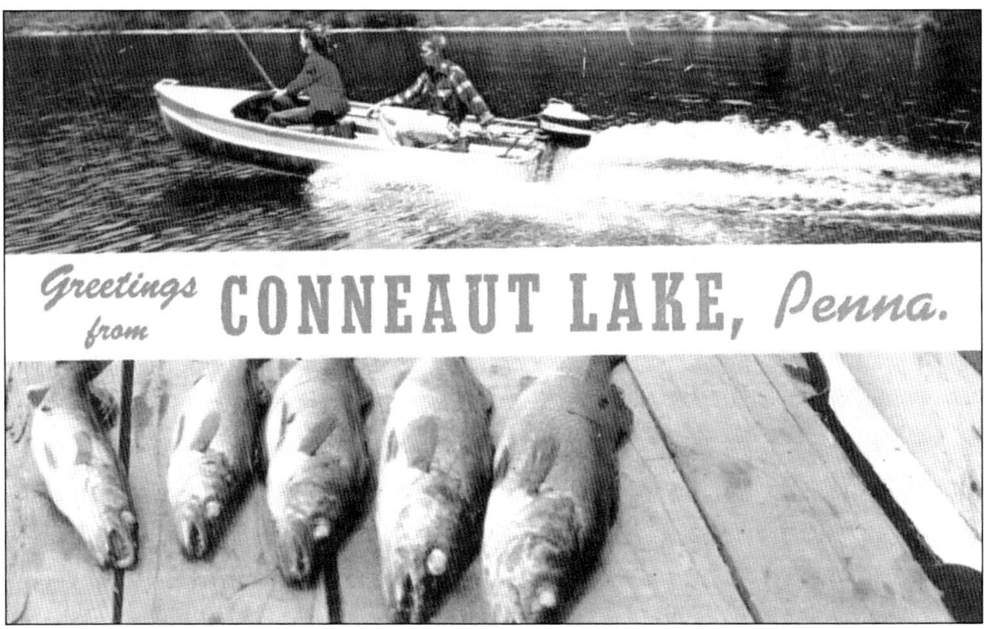

Five huge fish are pictured on the docks of Conneaut Lake.

Rad Huffman of Waynesburg shows off two fish he caught in Conneaut Lake in 2001.

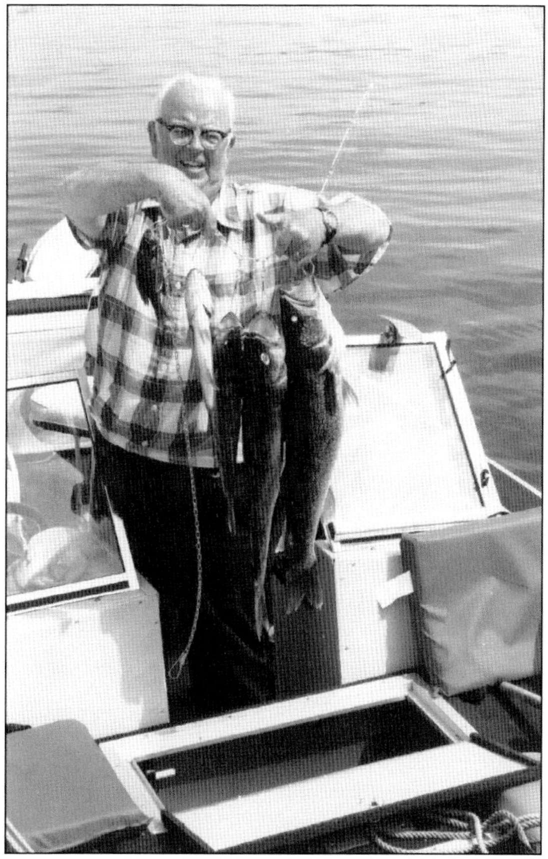

Members of the Skibo Club of Conneaut Lake take time for a photograph before hitting the water. Most of the uniforms had a large letter "s" on the front, while some had the Skibo name. The club enjoyed skiing on the lake during the summer months. (BH.)

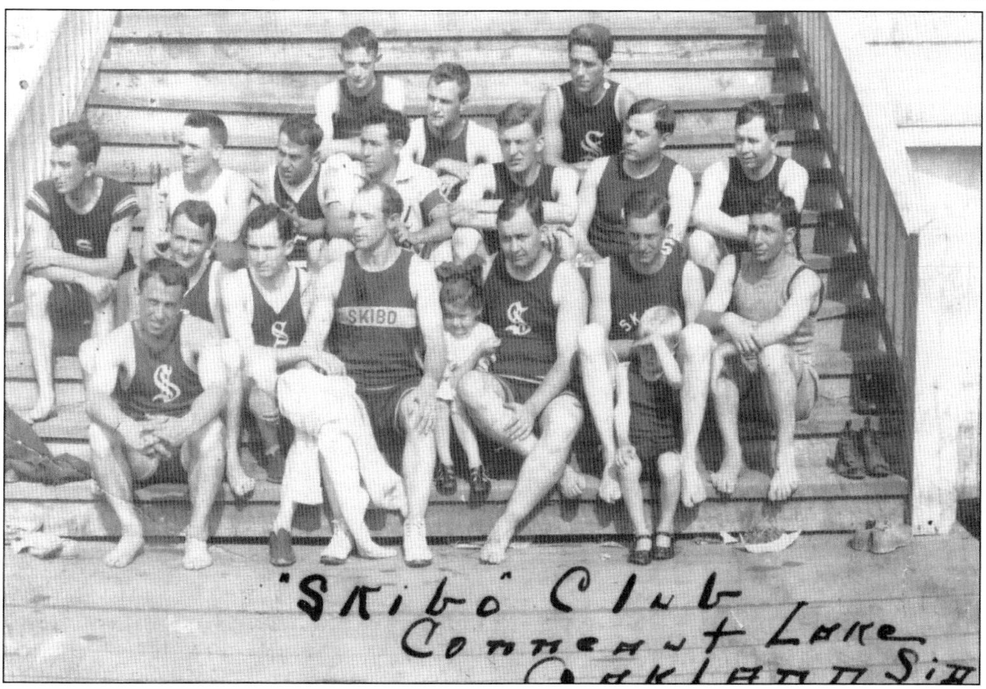

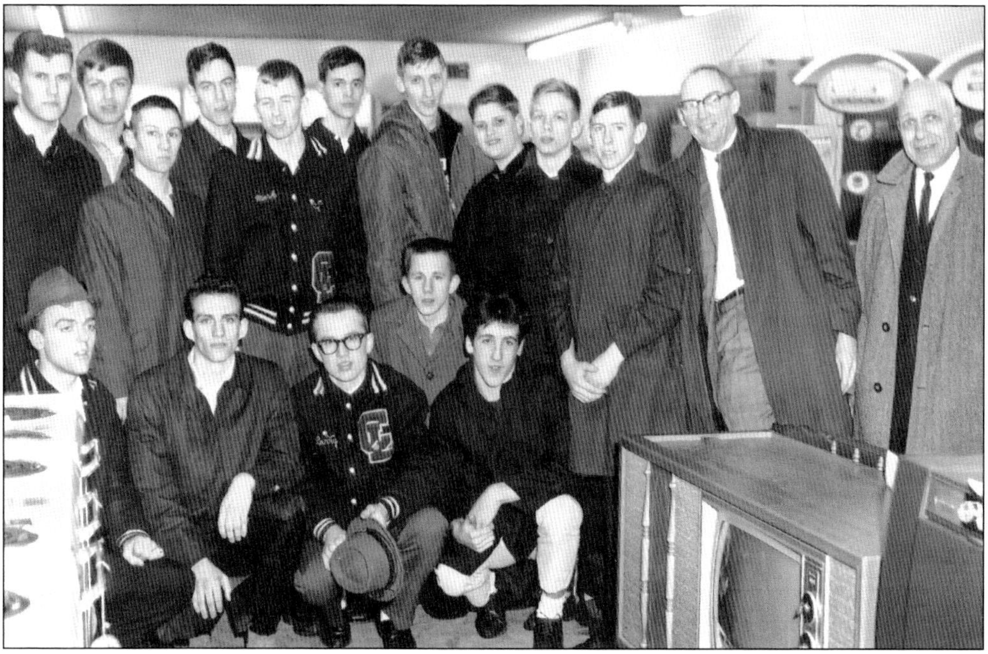

The state champion Class C basketball team from Conneaut Lake High School became the first county team to bring home a state title in 1965, following an incredible playoff series. Coach Don Weyel is second from the right. School principal Raymond Van Slyke, on the right, joined the victory celebration. (HLF.)

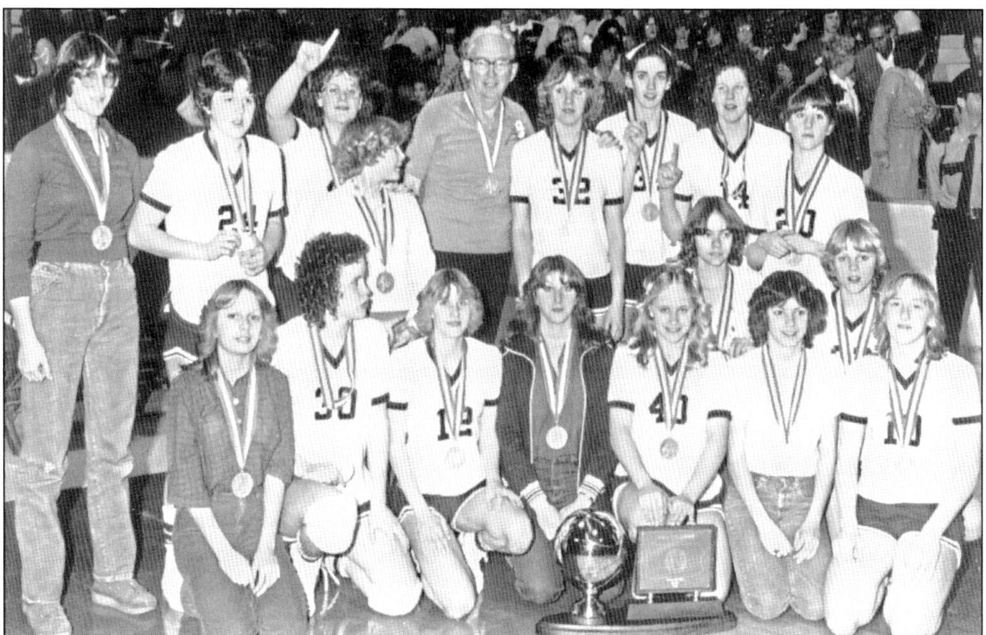

The girls from Conneaut Lake High School gave Don Weyel a special distinction when they won the girls' state basketball championship in 1981. Weyel is the first coach to have won a state championship with both the boys' and girls' teams. The photograph was taken right after the game as their fans were still in the gym. (HLF.)

Water slides are always popular among those swimming, and this photograph shows the slide on the east side of Conneaut Lake was no exception. This slide started on the beach and went out into the water, giving swimmers a real thrill as they hit the bottom, sliding into the cool water. (LFC.)

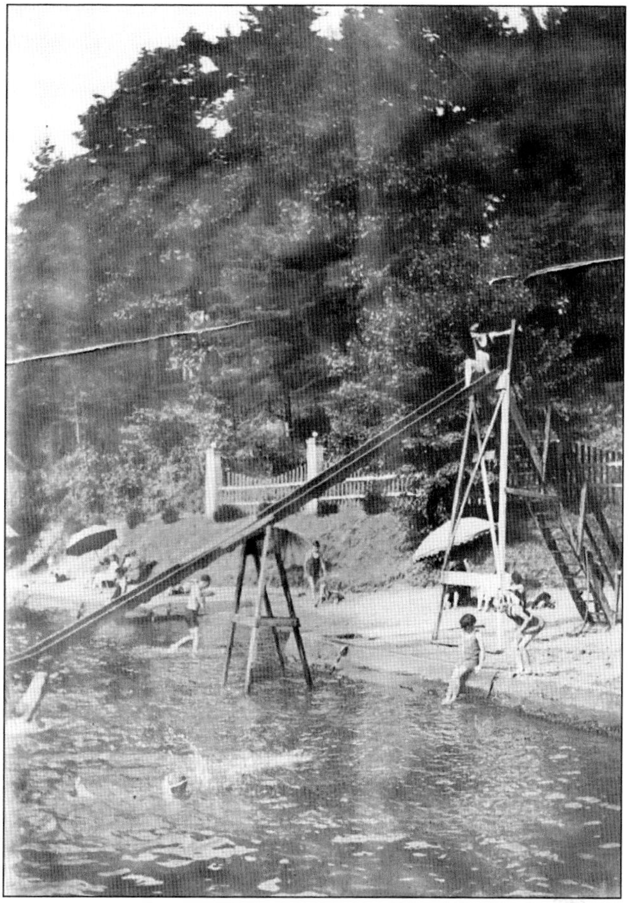

This postcard shows Oakland Beach Golf Clubhouse, as viewed from the No. 1 Fairway. The golf course, open to the public, had 18 holes nestled in the rolling hills of the east shore of Conneaut Lake. It is described as a "Golfer's Golf Course." It is still in operation in 2012.

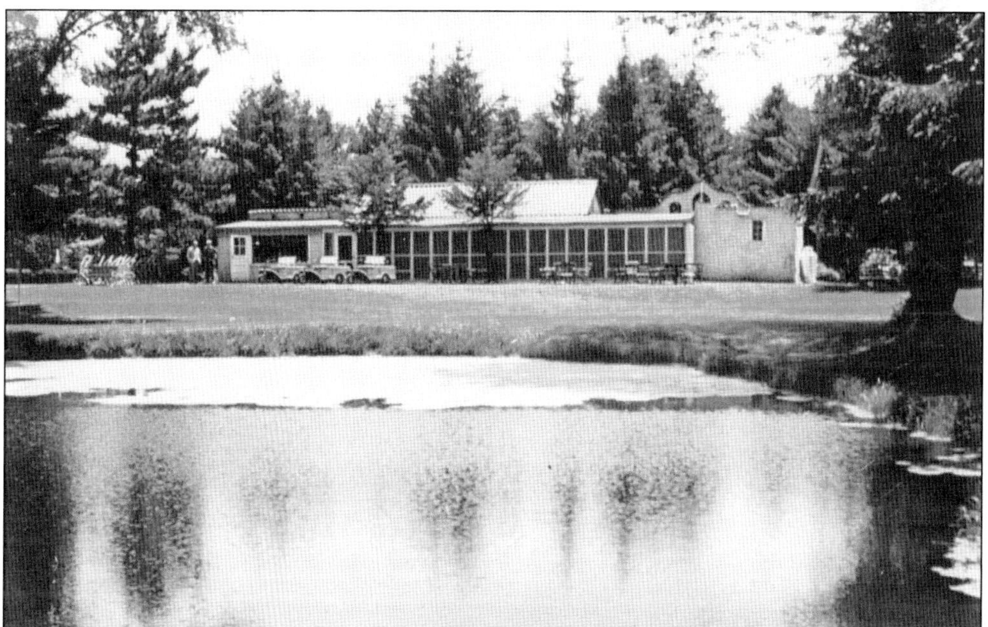

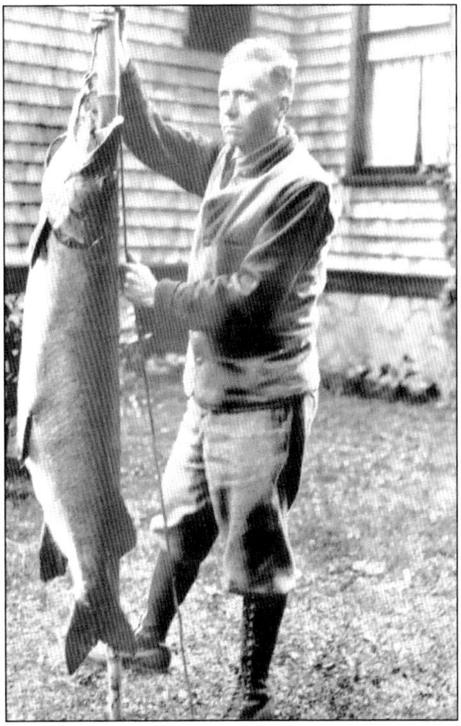

Col. Lewis Walker of Meadville shows off the huge Muskie he caught in 1924 in Conneaut Lake. It was 59 inches long and weighed 53 pounds, 4 ounces—a state record that stands in 2012. A replica of the fish is on exhibit at the Conneaut Lake Area Historical Society Museum.

Community teams battle it out in a fundraising basketball game at the community hall during the 1950s, when the teams wore blue jeans and white shirts instead of traditional uniforms. The teams consisted of young women who agreed to play basketball to raise funds for the community.

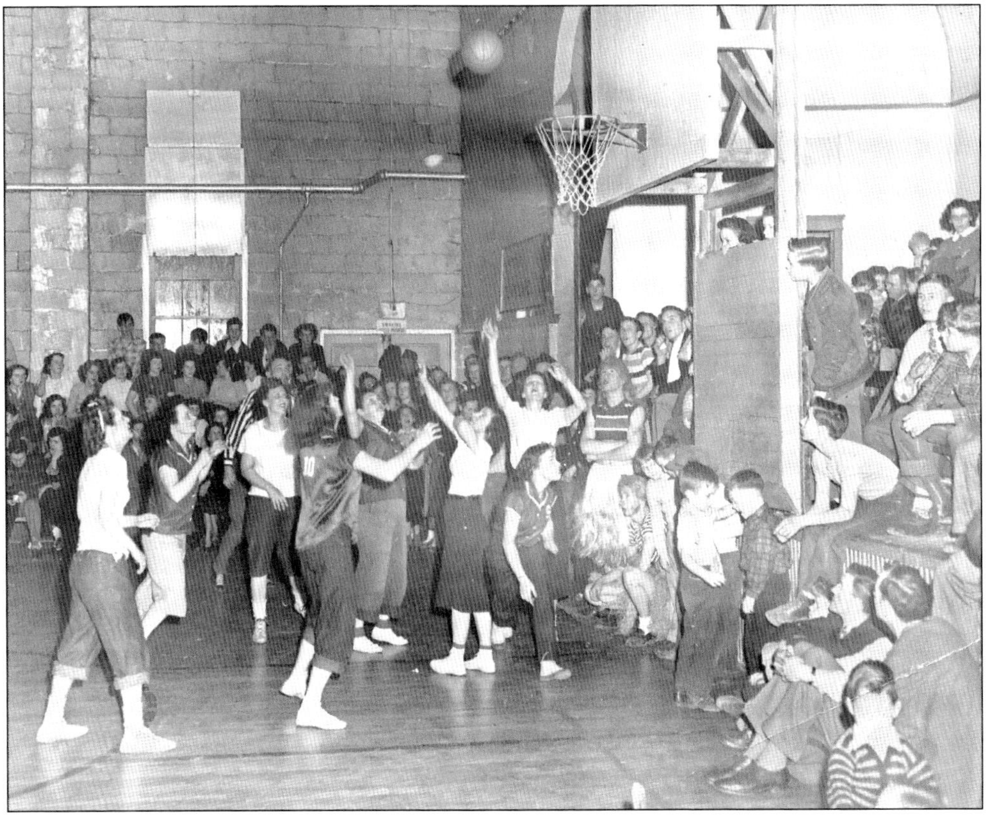

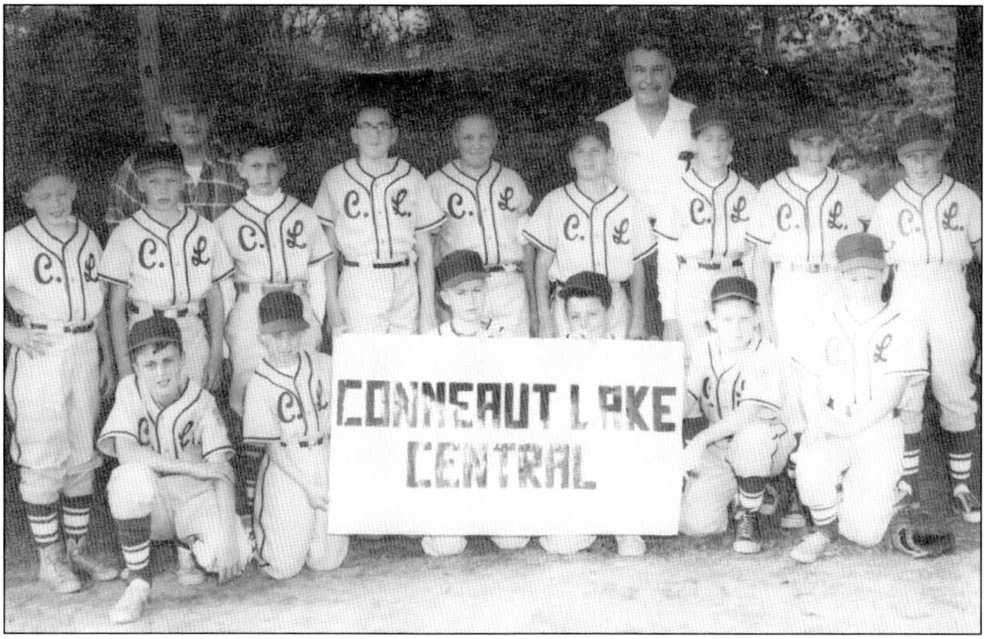

The Conneaut Lake Central Little League Baseball team is shown with the team pennant in this portrait from 1964. From left to right are (first row) Bob Andrews, Kevin VanHonk, Glenn Dillon, Heath Hanmore, Mark Cosner, and John Leasure; (second row) Timmy Osborn, Paul Christy, Paul Saulsbery, Keith Worley, Miles Beard, Ronnie Andrews, Mike Burchfield, Bob Christie, and Tom Griggs; (third row) John Carl, assistant coach, and Bill Lobins, coach/manager. Member Joe Vincent was absent.

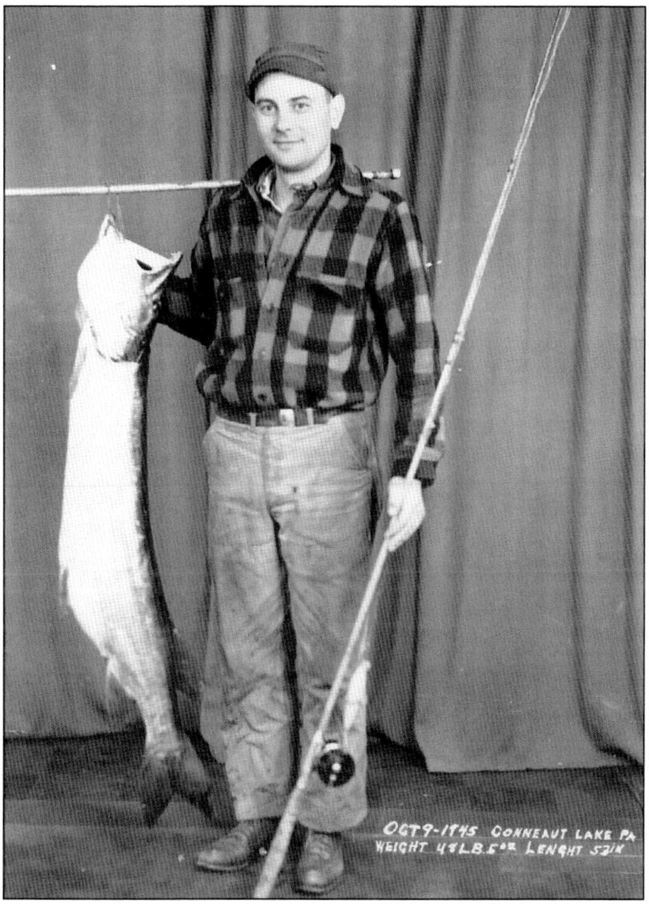

Mearl Klinginsmith landed this fish on October 9, 1945, in Conneaut Lake. This fish weighed 48 pounds, 5 ounces, and was 52 inches long. Klinginsmith also holds the rod he used for his big catch, one of many he claimed over his years of fishing in his hometown.

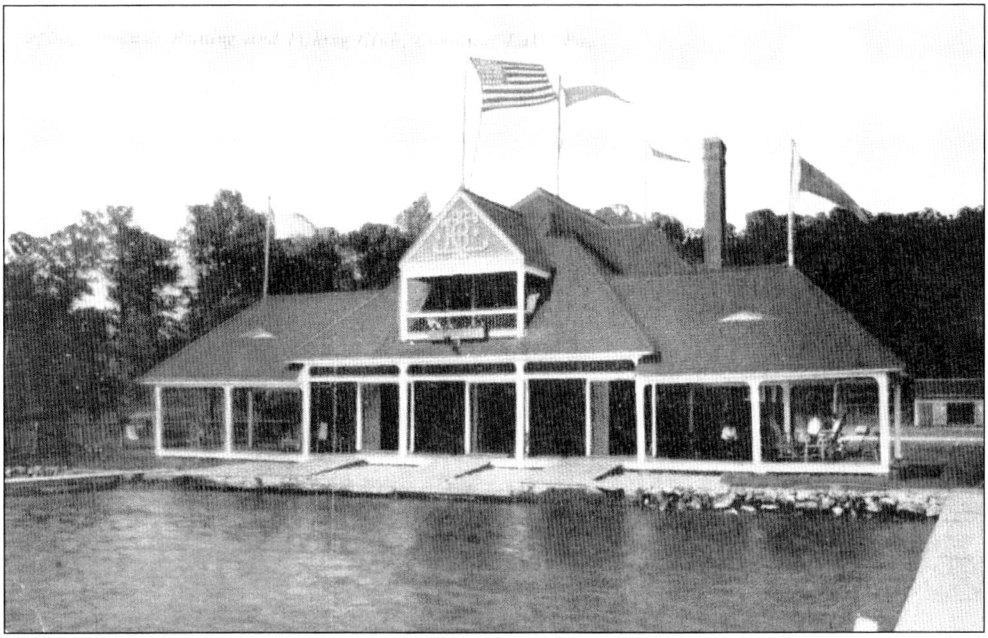

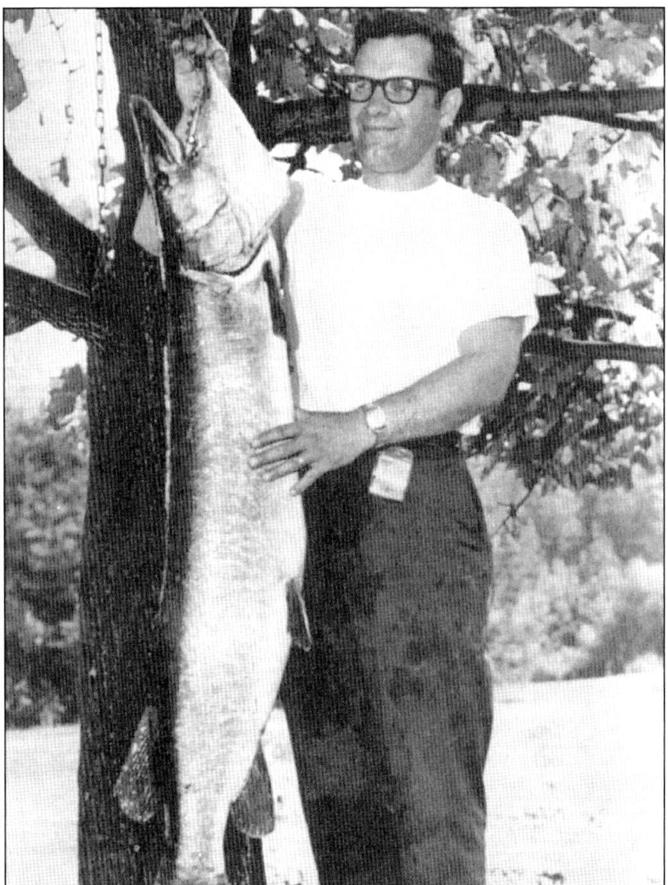

The Iroquois Boating and Fishing Club on the east side is a popular place to relax at after time spent on Conneaut Lake or go to for an evening out.

Gerald Munson shows off a 46-inch, 48-pound muskellunge caught at Conneaut Lake. Munson caught the fish with an artificial lure in 1970.

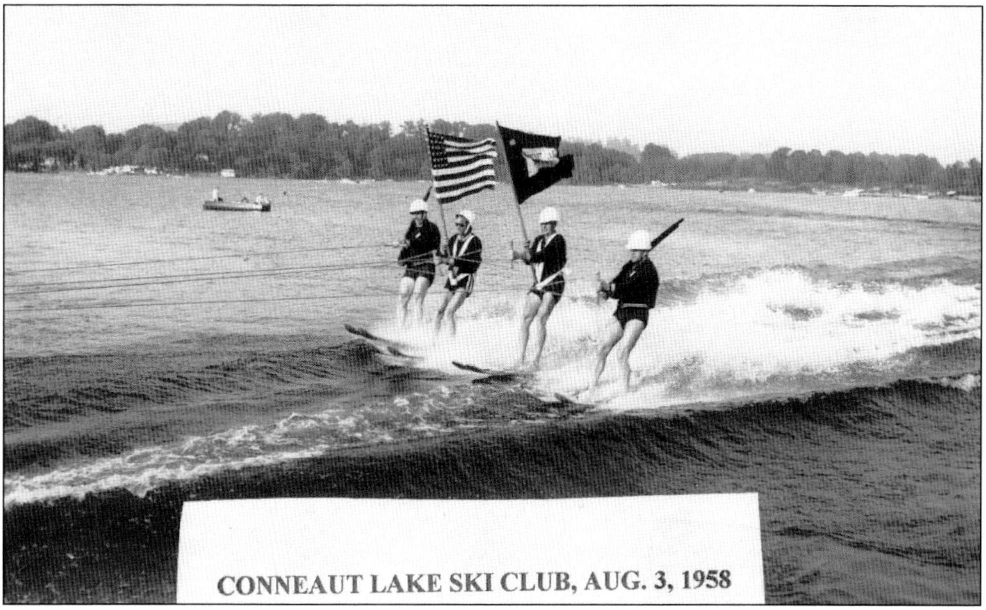

Four members of Conneaut Lake Ski Club formed a color guard, carrying the US flag and the club's flag. Others are carrying rifles while participating in a ski show on August 3, 1958. The shows included various members on skis, often forming pyramids, pulled by speedboats.

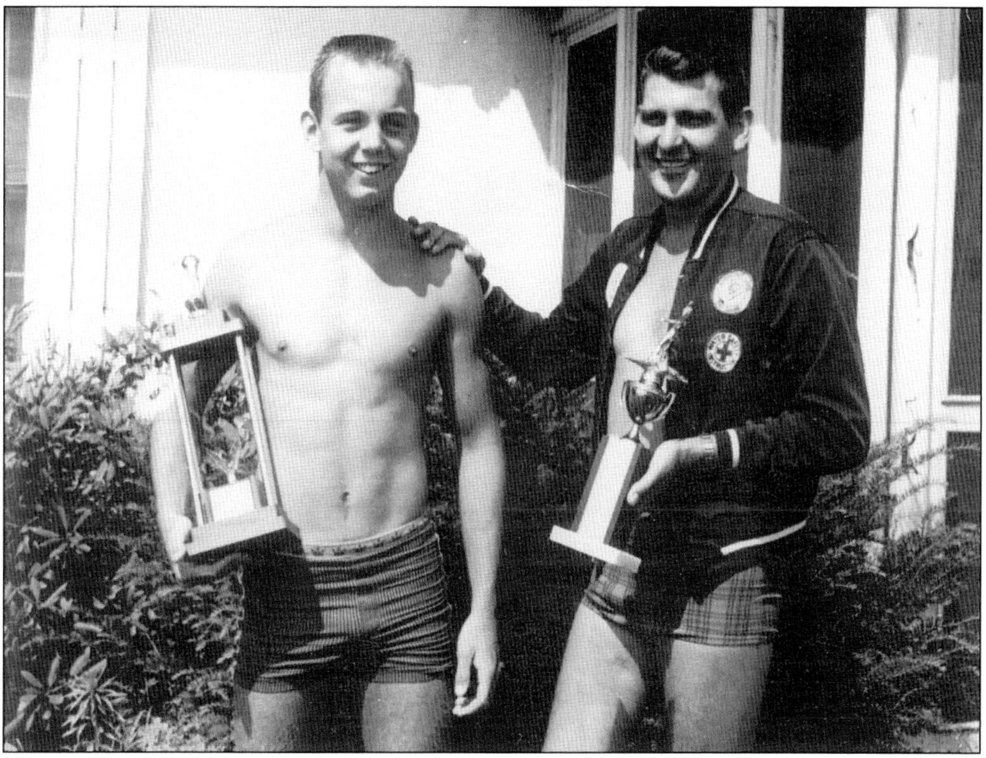

Audley Hays was just 15 years old when he set a world record in 1961 for barefoot skiing, staying up five minutes and 45.3 seconds. President of Conneaut Lake Ski Club Reid Bennett congratulates Hays, on the left. Hays won many skiing trophies.

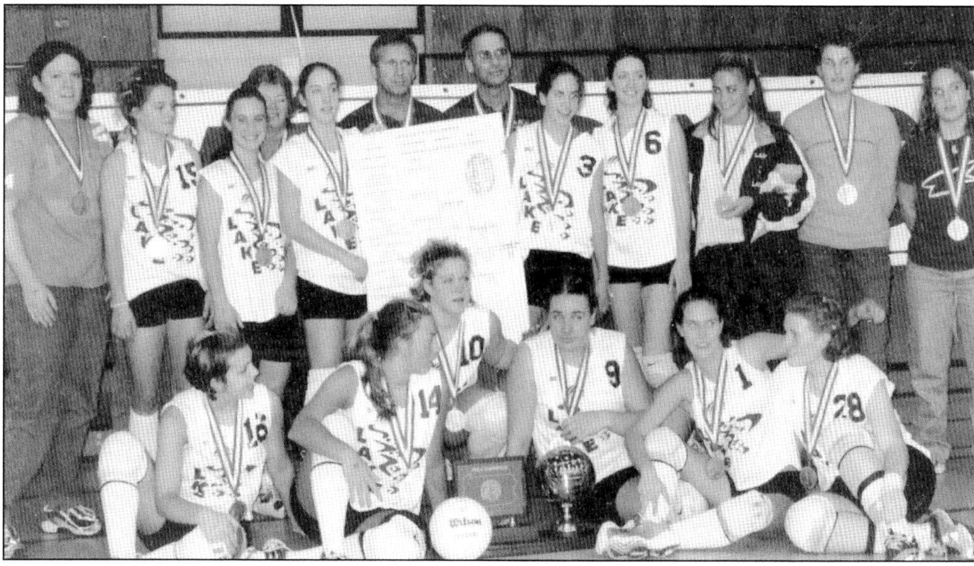

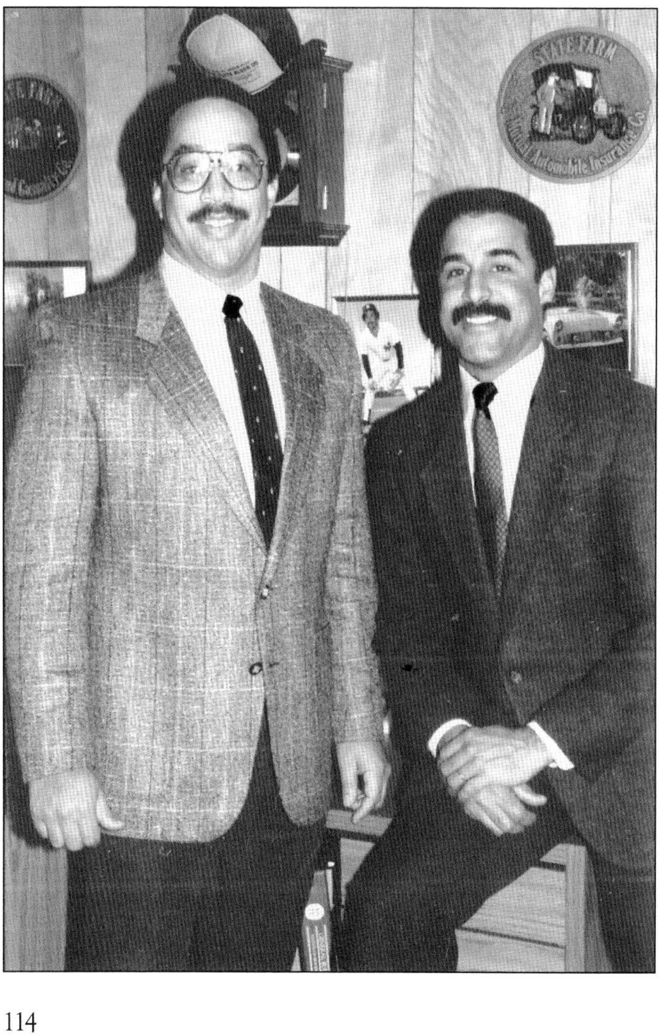

This photograph shows members of the Conneaut Lake High School girls' volleyball team, which took the Pennsylvania State Championship trophy in the year 2000. This was the first time the Conneaut Lake team won a state trophy.

Darryl (left) and Lynn Jones talk about their Major League Baseball careers in an interview from their home in nearby Harmonsburg. Lynn played for the Detroit Tigers and the Kansas City Royals. He won World Series rings as a player for the Kansas City Royals and as a coach for the Boston Red Sox. Darryl played with the New York Yankees before an injury shortened his career. (EM.)

Nine

Churches and Education

Five years after Abner Evans arrived in what is now known as Conneaut Lake, the first church was established in 1798. Called the Meetinghouse, it was a Presbyterian church but was used by other denominations as well.

Throughout the area's history, churches of many denominations, including those of independent nature, have been built. All the congregations of the early churches met in smaller quarters, private homes, community buildings, or other sites before constructing their churches. Today, churches in Conneaut Lake area include the following denominations: Presbyterian, Methodist, Catholic, Lutheran, Mennonite, and independents, such as Victory Fellowship on the east side. In nearby Geneva, the Advent Christian Church has closed. Other Geneva churches include a United Methodist and Pilgrim Chapel. Harmonsburg also has Methodist and Presbyterian churches.

Formal education, like spiritual life, has remained important to Conneaut Lake residents. Students met in various homes before the first school was built in 1799. The second elementary school was built in 1832; the high school grades went to the "Academy" at the Presbyterian church. In 1860, the third school opened at the corner of Water and Fifth Streets. In 1886, a school located on Fifth and High Streets opened for both high school and elementary grades. It was located at the present site of Zatsick's Golden Dawn Store. That building burned in 1952, and classes were held for the remainder of the year in various churches. A high school that was built in 1937 at Sixth and Line Streets became the elementary school in 1954. A new and expanded high school opened that year. Before the 1954 high school opened, the community hall was used as the gymnasium, and students walked from the Sixth Street school to the Third Street hall to take their physical education classes.

In nearby Greenwood Township, its elementary school was closed in 2007, and all the students transferred to Conneaut Lake. Major renovations were completed in 2005 to both the high school and elementary school.

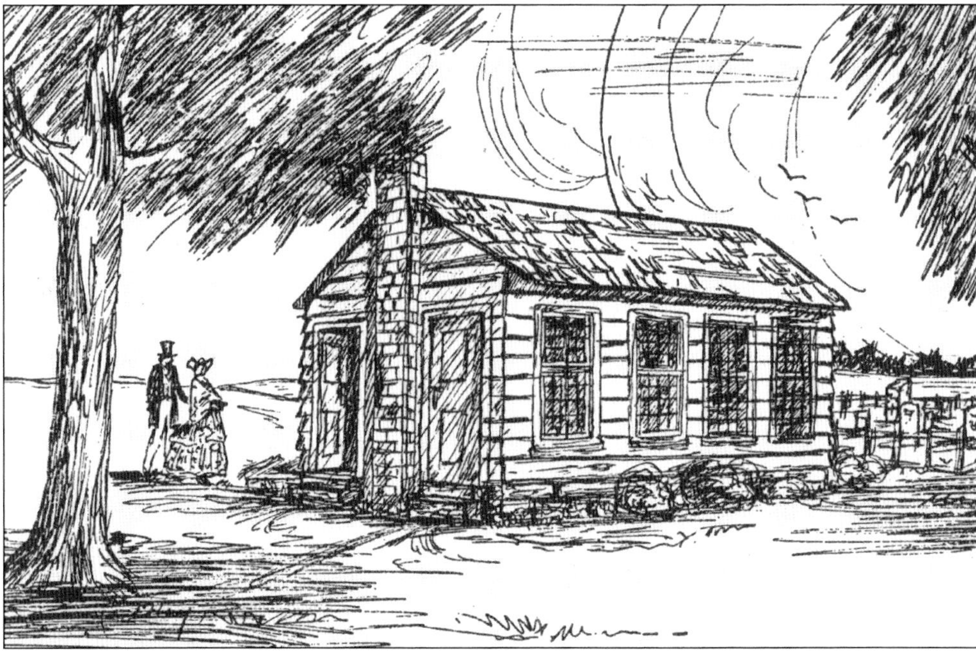

This artist's sketch shows the first house of worship in the village of Evansburg. A log cabin, built in 1798, was about 75 yards from the bank of the lake. Three large doors were on one end. Another door was on the side, opposite the pulpit. Benches were laid on blocks and trestles.

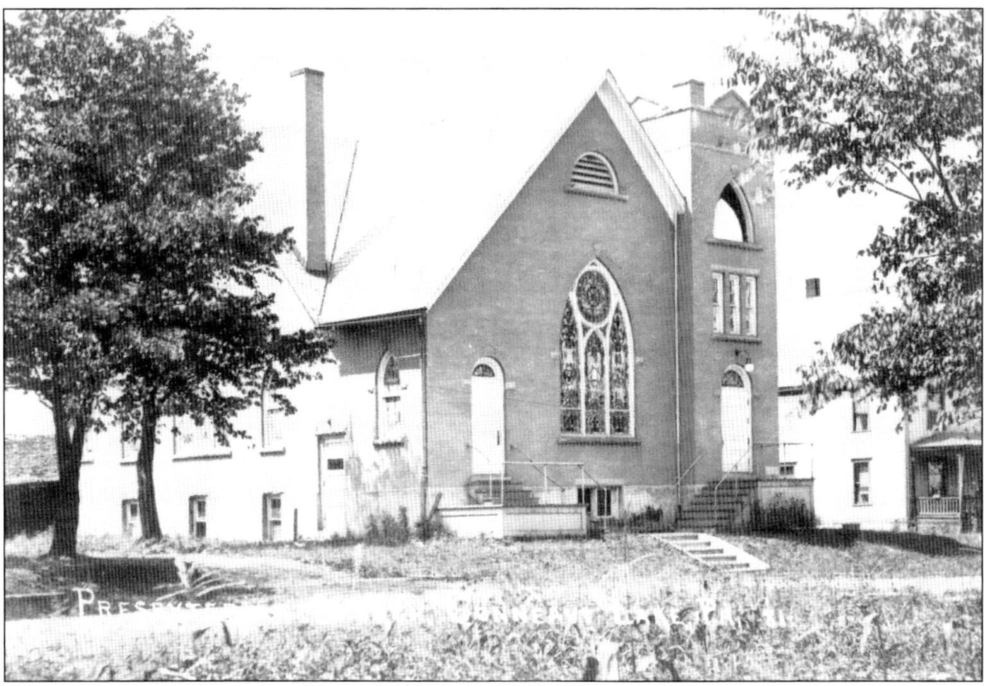

This postcard shows the Presbyterian church, erected in 1912 on Fifth Street. The church history dates back to 1799 when two young missionaries, Rev. Elisha McCurdy and Rev. Joseph Stockton, came into northwestern Pennsylvania. Several additions were made to the church in the late 1900s. (BH.)

This Methodist Episcopal (now Trinity United Methodist) church was founded in the early days of Evansburg, but a church was not built until 1839. The new church was completed in 1902, as shown in right photograph. The church was expanded in 1954 and again in 1977. The expansion included a new education wing, and the old church was torn down to make way for the renovated church. (BH.)

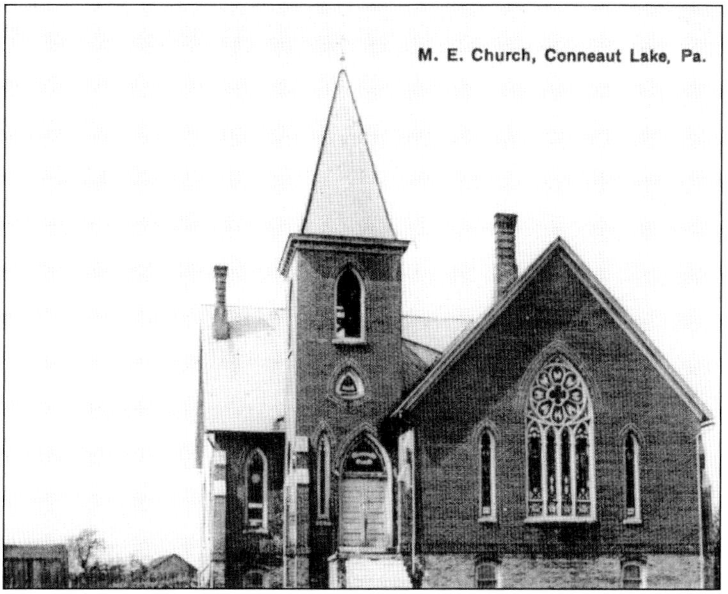

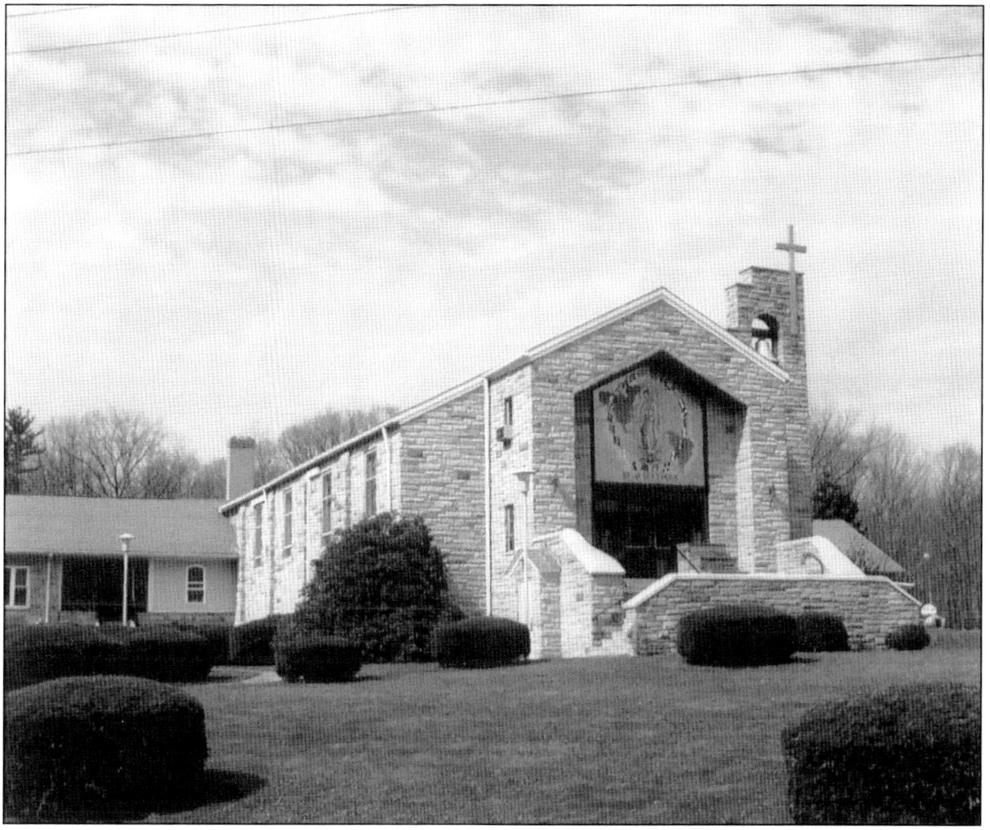

Our Lady Queen of the Americas Roman Catholic Church met in the community hall for Masses prior to building its new church on US 6 and Route 285 on the west end of Conneaut Lake. The church property also is the site of the Holy Ground Samaritans Thrift Shop, which also serves as a distribution center for food for those in need.

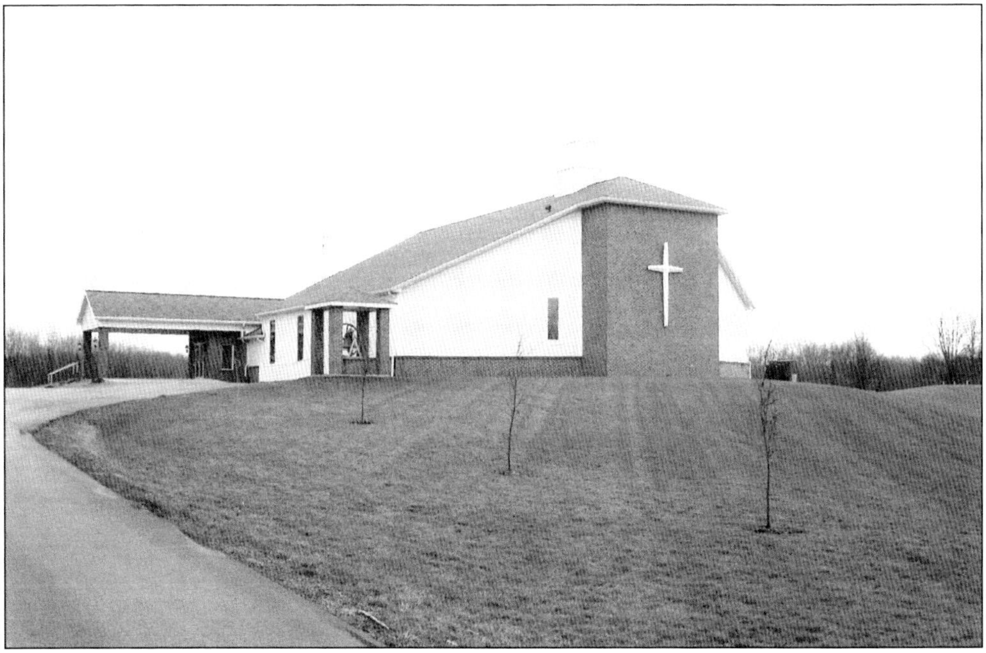

High Street Community Church, the former High Street Presbyterian Church, moved from its building on Fourth and High Streets in Conneaut Lake to its new location several miles south of town. The first service was held there in 2007. The church maintains the former building as well.

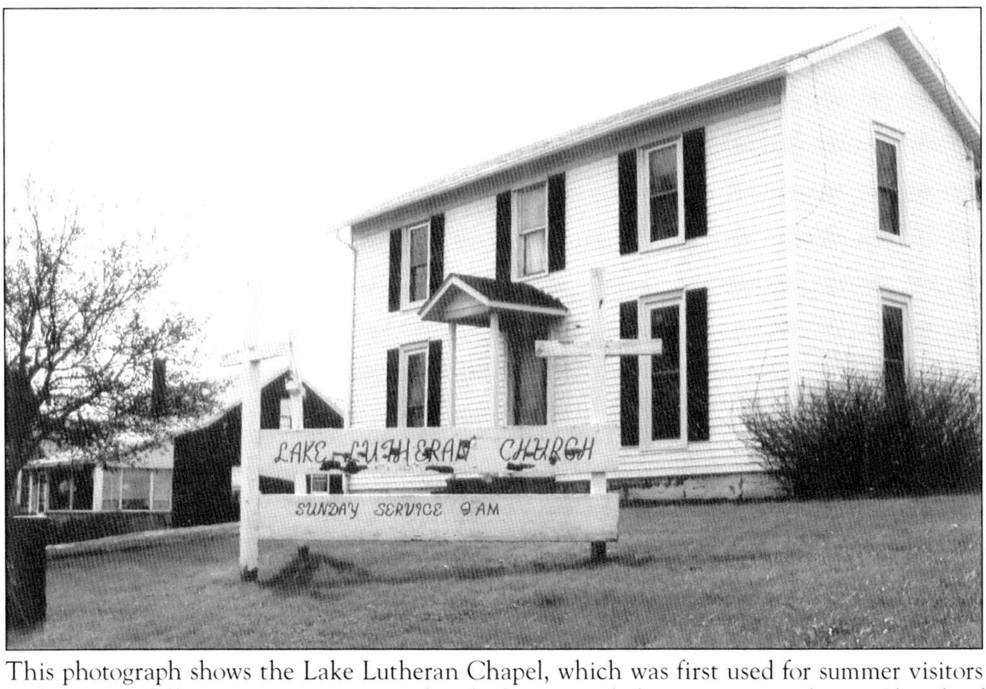

This photograph shows the Lake Lutheran Chapel, which was first used for summer visitors and now is a full-time ministry. Assisted with their growth from Trinity Lutheran Church of Meadville, the congregation met in a number of places when first formed, including a restaurant. The congregation purchased this home in 1973 and converted it into a church.

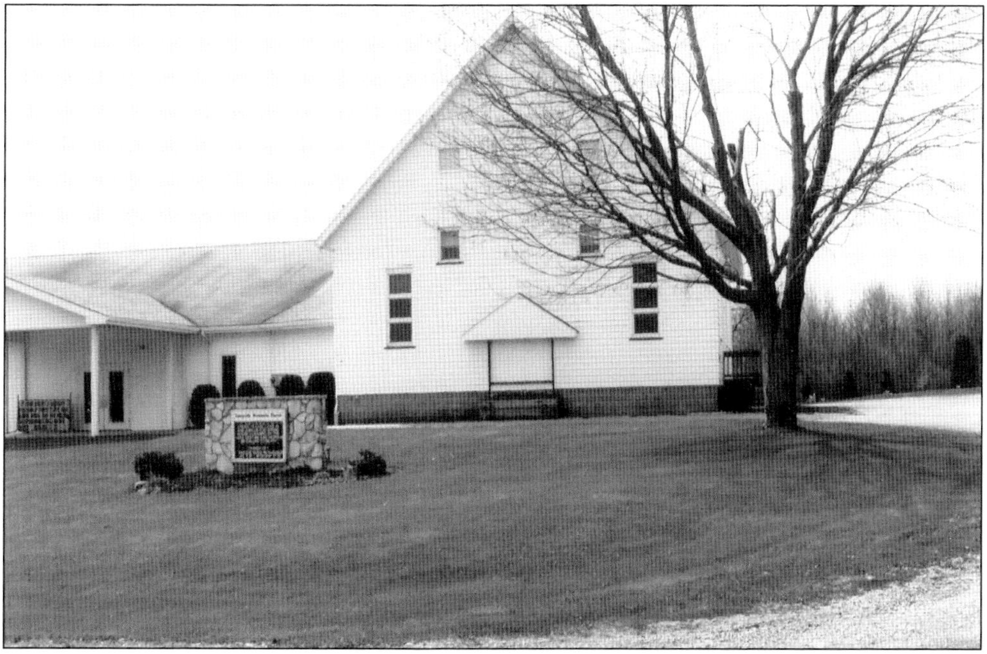

Beginning as a mission church by the Mennonites, this Sunnyside Mennonite Church is located on the east side of Conneaut Lake. In 1935, missionaries wrote to the bishop and told him of the need and the economic opportunities in the farming community of Conneaut Lake. Construction began in 1938; the building was dedicated on September 17, 1944.

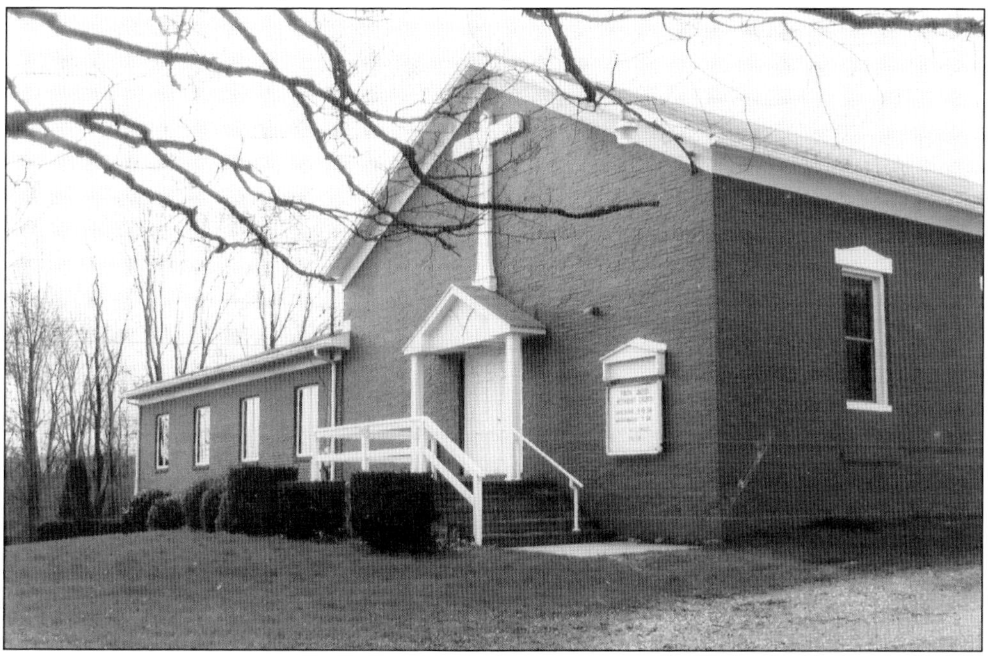

This photograph shows the Geneva United Methodist Church in Greenwood Township. It was previously the United Brethern church, built on land donated by John Gelvin. When the Methodist and United Brethern denominations merged in 1969, the church became the United Methodist. This brick church was erected in 1872 at a cost of $3,000.

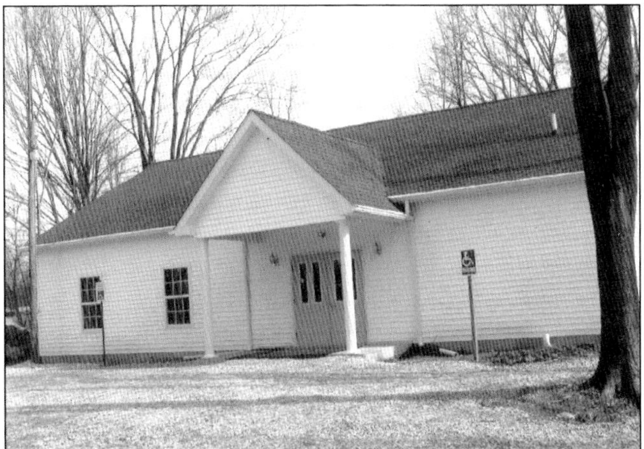

The Faith and Grace Fellowship Church, a nondenominational Charismatic church, was founded in 1996. The congregation met in various places until 2003, when a church was built on Leach Road, not far from Conneaut Lake. The first services in the new building were held on January 11, 2004.

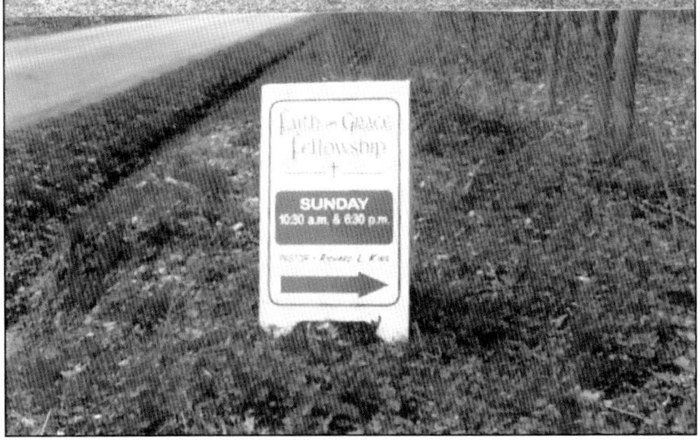

The Harmonsburg United Methodist Church, pictured here, was constructed in 1840 in the northeastern part of the village. The congregation previously used the Union church, which had been built in 1821 but was vacant. That building was traced back to the German Reformed church, which was one of the early churches that organized in the township.

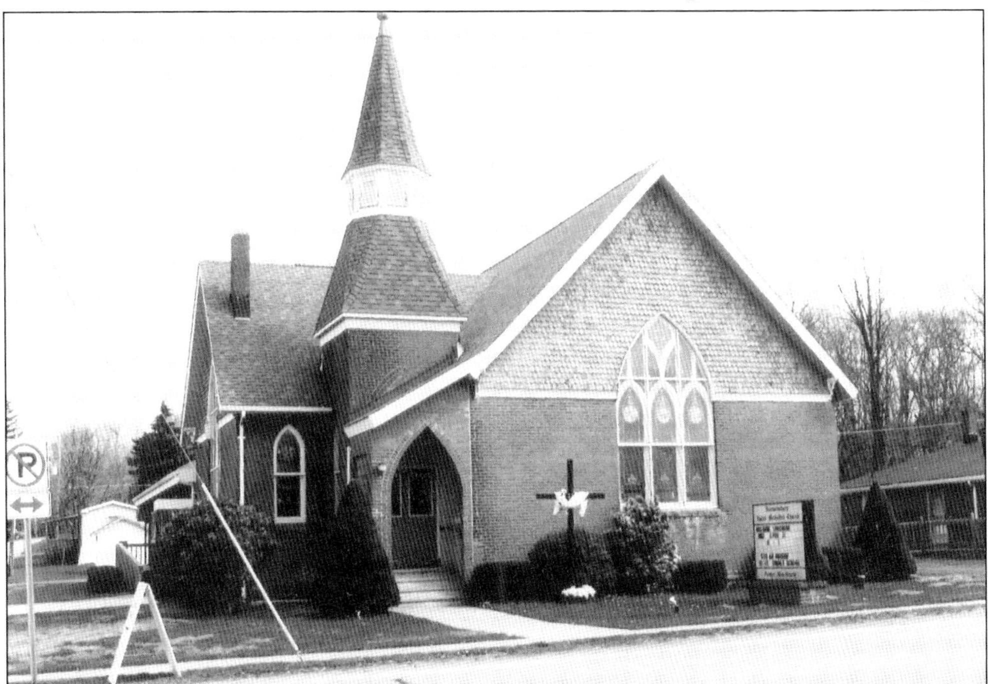

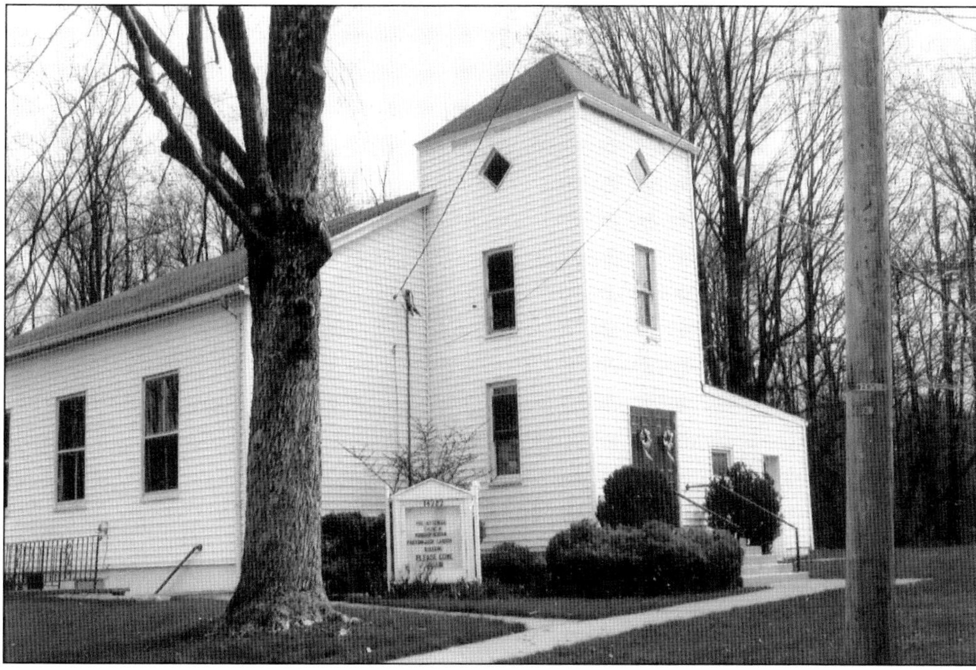

Organized by Rev. David McKinney, the Harmonsburg Presbyterian Church is shown in this photograph. Many of the members had formerly been connected with the Meadville Presbyterian Church. Early meetings were held in the Union church, but in 1844 a frame church was erected at cost of about $800, just north of the village. The church burned in 2008 but was rebuilt.

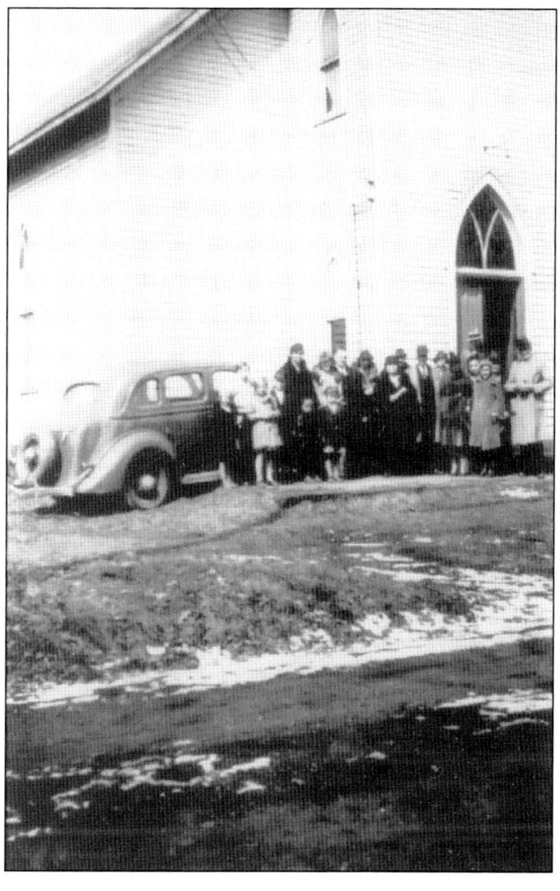

The Advent Christian Church, shown in this 1937 photograph, was located on Church Street in Geneva. It closed about 1950 and was subsequently sold to Northwest Specialty, a lumber company, and used as a warehouse. The interior featured a large Biblical scene. (GA.)

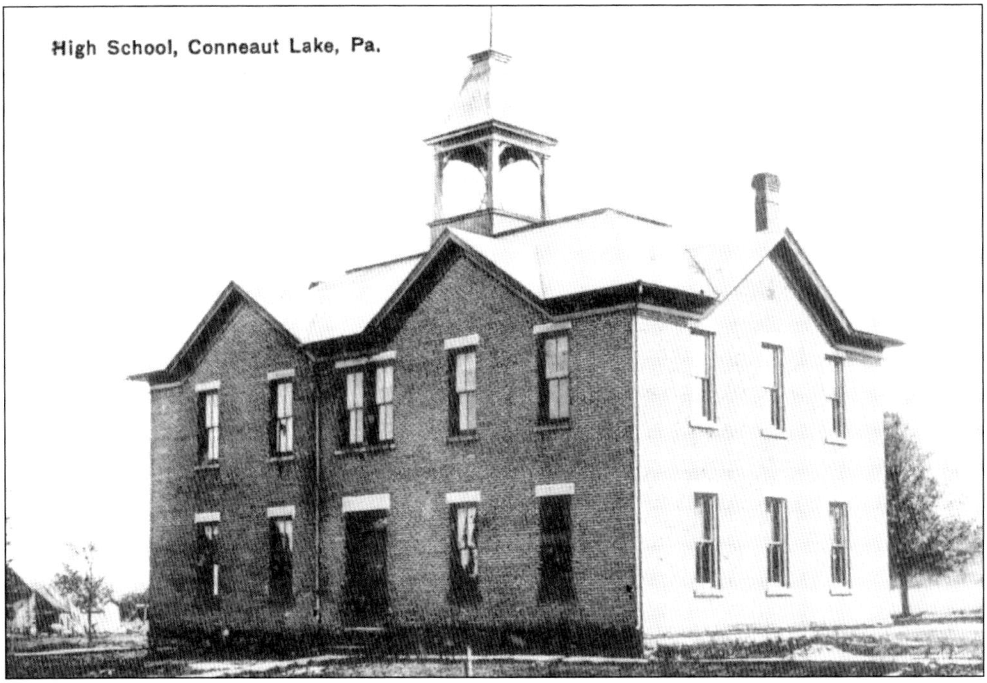

Conneaut Lake High School was housed in this building, constructed in 1886. When a new high school was built on Line Street, this building was used as an elementary school until it burned in 1952. At the same time, however, a new high school was under construction, so the Line Street facility then became the elementary school, as had been planned. (BH.)

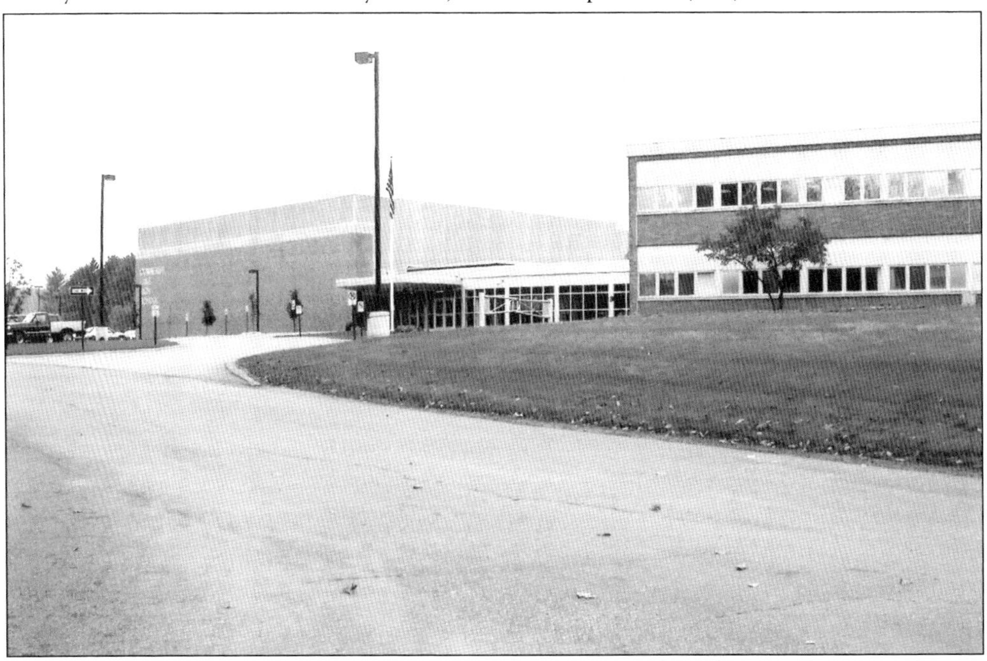

Conneaut Lake Area High School is shown in this photograph at the 2012 location, close to the intersection of US 6 and Route 618. The school opened in 1954 and has been renovated and expanded several times since that date.

Ten

Fire Departments and Fires

Like many small-town communities, Conneaut Lake has had to rely on volunteers. Conneaut Lake's first volunteer fire department, the Ringold Volunteer Fire Department, was named for its founder, an African American worker at the famed Huidekoper stock barns. It became the Conneaut Lake Volunteer Fire Department (CLVFD) in 1918.

At the time, the department's equipment consisted of buckets. Since the lake was nearby, bucket brigades were fairly effective, common practice in the area in the early 1900s. About 1906, a hand-drawn ladder cart and ladders were purchased. Following a 1909 fire, in which a large part of the town burned, the borough council put in a new water system and fire hydrants in 1910. Two hand-drawn hose carts were purchased.

Firefighters headed a campaign to construct a community hall with room to house equipment. The hall was completed in 1931 at a cost of $9,000, plus donated labor.

The first fire truck was bought in 1938; it was the first piece of motorized equipment in Crawford County. The department eventually outgrew the facility. After several subsequent moves, the CLVFD purchased the Wayside Inn, burned it, and constructed a new building on that site. The department also sponsored a junior fire department and a band and marching unit with majorettes in the 1950s. Changing times eliminated both of those activities.

Other departments serve nearby townships. Conneaut Lake Park VFD serves Sadsbury; and Summit and Greenwood departments serve their respective townships. In addition to the fire department, Conneaut Lake also has the volunteer Conneaut Lake Area Ambulance Service, started in 1977 by the Conneaut Lake Jaycees. Today, it is staffed with trained personnel and modern equipment on call 24 hours a day, seven days a week.

This chapter includes photographs of two of the town's most memorable fires, Hotel Iroquois and the Cow Shed.

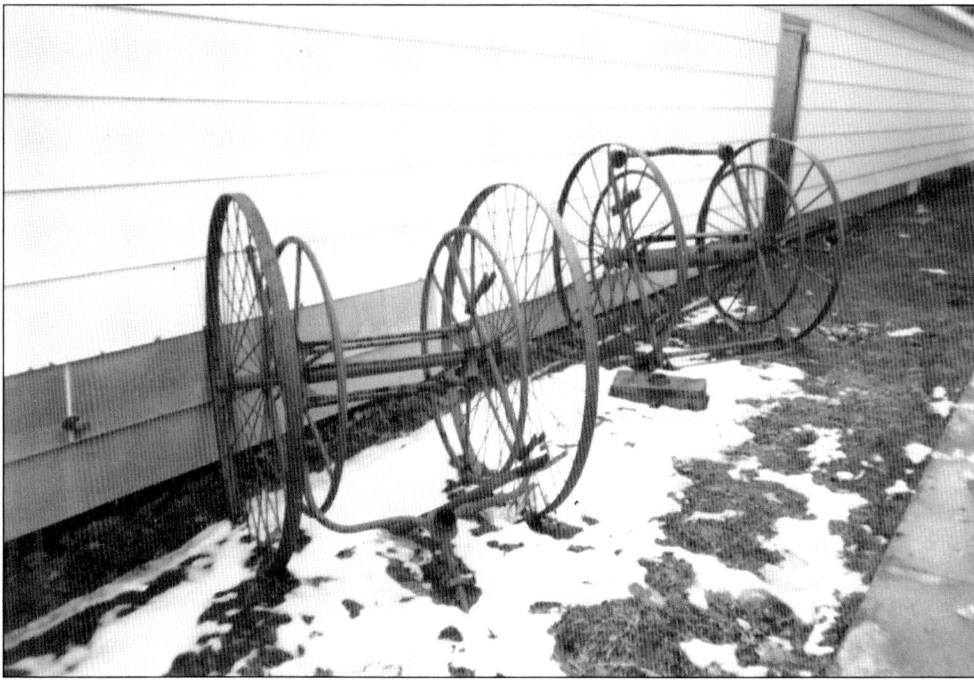

These hand-drawn hose wagons were part of Conneaut Lake Volunteer Fire Department's original equipment, purchased in 1909. At the time, the department had no fire truck. No longer in use, the wagons were preserved; one is on display in the Conneaut Lake Area Historical Society Museum.

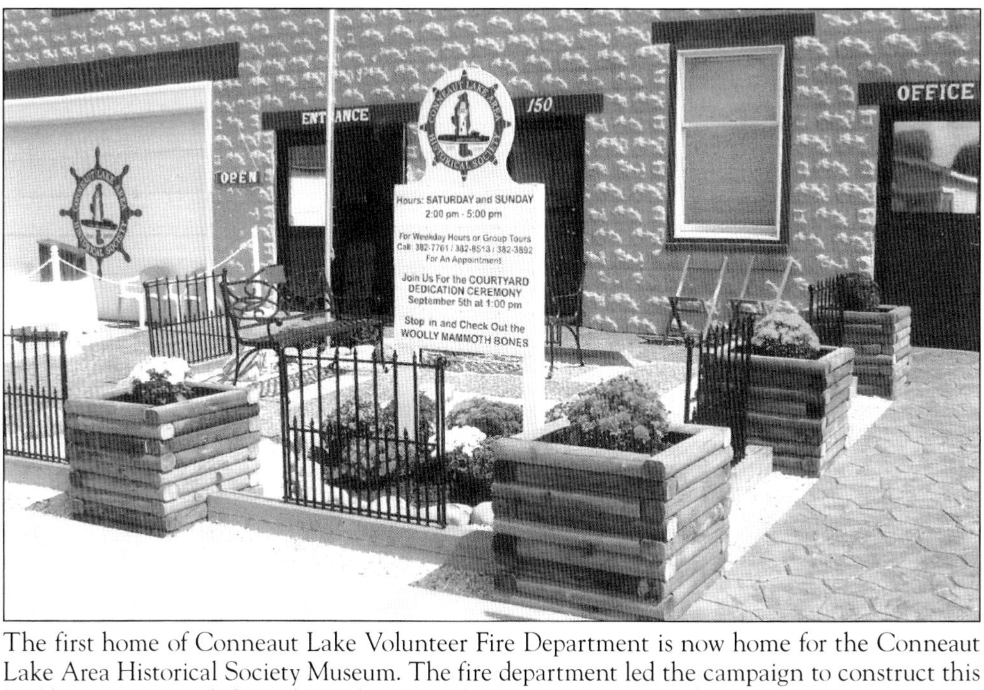

The first home of Conneaut Lake Volunteer Fire Department is now home for the Conneaut Lake Area Historical Society Museum. The fire department led the campaign to construct this building. It was used throughout the town's history as a meeting place for many organizations before becoming the historical society museum in 2003.

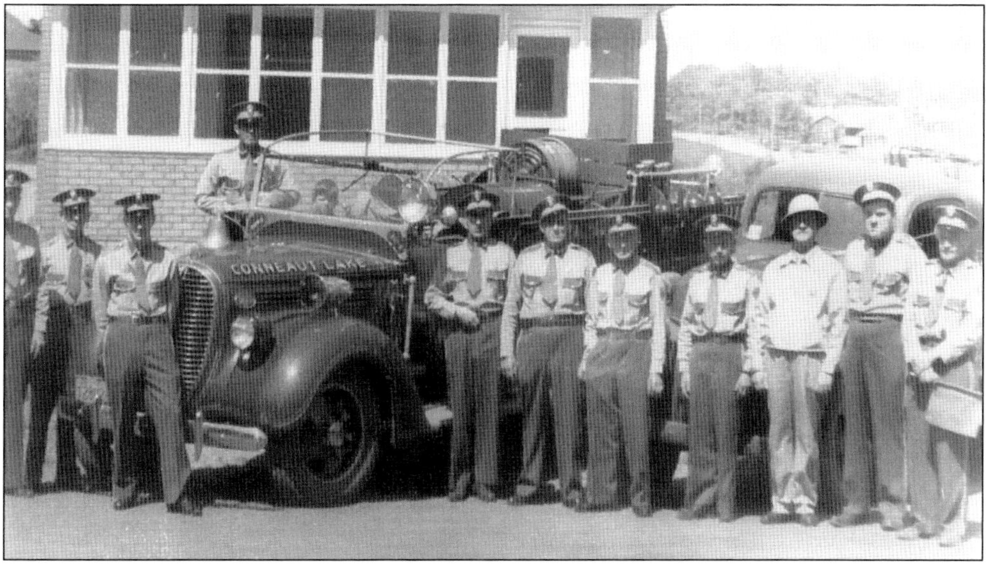

Volunteers from Conneaut Lake Volunteer Fire Department line up with their first truck in this 1938 photograph. From left to right are George Allio, Herb Schnepf, Raymond Lewis (chief), Albert Reed (driver), Raymond Reed (on truck), Alton Osbone, Charles Buckley, Harry Lewis, Reed Uplinger, Harry Moore, Stewart Highhouse, and Robert Miller.

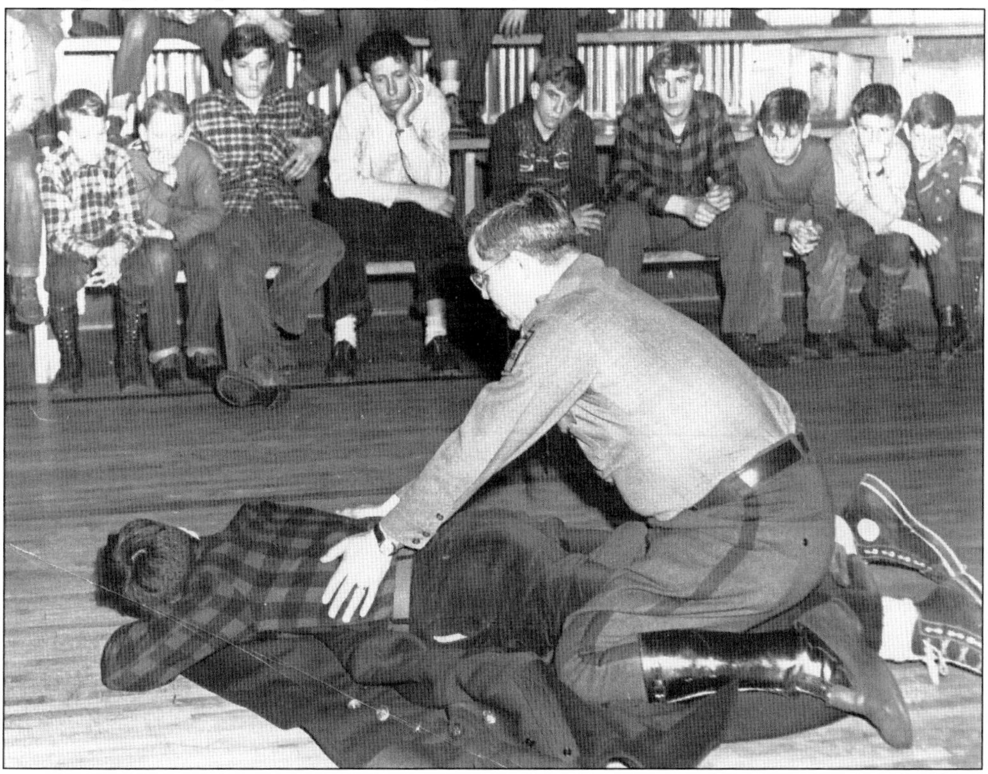

Sgt. Kenneth Leeper of the Pennsylvania State Police demonstrates the technique of cardiopulmonary resuscitation for members of the Conneaut Lake Junior Fire Department during special educational programs in the 1950s, designed to interest teens in serving their community.

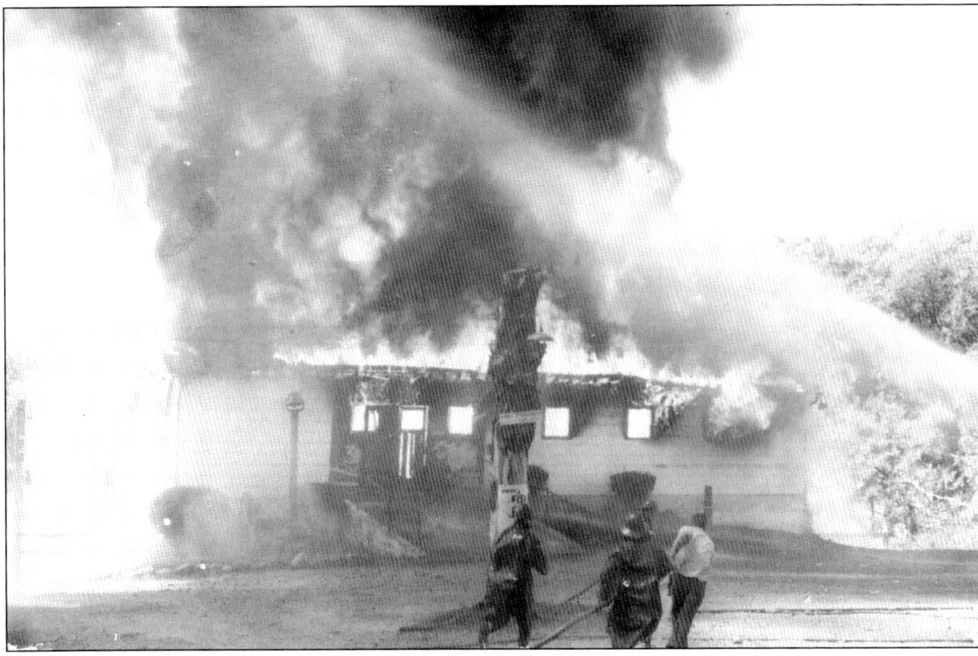

On Labor Day weekend in 1963, firefighters battle this devastating fire of the Cow Shed, a popular entertainment center. The Cow Shed was destroyed, but owners rebuilt it as part of the Stable Pit and Pub complex on Route 18, located on the east side of Conneaut Lake. (HLF.)

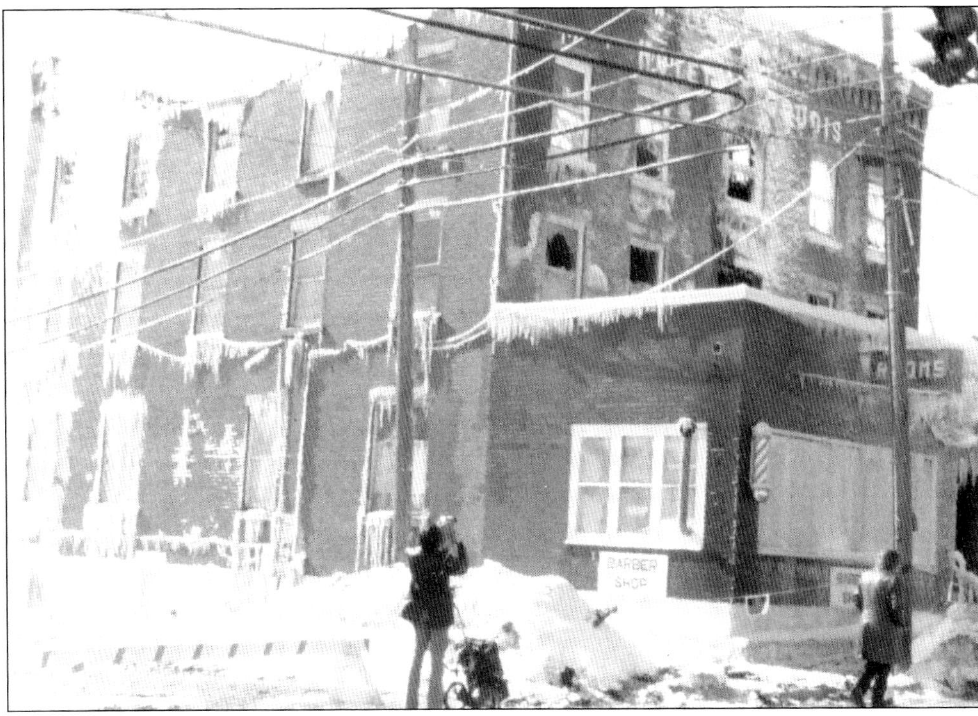

Ice covers the remains of what was left of Hotel Iroquois after a 1978 fire on Water Street. The multi-alarm fire claimed the life of a hotel patron and destroyed the building. It was the last hotel to operate in downtown Conneaut Lake. The owners did not rebuild.

About the Conneaut Lake Area Historical Society

Organized in 1999, the Conneaut Lake Area Historical Society's mission is to preserve Conneaut Lake area's heritage for future generations. The society has a 16-member board of directors and operates a museum at 150 North Third Street. The museum is the former community hall, built in 1931 by volunteers. It has been home to the local volunteer fire department. It includes a gymnasium, where Conneaut Lake High School's basketball team once played its home games. In addition, a stage supported band concerts, graduations, and other community activities.

The museum focuses on the area's history, including the woolly mammoth bones discovered in 1958 by workers preparing an area for docks. In addition, it is also home to the *Liberty the Second* speedboat, which capsized in 1922 as it prepared to participate in a race. The boat was brought up from the bottom of Conneaut Lake in 1985 by local divers, and the community raised more than $60,000 to have it restored. Other museum exhibits include a wide variety of artifacts from Conneaut Lake Park and many other aspects of the community's history.

All the items have been donated to the society, and volunteers complete all the work. The society is a 501-c-3 organization, meaning all donations are tax deductible. All of the author's royalties from the sale of this book will go directly to the Conneaut Lake Area Historical Society.

The society also is caretaker of the Barber Cemetery.

Consistent with our mission to preserve history on a local level, this book was printed in South Carolina on American-made paper and manufactured entirely in the United States. Products carrying the accredited Forest Stewardship Council (FSC) label are printed on 100 percent FSC-certified paper.

MADE IN THE USA